WAR OF NUMBERS: AN INTELLIGENCE MEMOIR

WAR OF NUMBERS

AN INTELLIGENCE MEMOIR

SAM ADAMS

INTRODUCTION BY COLONEL DAVID HACKWORTH

STEERFORTH PRESS

SOUTH ROYALTON, VERMONT

Library of Congress Cataloging-in-Publication Data
p.   cm.
Includes Index
ISBN 1–883642–23–X
1. Vietnamese Conflict, 1961–1975—Secret service—United States.
2. Adams, Sam, 1933–1988. 3. United States. Central Intelligence Agency—
Officials and employees—Biography.
I. Title.
DS559.M44A33   1994
959.704′38—dc20   93–50207   CIP

Manufactured in the United States of America

First Edition

To Colonel Gains B. Hawkins
and to my sons, Clayton and Abraham

"My dear Spencer, I should define tragedy as a theory killed by a fact."

—Huxley

CONTENTS

INTRODUCTION

WALTER CRONKITE SUMMED up the national mood in the third year of U.S. involvement in the Vietnam War when he said during the 1968 Vietnamese Tet Offensive, "What the hell is going on? I thought we were winning the war."

Thousands of books have been written about the Vietnam War. Yet this unfinished memoir by Sam Adams could well be the most important of them and the most damning indictment of the "best and brightest" who engineered the war, from the White House policy makers to those top military and intelligence brass who lied about the war from womb to tomb. *War of Numbers* gives the inside story, chapter and verse, outlining why America's intelligence community is as sick as a junkyard dog that's gotten into the rat poison.

Had the truth about the enemy's strength and intentions been revealed before the Vietnamese New Year in 1968, 2,200 American lives might have been saved and tens of thousands of other American casualties could well have been prevented. A flawed and manipulated intelligence system cut these brave men down almost with the precision of machine gun fire. How many names are on the Black Wall of the Vietnam memorial in Washington today because of a corrupted intelligence machine? When commanders expecting 100 men to attack were hit by a thousand instead, it was the grunt who paid the grim price for fraudulent bookkeeping.

War of Numbers is about one man's effort to get the truth to the grunts and their sergeants, captains, and colonels who fought the war down in the blood and mud and who needed to know the straight skinny about their Vietnamese enemy.

The man who made this effort was Samuel Adams, a young Central Intelligence Agency (CIA) analyst who could not be bought or shut up by threat of ruining his career, but hung on like a pit bull to his gut conviction that persons on high were cooking the books on enemy strength in Vietnam. Adams had the passion, moral courage, and integrity of Oliver Cromwell just after he got up from his knees from prayers, a most uncommon trait in any bureaucrat. In his friendly way Adams took on his bosses toe-to-toe, from CIA director Richard Helms on down the corrupted go-along-to-get-along chain-of-command within the CIA, the Pentagon, and the White House. He gave fits to the men appointed by President Lyndon Johnson to top jobs, and he presented the same dogged demand for honest accounting to Generals William Westmoreland and Phillip Davidson (the Theater Intelligence Officer for American forces in Vietnam) and platoons of deceptive colonels who forgot their solemn oaths to defend their country.

In *The Art of War,* written over 2,500 years ago, Sun Tzu said, "if you know the enemy and know yourself, you need not fear the result of a hundred battles. If you know yourself but not the enemy, for every victory gained you will also suffer a defeat. If you know neither the enemy nor yourself, you will succumb in every battle." Had Sam Adams been successful in getting the truth out, tens of thousands of lives would not have been shattered in Vietnam. His report would have clearly told Walter Cronkite who was winning and who was losing.

Across the U.S.A. in 1968, television images of the Vietcong's massive and coordinated assault struck the American people with perhaps as great an impact as the Japanese surprise attack on Pearl Harbor. The terrible battles fought simultaneously across Vietnam in early 1968 shocked, confused, and depressed the public. They had been assured for months by President Johnson, the Ambassador to Vietnam Ellsworth Bunker, and the

American commander in the field, General Westmoreland, that we were winning the war in spades and that the Vietcong were about to go down for the count.

The Tet offensive was a stinging tactical defeat for the Vietnamese insurgents when measured by Western military standards. Yet the TV was telling a different story. The small screen clearly showed the Vietcong as a potent and skillful force, and the communists as far from being defeated. The American people realized they'd been led down the primrose path, conned by political double talk. The sight of Vietcong holed up in the U.S. Embassy in the middle of Saigon told the American people with one picture all they needed to know. That picture put a lie to Westmoreland's pronouncement in the fall of 1967 that "whereas in 1965 the enemy was winning, today he is certainly losing."

After years of solemn assurance that the Vietcong faced imminent defeat, the American people were dismayed to discover the enemy all over the place like ants at a barbecue. How could America's top officials not know that North Vietnamese General Vo Nguyen Giap was going to launch a complex and massive attack involving hundreds of thousands of Vietcong and North Vietnamese Army (NVA) soldiers striking within a 24-hour period in virtually every major city in South Vietnam? How could our multi-billion dollar, highly sophisticated intelligence community have failed to see this attack coming?

Ironically, as the reader will see in the gripping pages that follow, just ten weeks before the Tet attack, the CIA analyst Joe Hovey had predicted from Saigon: "All-out offensive . . . January to March 1968 . . . urban centers." Hovey's bull's-eye analysis had made the rounds among the CIA's top brass and was even dispatched to the White House, where President Johnson read it 15 days before the attack. However, a note from George Carver, a top CIA official, shot down Hovey's warning. Carver said Hovey was "crying wolf."

Throughout the war, the intelligence and military top brass sometimes seemed incapable of getting anything right. In 1965, a CIA branch chief, Ed Hauck, said, "The Vietnam War's going to last a long time. In fact, the war's going to last so long we're going to get sick of it. We're an impatient people, we Americans, and you wait and see what happens when our casualties go up, and stay up, for years and years. We'll have riots in the streets, like France had in the fifties. No, we're not going to 'clean it up.' The Vietnamese Communists will. Eventually, when we tire of the war, we'll come home. Then they'll take Saigon. I give them ten years to do it, maybe twenty." What a heart breaker that this wasn't said to the members of the U.S. Congress on national TV! Communist tanks rolled into Saigon ten years to the month after Hauck made his prophetic statement.

Intelligence failures are no anomaly in American history. Since the Civil War, the U.S. intelligence community has dropped the ball as often as a freshman high school football team in its first game. During World War II, our spooks didn't see the Japanese coming in 1941 and missed the massive Nazi attack in the Ardennes in 1944. These blunders, which cost thousands of lives, were followed by the failure to identify the June 1950 North Korean invasion of South Korea, or the fact that five months later, a million man Chinese army entered the war and surreptitiously slipped behind U.S. forces deployed near the Yulu River, cutting them off. Only brave men prevented America from suffering one of its worst military defeats. Korea was followed by more intelligence failures, from the Bay of Pigs in Cuba in 1961 to Tet in 1968 to the 1979 failure to foresee the revolution that dethroned the Shah of Iran. Intelligence blunders continued in Beirut and Grenada in 1983, followed by the "let's get Noriega" fiasco in Panama in 1989. But the biggest screw-up made by America's inept multi-billion dollar intelligence machine over the four-decade-long Cold War was probably its failure to realize that the Soviet Union was finished well before its Iron Curtain came tumbling down like Humpty Dumpty. Even after the Berlin Wall disappeared in a night, the CIA director, the Secretary of Defense, and the Chairman of the Joint Chiefs of Staff wouldn't concede that the Cold War was over. For months afterward they continued to chant, "the Russians are coming."

It's obvious from these examples that from 1945 to the end of the Cold War, the U.S. intelligence community has been too often out to a very long, multi-martini lunch. Yet there has been little improvement since the cold war ended. When Saddam Hussein invaded Kuwait in 1990, the intelligence community—miracle of miracles—finally got it on the nose. They predicted the exact date, but failed to determine Iraq's strength or its disposition of nuclear and chemical capabilities, and from Desert Shield to Desert Storm, U.S. intelligence seldom got the Iraqis' military intentions, strength, or disposition right. Subsequent to the invasion, they reported that a half-million man Iraqi army—"the fourth largest in the world"—was deployed in and around occupied Kuwait, when in fact we now know that less than a third of that figure was on the battlefield. The intelligence community greatly inflated the Iraqi military strength, whereas in Vietnam, as this brilliant book describes, the enemy's size was purposely deflated by almost fifty percent. In both cases, as throughout the cold war, intelligence estimates were juggled to suit political purposes.

The Desert Storm commander, General H. Norman Schwarzkopf, told Congress in 1991 that military intelligence in the Gulf War was both a triumph and a failure. In the Gulf, I believe, the failures overwhelmed the triumphs. The Republican Guards' will to fight was overrated, as was the Iraqi Army's combat effectiveness. Intelligence also failed to pinpoint the number of Iraqi Scud missile launchers or to estimate the effectiveness of the naval blockade and economic embargo. Satellite systems provided an unprecedented amount of information, but it was often late in reaching the user. Cloudy days made observation spotty, bomb-damage assessment was both delayed by foul weather and far from accurate. Iraqi military codes were cracked early in the game, but the shortage of skilled translators impeded the flow of radio intercepts, and lack of access to the Iraqi leadership doomed the allies to ignorance of Saddam Hussein's true intentions. One general said he had stacks of satellite imagery, but would swap it all for "one good spy on the ground."

The significance of Sam Adams's book is that it clearly shows from the intelligence grunt's perspective how and why the CIA and top military brass—with White House encouragement—misled the Congress, the press, and the American people before the communist 1968 Tet Offensive by juggling the figures for enemy strength in Vietnam. Westmoreland and Davidson have argued that Adams's figures were inflated, and that even if true they wouldn't have affected the way the war was fought. Davidson wrote in his revisionist history, *Vietnam at War,* "In a military sense, the whole controversy was piddling, reminding one of Alexander Pope's ironic aside that 'mighty contests arise from trivial things.'" Among the "trivial things" Davidson almost casually mentions was, in this case, the communist order of battle (OB), a tabulation of the enemy's strength. The "piddling" thing was the disappearance of almost 300,000 communist soldiers from Davidson's intelligence books.

The Saigon brass in their plush villas didn't believe that a VC youth of twelve who mined jungle paths and scouted for main force troops, or a fifty-year-old woman who tended VC wounded, should be counted as combat or support troops. They didn't understand they were as much a part of the VC Army as any of the half dozen aides who kept Westmoreland's villa operating efficiently. The paradox was that though the generals insisted these non-regulars be arbitrarily dropped from the OB, when killed, they were included in the body count.

As described in detail by Adams, the American military in Vietnam removed whole units from the OB, including the "self-defense" militia guerrillas who are key players in irregular warfare. In Vietnam, the local militia made up the replacement pool for the regular units. When a main force unit got bloodied, the local militia filled it back up, so virtually overnight the unit was fit to fight. Throughout the Vietnam War, American commanders were amazed at the speed with which main force units could recover from a beating. The local militia also provided valuable intelligence services, guided and scouted for main force units when they operated on their home turf, and provided logistical support such as raising food, tending the wounded, or sheltering VC soldiers. They set the mines and booby traps that were responsible for an estimated sixty percent of all U.S. casualties. Westmoreland has often been accused of fighting WWII all over again in Vietnam, which may explain why he didn't want to count one of the main players in a guerilla war.

Not counting them is like a jeweler not counting diamonds because they're small. Westmoreland's fatal flaw was fighting an unconventional war with a conventional mind-set.

Adams argues that Westmoreland dropped around 300,000 local militia from the order of battle prior to the Tet surprise in order to prove the U.S. was winning. Westmoreland feared that his other perceived enemy, the U.S. press, would find out the true figures and expose the pre-Tet truth: our forces were not whittling the enemy down and we were losing the war in Vietnam. To leave the local guerrillas on the books contradicted the image of success promoted by Westmoreland and President Johnson. Westmoreland had his deputy, General Creighton Abrams, cable the White House to say that an increase in the OB would contradict the "image of sucess" they had been promoting, and would provoke the press into drawing "an erroneous and gloomy conclusion" over the progress of the war. This was the same manipulative game of changing the facts to present a winning picture that Westmoreland's predecessor, General Paul Harkins, had played, and what had sucked American combat forces into Vietnam in the first place. The Vietnam War, from beginning to end, was an enormous deception.

War of Numbers is one hell of a good tale about life inside the CIA and the struggle over the worst intelligence failure of the Vietnam War, but the book also gives the reader a good look at what the man, Sam Adams, was made of. His life was all about integrity and moral courage. He refused to bow to pressure and lie about the order of battle figures as a way to move onwards and upwards, and when his superiors went ahead and faked them anyway, he refused to let the issue die. Instead, he rattled every cage in Washington, from Congressional committees to the CIA's Inspector General, kicking on doors all the way to the White House. What Adams had in abundance—the guts to stand up and be counted—has always been in short supply. Perhaps his stalwart example of moral courage will bring a comeback in a value that seems to have almost disappeared from the American scene.

Sadly, his analysis proved accurate. The Communist forces which attacked during Tet came from a force double the size estimated in the official order of battle. Good men down on the ground paid the ultimate price for not knowing the enemy's real strength. It is a tragedy that Sam Adams didn't finish this work before he died suddenly at the age of fifty-five in 1988. It might have ended the controversy over who told the truth in Vietnam, and exposed the rivalries which infected the U.S. intelligence community throughout the cold war.

Adams stopped writing his book in the early 1980s to work on the CBS documentary which resulted in the Westmoreland lawsuit. (The case never went to jury; after great effort and expense Westmoreland dropped his suit at the last minute and CBS said it never intended to cast doubt on his patriotism.) Perhaps Sam Adams didn't resume writing because he believed the truth had already emerged. There's no question he had driven William Westmoreland, Phillip Davidson, Daniel Graham, Walt Rostow, Dean Rusk, Robert McNamara, and a host of lesser figures nuts. He forced them to sit in lawyers' offices for hours at a time and testify under oath about secrets they had intended to carry to the grave. The incredible thing was that Sam Adams was not a senior bureaucrat but a minor intelligence analyst, a mere grunt in a huge secret bureau that was a law unto itself, seemingly accountable to no one. A friend of Adams's said, "I sometimes think that Sam was sent to this earth by God specifically to hound these people for their sins, and especially for the sin of having put their name to something which they knew was not true."

Looked at from that point of view, Adams's life was a great triumph, a David and Goliath story in which Goliath, while not slain, was covered with public shame. The history of the world is filled with similar episodes in which men who could not change the facts changed the paper; but in no other case did the whole sordid story emerge in all its factual detail as it did with the OB controversy. High officials are accustomed to telling clerk analysts to screw off, and the clerk analysts generally skulk from the room and history forthwith—but Adams, far from slinking off, subjected those officials to moments when they were heartily sorry they had ever been born.

Unfortunately, Adams didn't see it as a triumph. He was never bitter, but he felt the exhaustion of utter defeat. Adams believed historians would ignore or revise the truth, and this has certainly been the case until now. Westmoreland, Helms, Davidson, Carver, Graham, and many others are in good jobs or comfortable retirement; the liars and number-fakers have prospered and risen and enjoyed celebrity status, while Sam Adams and his friends—the people who stuck their necks out, who ignored the threats, who broke with friends and told the truth—all of them were forced out of jobs, ostracized, demoted, ignored, treated like creepy complainers and malcontents, and the lives of one or two of the men who risked the most were completely shattered by the ordeal. Shortly after telling a friend he felt he'd achieved nothing, Adams died, leaving his unfinished memoir behind.

I believe Sam Adams could have died of a broken heart. He was a true patriot who perhaps felt, in the end, he had failed. Yet this unfinished work gives an outsider an inside view of the shabbiness of much CIA intelligence work during the Vietnam War. It certainly proves that Adams won not only the battle of the cooked books, but the war against the deceivers. This book is about true grit, about men and women who stood tall during a dark period in U.S. history.

We have a right to hope that Sam Adams's legacy will be twofold: first, that other writers will pick up the torch he once held high and illuminate more facts in one of the great failures of our country's intelligence history. We can hope that these future writings will spark much more vigilant congressional oversight of America's intelligence services. And secondly, we can hope that Adams's legacy will lead to desperately needed reforms which will cut out the blubber, the duplicated efforts and the rivalries from all the different intelligence agencies and streamline them into one lean and mean superior intelligence community at last. For as history has shown, they've seldom gotten it right in the past.

Sun Tzu said that no war could be won without good intelligence. He wrote, "Spies are the most important element in war, because upon them depends an army's ability to move." To be kept in ignorance of the enemy by crooked operators who cook the books or by an ineffective intelligence service is worse than sending young men into battle without ammunition. This book vindicates Samuel Adams. The President of the United States should name the U.S. Military Intelligence School after him.

—Colonel David Hackworth
Whitefish, Montana, 1993

PUBLISHER'S NOTE

FOR THE LAST FIVE YEARS of his life, Sam Adams—Samuel A. on his paychecks at the Central Intelligence Agency but invariably Sam to all who knew him—told family, friends, and his publisher that he had nearly finished his memoir of his years with the CIA. This was a white lie born of writer's block; he had set his incomplete manuscript aside in the early 1980s to work on a television documentary. What Adams had written was found in manila envelopes after he died suddenly of a heart atttack in 1988, shortly after moving to Vermont. Adams's original publisher felt that the surviving manuscript, vivid as it was, needed both a conclusion and a defender, and that Adams, dead, could provide neither. Other publishers said much the same. Steerforth decided the book was too good to lose, and found an eloquent champion to introduce the work and speak for it on publication—Colonel David Hackworth (U.S. Army, Retired).

The book which follows was written by Adams. No new material has been added. The text has been carefully edited for style and consistency, in the manner usual with book manuscripts. A few minor changes have been made for reasons of clarity, or to drop repetitive material. Adams's failure to finish the book on his own had its source in the staggering quantity of official documents declassified during the three-year legal struggle over libel charges brought by General William Westmoreland, described briefly by Adams in his introduction. Adams felt he ought somehow to accomodate this ocean of material in his book but could not bring himself to begin. Steerforth felt the value of Adams's book was to be found in the personal note he strikes on the first page and sustains throughout; nothing else like it exists in the literature of intelligence. *War of Numbers,* therefore, remains Adams's account of the great adventure of his life—not a scholarly attempt to incorporate and weigh the vast documentary record of intelligence during the Vietnam war, now part of the public record as a result of Adams's efforts.

The preface and the first seven chapters of *War of Numbers* were written by Adams as a single work. Chapter 8, "Cambodian Replay," was intended for magazine publication, but failed to find a home. Adams was doing extensive additional research on this subject when he died. Chapter 9 consists of a chronology and a draft of Adams's conclusions, apparently intended to close his book. The Appendix is based on a late chronology of Adams's reconstruction of what took place on MACV's side of the numbers controversy. It was intended by Adams as a working document but it complements his own story well, and ends on a note of closure which strikes the editor as a fitting conclusion to his book.

PREFACE

CENTRAL INTELLIGENCE AGENCY employees don't normally walk off with top secret documents, stash them in a wooden box, and bury them in a neighbor's woods. I did. This book tells why. The immediate reason the documents went underground was a letter from Admiral Rufus Taylor, the agency's otherwise kindly deputy director, who intimated that the CIA would be better off without me.

"Your suggestion of a board of inquiry," he wrote, "into what you describe as past failures" would "take the time of busy people in the White House," and would "seem to be more wasteful of time and effort than may be the very conditions you deplore . . . I suggest to you," he concluded, "that if you cannot abide the decision implicit in the above, you cannot continue to consider yourself a helpful member of the intelligence team here at CIA, and should, therefore, submit your resignation."

Well, that was that: no board of inquiry. And after the damnedest set of misdeeds that U.S. intelligence had ever strung together. The letter was Admiral Taylor's last official act. On the CIA headquarters' seventh floor that afternoon, he shook hands with well-wishers congratulating him on his final day in the government. The date was 31 January 1969, a year and a day after the Vietcong Tet Offensive swept South Vietnam, causing a near political cataclysm in the United States. Admiral Taylor shortly made off for retirement in Florida.

Despite his letter I had no intention of quitting. Instead, I removed from my desk a manilla folder of classified documents, slipped the folder into that day's *Wall Street Journal,* walked past the guard at the agency's west-side exit, and drove home.

Two years earlier I would never have dreamed of removing such documents from the CIA. Agency regulations, backed by God-knows-what federal statutes, forbade such a thing. Furthermore, it was against my habit. At the close of each day since joining the agency in March 1963 I had performed the ritual of tugging at the file drawers to make sure they were locked, pushing paper bags of classified trash down burn chutes, and even checking the floor around my desk for stray scraps of paper. Admiral Taylor's letter modified my outlook on security, and for good reason.

"Suggestions" to resign, such as the admiral's, are often followed by pink slips. And if I were fired, all the documents I'd collected about the odd goings-on around the Tet Offensive might vanish. Future boards of inquiry, if any, might have to depend on people's memories; disputes over facts would become one man's word against another's. Clearly the documentary evidence had to be preserved.

Many days and envelopes later, I began to worry that the CIA might search my house. I decided to bury the papers. Wrapping them in a plastic leaf bag, I put the bag in a wooden box—it had once held twelve bottles of cheap Spanish wine—nailed the box shut, and headed for my neighbor's woods. It took me an hour with pick and shovel to get the box a foot and a half underground.

In hindsight, I was overreacting. My career at the agency was to last four more years. During that time I received twelve more "suggestions" to resign. They were never followed up, however, and when I finally quit the agency in May 1973, it was of my own accord. All that time the wooden box lay buried in the woods.

It stayed there during the summer of 1973 as I went from congressman to congressman trying to explain what had gone wrong with U.S. intelligence during the war. No one on the hill seemed interested. The last U.S. soldiers had left Vietnam in March of that year and apparently the rehashing of old mistakes—no matter how serious—was like trying to raise the dead. In August I called it quits with Congress. I decided to write a book about my years with the CIA.

Near where I lived is the small Virginia town of Purcellville, with a solid stone library built in the thirties. Its head librarian, the late Mrs. Jean Carruthers, said I could set up my typewriter in the library basement. There I started the first draft of what eventually became this book. The first draft was less than perfect. Angry at what had gone on at the CIA, I wrote it off the top of my head—contrary to my usual practice—without research or recourse to documents. Thank God for Mrs. Carruthers. With red hair, strong opinions, and a sympathetic ear, she did me the service of listening to what I had to say, and better yet, agreeing there was something to it. I talked to her a great deal. Gradually my anger began to subside.

The palaver with Mrs. Carruthers might have continued indefinitely had not a friend, John Gardiner, told an editor of *Harper's* magazine that there was someone in the Purcellville Library cellar with an unusual story. The editor, George Crile, tracked me down in late 1974. I wrote the article for *Harper's* early the next year. Recounting my career at the agency, the article appeared as the cover story of the May 1975 issue. It hit the stands a few days before the fall of Saigon, and as a result, I expected it to make a big splash. It didn't. Saigon's collapse apparently made people want to forget about Vietnam. The May issue was a poor seller.

The article had important results, however. The first was that it convinced a publisher to offer me a contract for my book. This contract changed my attitude toward writing. I discarded the first draft, and began a second, this one on the basis of solid research. With this in mind, I decided to dig up the document box. With crowbar and shovel I trudged off to my neighbor's woods, confident it would be easy to find because of three red thumbtacks I'd stuck in trees surrounding the small clearing where the box was buried.

Unfortunately, the red thumbtacks were gone. I frantically paced the woods, cursing myself for not having used better markers. After an hour's fruitless search, I returned to the spot I'd originally thought was right and stabbed the ground with the crowbar. There was a hollow thump. I looked up at a nearby tree and saw a thumbtack, only it had faded to brown. Unearthing the box, I took it to my attic. When I opened it, I almost wept. The leaf bag had sprung a leak. The papers were a mass of black slime. Hopelessly, I spread the wads of slime on the attic floor to dry.

Weeks later, more out of curiosity than anything else, I returned to the attic with a kitchen knife, stuck it into one of the now-dry wads, and twisted. The wad split in half. The writing on the paper was perfectly preserved! Only the edges were eaten away. Giving a short prayer of thanks to whomever invented margins, I spent the next four days in the attic. Like an archaeologist, I pried papers from the wads sheet by sheet. Almost 95 percent of them were legible.

The *Harper's* piece had a second result. It came later that summer when an investigator for the House of Representatives, Greg Rushford, appeared on my back porch and asked me, my God, was what I'd said in *Harper's* really true? I said yes. A short while later, the so-called Pike Committee on Intelligence (named for its chairman, Congressman Otis Pike), decided to investigate charges the article had made about the faking of U.S. estimates of Vietcong strength before Tet. I offered the committee my documents—but with a string attached: that the CIA be permitted to review them first. No way, said the committee, jealous of its prerogatives. So I didn't turn them over, but let Rushford see them instead.

Although the committee eventually wrote a report that supported the charges made in the *Harper's* piece as substantially correct, I felt that their investigation was scarcely the board of inquiry I'd hoped for.* Besides myself, only one other intelligence analyst—an obscure

---

*Never formally issued, the Pike Report was leaked to the *Village Voice,* which published it in 1976. The furor over the leak far overshadowed what the report said.

ex-Army lieutenant named Richard McArthur—had testified about how U.S. intelligence falsified the enemy strength estimates in 1967 and 1968. I knew that hundreds of other people had been involved in the falsification. Therefore, I decided to launch an investigation myself. I tossed out most of the first draft of my book, and picked up the telephone to make the first of what became thousands of calls.

This time I decided to do things the way I had at the agency— methodically and with precision. Using every conceivable source of information—documents, checkbooks, phone records, even medicine bottles, I constructed a day-by-day chronology of my ten-year career at the CIA. I made separate chronologies for specific subjects, such as the enemy strength estimate. With this basic framework complete, I had a place to put every newly acquired fact.

My initial investigation took five years to complete. There were some three hundred interviews, many of which took several weeks to prepare for. The hardest problem was finding people who would talk. Since the Pentagon refuses to give out names, the most useful device in finding contacts was Christmas-card lists. I went to such places as California (to see Joe Hovey), New York (to see George Hamscher), Florida (to see Joseph McChristian), a bowling alley in McLean, Virginia (to see George Allen), and London (to see James Meacham). Perhaps the most helpful material that I came across was a batch of 322 letters home written by James Meacham to his wife Dorothy over a twelve-month period between 1967 and 1968. The first really unexpected material I found was during an interview with Bernard Gattozzi, once a lieutenant in General Westmoreland's headquarters, now an official for the Department of Justice. By late 1980 I was in the home stretch of my book and had compiled a chronology of doings in Westmoreland's headquarters, a chronology that if typed out would have been some seven hundred pages long.

At one time I planned to call my book "To Square a Circle." That title (which my editor axed because it sounded too much like a mathematics textbook) derived from the opening line of a cable that my CIA boss, George Carver, sent to agency headquarters from Saigon right after he had caved in to the Military Assistance Command, Vietnam (MACV) during the September order of battle conference at Westmoreland's headquarters in 1967: "We have squared the circle," he wrote, ". . . We now have an agreed set of figures."

Carver used the unusual phrase because of his familiarity with the life and works of Thomas Hobbes, on whom he had written a thesis at Cambridge University. Hobbes, the seventeenth century philosopher and geometrician who wrote *Leviathan,* had spent an inordinately long time trying to solve the geometrical problem of squaring a circle. Hobbes tried and tried, but finally concluded it couldn't be done. Thus Carver—who was intimately familiar with Hobbes' effort—was saying in effect, "I have achieved the mathematically impossible."

In the fall of 1980 who should pop up in my life again but George Crile, no longer an editor for *Harper's* but now a producer of documentaries for CBS News. "What have you been doing with yourself since I saw you last?" he asked. I told him about the interviews and showed him the order-of-battle chronology. Apparently he was impressed with what I'd turned up because in December he submitted a formal proposal for a documentary to CBS Reports, a division of CBS News. The proposal centered on the possibility of getting some of my sources to repeat their stories on camera.

CBS News gave a tentative okay early the next year and allowed Crile a small budget to see what he could do. Crile hired me on as a consultant, in part to persuade my contacts to come on camera and in part to describe my own activities in the month surrounding Tet.

The CBS front office was skeptical that we could get anyone to talk, believing that it was one thing for former intelligence officers to share their stories privately with one of their own and quite another thing to go public on national TV. At first this skepticism seemed well founded, as Crile and I received a number of refusals. Eventually seven former intelligence officers whom I had already talked to (George Allen, George Hamscher, Gains Hawkins, Joseph Hovey, James Meacham,

Richard McArthur and Joseph McChristian) agreed to appear. At the last minute Bernard Gattozzi—for reasons I fully sympathize with— declined to come on, and I had to search out a replacement to tell his story. The replacement was Russell Cooley. Crile, together with Mike Wallace, extended the list by interviewing two others, Daniel Graham and General William Westmoreland. The resulting documentary, called "The Uncounted Enemy: A Vietnam Deception," appeared on 23 January 1982, a Saturday night. It ran against the "Steve Martin Comedy Hour" and received the lowest ratings of any national program for that week. A few days later Westmoreland held a press conference in rebuttal, there was a short flurry of newspaper articles about the show, and the story of American intelligence surrounding Tet seemed headed back into obscurity.

But that May the issue was rekindled when *TV Guide* ran as its cover story an accusation that the documentary had "smeared" General Westmoreland. Although the story claimed to have no problems with the substance of the broadcast, it charged that CBS had made several mistakes in putting together the documentary. Whereupon, CBS shot itself in the foot by taking the article seriously and running an investigation which found that some of the charges were valid. The article apparently convinced General Westmoreland that CBS had defamed his honor, and he sued the network for $120 million. As consultant to the show, I became a named defendant in the case *Westmoreland v. CBS Inc. and Mike Wallace, George Crile, Van Gordon Sauter, and Samuel Adams.*

My reaction to the lawsuit was profound surprise, rapidly followed by elation. Realizing that such a suit would involve the subpoena of documents and the sworn testimony of all the parties concerned, I felt that at last I could get to the bottom of what happened. Here, paradoxically, was my long sought board of inquiry. Since the suit was too big for in-house CBS lawyers to handle, the network hired the famous Wall Street law firm of Cravath, Swaine and Moore.

The discovery process of the lawsuit exceeded my most sanguine expectations. It was a researcher's dream. Subpoenas were issued to every conceivable government agency, dozens of archivists combed the files for relevant documents, and a number of intelligence officials were put under oath.

Once again, as a consultant, I guided the document search, wrote out the questions to be asked, and attended most of the depositions. Among the depositions I attended were those of all the living principals of the war, including then Secretary of Defense Robert McNamara, Secretary of State Dean Rusk, Head of the National Security Council Walt Rostow, CIA directors Richard Helms and William Colby, and of course General William C. Westmoreland. My role was to frame questions for the deposees. My position was virtually unique—a midlevel CIA researcher with a rank roughly equivalent to army major, guiding what became the only major investigation of the Vietnam War. The trial ended on 18 February 1985, when General Westmoreland withdrew his suit a week before the case was scheduled to go to the jury.

The lawsuit brought to light the facts of the events around Tet but it left unanswered the main subject of the book I wanted to write: Who the hell were we fighting out there?

Answers to this question were to be found at CIA headquarters in the form of captured enemy documents. Prior to my resignation, I discovered that the issue of actual enemy numbers was peripheral to the real strengths and weaknesses of the Vietcong. The main enemy strength lay not in the number of troops deployed but in other areas that U.S. intelligence had hardly considered. While other people worried about the "big issues" of the war, as riots broke out on the streets at home, and as American soldiers continued to fight in Vietnam, I read the Vietcong documents. In them I was to answer to my own satisfaction the question about who we were fighting. Perhaps the recounting of what these documents said will help others understand why America lost the war in Vietnam.

1 THE SIMBAS

SEVEN DAYS AFTER I sat down at the CIA's Congo desk, a rebellion broke out in Kwilu. It was January 1964, and according to an urgent coded message from the agency's Leopoldville Station, the revolt's leader was the Congolese politician, Pierre Mulele.

"Who's Pierre Mulele?" I asked my new boss, Dana Ball. "Damned if I know," he said. "But you better write up this Kwilu ruckus before it gets out of hand. How about doing a quick piece for tomorrow's Bulletin?"

By "Bulletin," he meant the Central Intelligence Bulletin, put out each morning except Sunday at CIA headquarters in Langley, Virginia. That's where we were, agency headquarters, in one of a row of sunlit cubicles on the sixth floor. Dana was chief of the Southern Africa Branch, which I had just joined. He was short, with salt-and-pepper hair, a tweed suit, and a master's degree from Johns Hopkins. His father had run a hardware store in New Hampshire.

I set to work. First I checked the National Geographic map scotch-taped to the partition wall next to my desk to see exactly where Kwilu was; it was a province whose seat was 247 miles east of Leopoldville, the Congo's capital. Then I phoned Biographic Register downstairs to find out what they had in their dossier on Mulele: a good deal—he'd trained as a guerilla in communist China before becoming the Congo's minister of education and fine arts. Next I got from the Congo desk's built-in safe drawer the Leopoldville Station's latest aardwolf on the Congo's prospects; the prospects were grim, the aardwolf said—"aardwolf" being the agency's code word for a think piece from the field. And finally I wrote out an article in longhand on a single sheet of legal-size yellow paper.

The aardwolf set the tone of the piece, which put forth the basic facts of the revolt, such as I could make them out, and concluded that the Congo government—whose main backer was the United States—was so shaky and inept that even a small rumble in a far off place like Kwilu "would probably be difficult to contain." The branch secretary, Colleen King, a pretty twenty-one-year-old from North Dakota, typed it up, and I handed it to Dana.

"Close enough for government work," he told me after he'd crossed out several words with his fountain pen. "Now you call up State and Defense to see what they have to say. Bet you a dollar State's going to weasel. It's a fact of life around here you might as well get used to. The department doesn't like climbing out on limbs."

Checking Bulletin articles with the State Department and Pentagon was standard procedure, because the Bulletin was supposed to be fully agreed upon before it left the CIA building early the next morning. At that time special couriers rushed it to the top hundred or so people in the government, including President Johnson, so they could read it before breakfast. I picked up the telephone on Dana's desk and began dialing.

"OK by me," said the woman who handled the Congo for the Defense Intelligence Agency at the Pentagon. "I'm only surprised Leopoldville didn't go down the tubes a couple of months ago."

"I think you ought to tone it down," said the Congo analyst at State. Leopoldville aardwolfs were often alarmist, he explained, and besides, the Congolese were always holding little revolts that never got anywhere.

"What do we do now?" I asked.

"Fix the conclusion. The conclusion's too strong," he said. We talked it over for the next five minutes or so, and finally changed the phrase that the rebellion would "probably be difficult to contain" to it "may well prove hard to handle."

"What'd I tell you?" Dana said. "You could predict sunrise tomorrow morning, and State would want to explain why it might not. But no real harm done, I guess. Run it on down to the PA." I left Southern Africa, walked past Southeast Asia (the next cubicle down the line), and entered a carpeted office with a sign on the door that read Production Assistant.

"Christalmighty," said the PA, when he saw the article was about the Congo. "Here we go again." I went back to my desk to answer the telephone.

The phone rang constantly for the rest of the afternoon as the Kwilu piece went from office to office. The map section called to find out if the article needed a map. ("Yes, it does. I'll be down right away.") The Asia-Africa area chief called to ask whether the Russians were involved. ("Not yet, Mr. Dubberstein, as far as I can tell.") A man from the front office on the seventh floor wanted to know how to pronounce Mulele. ("Mu-lay-lay, sir, accent on the second syllable.") And so on. I left work at the regular hour, four-thirty.

When I got back to headquarters the next morning at just after eight, I stopped by Colleen's desk to see if my Kwilu piece had actually made the Bulletin. "Howdy, Sam," she smiled, as she handed me the latest edition, which was labeled "Top Secret." I opened it up and almost collapsed. My piece was the lead item!

"Home run first time at bat," I crowed. It was phenomenal luck. Most new analysts in the CIA's research department—called the Deputy Directorate of Intelligence, or DDI for short—spent upwards of a year before they got in the Bulletin. Others, like the Swiss analyst, never made it at all. Here I'd been on the job only eight days and already the president of the United States was reading my stuff before anyone else's. I grinned at Colleen, expecting her congratulations. But she had her head buried in the *Washington Post*. And when I walked into Southern Africa, nobody there mentioned my achievement either.

Of course on reflection it came to me why everyone was so blasé. Congo disasters were the branch's meat and potatoes. My forebears at the desk—among them Dana, before he made branch chief—had written so many Congo pieces that its "country book" (the blue loose-leaf notebook where the articles collected) was thicker than all the rest of Southern Africa's combined. In fact it was one of the fattest in the whole DDI.

There were many causes for the book's size. The main one was the Congo's problem of being both rich and weak at the same time. Its wealth came from minerals—cobalt, zinc, and vast amounts of copper, mostly in Katanga, the country's southernmost province. Its weakness came from the fact that Belgium, which had granted the Congo independence just three and a half years before, had done almost nothing to get the place ready for self-government. Of the Congo's fifteen million people on independence day, less than twenty were college graduates. The highest rank the Belgians had allowed a black to reach in its colonial army was sergeant. And to many of the country's two-hundred-odd tribes, the word *Congo* was only a figure of speech, foisted on them by outsiders.

I'd read through the country book as a way to learn about the Congo's recent history. Its first page was dated 30 June 1960, the day of independence. For weeks after it had almost daily entries—5 July, for example, when the Congo army mutinied; 11 July, when Katanga Province seceded with the copper mines; and so forth, one crisis after another, culminating in early 1961 with the assassination of the Congo's first prime minister, the left-wing nationalist, Patrice Lumumba.[1] Lumumba's body was scarcely cold when a rebel regime invoking his name and backed by the Russians set up shop in Stanleyville, a city in the interior. The Stanleyville government was even shakier than the one in Leopoldville, however, and it lasted less than a year.[2] Then in December 1962, an American-financed army of United Nations soldiers invaded Katanga to

end its secession. By July 1963, the U.N. had won, and since then the
Congo had enjoyed six months of unaccustomed quiet—that is, until
Kwilu erupted. Still in the Congo, the U.N. troops were scheduled to
leave in June.

"Damn Mulele's jumped the gun," said Dana.

I spent the rest of January and the first part of February adding
Bulletin items to the country book as the Kwilu rebels tore up the rest
of the province. Leopoldville sent its best unit, an Israeli-trained parachute battalion, to try to stop them. Instead the battalion beat up the
locals and stole chickens, and in revenge the rebels killed the priests and
nuns. By mid-February, most tribesmen had gone into hiding, and the
idea of rebellion had grown contagious. Colleen began dropping cables
in my in-box which said that people in other provinces hankered to join
the fray. Among them were reports that Chinese and Russian diplomats
in nearby African countries were setting up smuggling nets to run guns
to the rebels. The Russian "diplomats" belonged to the Soviet KGB,
the Chinese ones to Peking's Ministry of Public Security. In those days,
these organizations were the agency's chief rivals.

By late February, the Congo situation had gotten so bad that the
Leopoldville Station wrote another aardwolf. The new aardwolf said
that signs of unrest had become so widespread that a general revolt was
now a distinct possibility. Even the State Department analyst had grown
worried, but he wasn't half as uneasy as I was.

My main problem was that I knew so little about the Congo. I'd
learned about imperialism at Harvard, from which I had graduated in
1955. And I had written a short paper on the Congo economy after
joining the agency in early 1963. But since then I'd spent most of my
time in training, much of it on the "Farm," the CIA's boot camp near
Williamsburg, Virginia.[3] The Farm had courses on how to hire spies,
pick locks, and steam open envelopes, but not on how to analyze the
Congolese. I'd have to pick that up as I went along. Getting ready for
the rebellion was like cramming for an exam. The first thing to do was
guess the main questions. The most urgent of these, I reckoned, were

which people had become rebels, and which were about to. To deal with the subject systematically, I fetched from supply downstairs a stack of three-by-five index cards and a small black cardboard box to put them in. When I got back to my office, I printed the word "Rebels" on a gummed label, stuck the label on the lid of the box, and began to fill out three-by-fives.

In the upper right-hand corner I wrote "MULELE, Pierre," and below that the date, what he was up to, who his henchmen were, and which outside diplomats he had applied to for guns. Then I filed the card in the box. Cards on "GBENYE, Christophe," and "SOUMIALOT, Gaston" shortly joined Mulele's, until I had three-by-fives on almost seven hundred insurgents. Some rebels had several cards. The one with the most by far was "TSHOMBE, Moise."

Moise Tshombe was not your normal rebel. He had led the Katangan secession before the U.N. chased him out of the province, and whereas most other Congo insurgents claimed that they were "marxist" or "third world," he said he was "pro-western" or "anti-communist." In fact he had once owned a hotel, several stores, and some plantations, and during the breakaway he had taken money from the Belgian businessmen who still ran Katanga's big copper mines. With part of the money, he had hired white mercenaries. With another part, he had financed (or so people suspected) the murder of Lumumba.[4] Naturally most African governments assumed Tshombe was a front man for European mining interests and therefore hated him. Washington went along with the prevailing view, and our policy toward the Katangan was to avoid him at all costs. My first three-by-five entry on Tshombe indicated he was in exile in Spain. The next half dozen showed that the State Department wished he'd damn well stay there.

Dana's attitude toward the growing revolt was abnormally calm. Instead of leaning over my shoulder to supervise—the natural inclination of an old hand towards a new one during periods of excitement—he left me increasingly to my own devices. After a while he even stopped editing my Bulletin pieces. But he continued to offer advice. One piece he kept repeating.

"Keep your eye on the tribes," he said. "The pols in Leopoldville are windbags almost as big as the ones in Washington. But there's a difference. In the Congo, nobody gives a hoot what they say. Over there it's the tribes that count. How far this revolt gets depends on how the tribes line up." Once he'd gone on to explain that in other African countries tribal power waned as central governments grew stronger. "But that's not true in the Congo. Not yet."

I took Dana's advice. By the end of March, I had three-by-fives on each of the Congo's two hundred or so ethnic groups, and had filed the cards alphabetically (Azande, Babwe, Bafulero, etc.) in a box marked "Tribes." Then on a weekend when I had the duty and the Congo was fairly quiet, I cross-indexed the tribes and the rebels. It was a big help. By Sunday afternoon I had formed what were to become three strong convictions.

The first was that Dana was right about the tribes. Looked at through their eyes, the Congo's troubles became much clearer. For example, some rebels were really people who had had run-ins with a local chief. Others were tribesmen kept out of the provincial courthouse by rival tribes from up river. And although the Congolese politicians sometimes described themselves by Western terms (such as "radical syndicalist"), their disputes were local. The one opinion most people agreed on was that the Leopoldville government—bumbling, corrupt, but armed with Belgian-made automatic rifles—ought to stay out of tribal business.

The second conviction was that any big revolt was bound to be fragmented. The Congolese spoke too many languages. Villages ten miles apart might be as distinct, say, as the Italians are from the Swedes. To expect large numbers of them to point their guns or spears in the same direction seemed highly unlikely.

The third conviction—unlike the first two, which were widely shared—came as a surprise. It was that Moise Tshombe was a lot more than a front man for European businessmen. His tribal lineage showed why. Although many people knew that Tshombe was a Lunda (Katanga's dominant tribe), it was less well known that he had relatives who were Yeke (another big one), or that his family tree had branches throughout the province. Furthermore he had organized his Katangan political party along strict ethnic lines. The only other big-time Congolese politician to have done so was Joseph Kasavubu, the Congo's president since independence. It was no coincidence that Kasavubu's tribe was the Bakongo, the one around Leopoldville.

In early May, my crash course in Congolese anthropology came to an abrupt halt. The rebellion rapidly began to widen.

The first place to kick over the traces was nowhere near Kwilu, but seven hundred miles away, Kivu Province on the Congo's eastern frontier. The local tribe was the Bafulero. I consulted the B's in the tribal box, and through cross-indexing found that a Bafulero chief was in contact with the secret police of Burundi, the small country next door; that Burundi's king, Mwami Mwambutsa IV, had lately admitted some Chinese communist diplomats; and that the Chinese had checked into Burundi's main hotel, the Paguidas, only ten miles away from the Bafulero's main tribal grounds in the Congo. Scarcely had I sorted out this information when reports came in to the effect that tribes to the Bafulero's south, along the shores of Lake Tanganyika, were shouting a new revolutionary slogan. "Hail Mulele," they said. "We are the Simbas." (*Simba* is the Swahili word for lion.) "Also the name of the local beer," said Dana.

By the end of May, the whole eastern Congo was aboil. Province bureaucrats began not showing up for work, telephones went dead, and the American Consulate in Stanleyville—there since the rebel regime went under in early 1962—fired off a cable that the local Congo army garrison was about to go over the hill. The consulate had five staffers, of whom four belonged to the CIA.*

In Leopoldville, the U.S. ambassador, an African specialist named G. McMurtrie Godley, had closeted himself with President Kasavubu to

---

*It was always hard to attract staffers to the city. A State Department post report of 14 January 1963 listed as one of Stanleyville's few advantages the fact that "Tarantulas and poisonous snakes are infrequently encountered in the city itself." The report omitted the suburbs, however, and headed its "suggested reading list" with Joseph Conrad's *Heart of Darkness*.

advise him how to head off the revolution. "You ought to broaden your political base," said Godley, and suggested replacing the nobody then prime minister with someone more charismatic. Godley telephoned a long list of possibilities to Washington, marking off the further-out Marxists and of course the Katangan exile and pariah of Africa, Moise Tshombe. Fortunately, as other State dispatches pointed out, Kasavubu would never be so wrongheaded as to pick Tshombe as prime minister.

Dana and I were considering the same problem back on Langley's sixth floor. "How's Leopoldville going to pull this one out of the hat?" I asked him.

"What you've got to try to do," said Dana, "is think like Kasavubu. The one thing that hasn't changed since independence is that wily old bastard's still president. He's a smart man, and remember, his neck's the one on the block, not Godley's."

Once again, I followed Dana's advice. I tried to look at the Congo from Kasavubu's vantage point instead of Godley's. The more I thought, the closer I came to a disturbing conclusion. I tried it out on Dana the next morning.

"If I were Kasavubu," I said, "I'd appoint Tshombe premier. Maybe black Africa can't stand him, and neither can Godley, but Tshombe has more to offer Kasavubu than anyone else." I listed Tshombe's assets: best of all, his solid tribal base in Katanga, but also access to money, and even a small army he'd marched to nearby Angola after the Kantangan secession failed. "Finally," I said, "he's more dangerous as an out than an in."

"Probably so," said Dana. "Why don't you write it up for the Bulletin? Before you commit yourself to paper, however, you better check it out with the other side of the house. For all I know, the DDP's trying to keep Tshombe out of Leopoldville. We'd look like damn fools if we said he'd become premier, and the spooks had him tied to a chair in Madrid."

DDP stood for the Deputy Directorate of Plans, then the official euphemism for the CIA's clandestine services.[5] DDI analysts normally referred to it as "the other side of the house" because the DDP occupied the CIA building's other main wing. From it the DDP ran the agency's secret operations via its "stations," such as the one in Leopoldville. Besides recruiting spies, the stations' job was to conduct "covert operations," which in this instance could mean preventing Tshombe from becoming prime minister. I hurried down the sixth floor's long office-lined corridor between the two wings to see what plans, if any, the DDP had regarding the Katangan.

"Tshombe?" asked the DDP Congo desk chief, arching his brows. He turned to his deputy. "Number two, what was the word that State Department gentleman used to describe Tshombe at the Congo meeting this morning?"

"Anathema," said the deputy.

"Exactly. Anathema. You know what that means. Can't touch him with a ten-foot pole. We don't mess with anathemas in this office, son," he told me. I thought he might be evading my questions so I kept at him for twenty minutes. Finally he said flat out that they had nothing going on Tshombe one way or another. I hustled back to Southern Africa to write my Bulletin piece.

It was short. It said that pressures from the growing rebellion would soon convince President Kasavubu to name Moise Tshombe—loathed in Africa, but strong in Katanga—as the Congo's next premier.

"Now the fun begins," said Dana. "Remember we've got to coordinate this item with State." I read the article to the State analyst over the phone.

"You don't really believe that, do you?" he groaned. I did, and told him why. We argued back and forth for more than an hour, the department analyst saying that Kasavubu had enough problems without taking on a hot potato like Tshombe. Finally Dana waved at me to stop. "To hell with it," he said. "Let State take a footnote."

"Dana Ball says for you to take a footnote," I told the analyst.

"You mean it's come to that?" he answered unhappily.

"I'm afraid it has," I said. He read out a short statement disputing my article. I copied it down and stapled it to the bottom of the draft.

"Let's go," said Dana rising from his seat. "We've got to clear it with the front office." Footnotes to the Bulletin were extremely rare. They came only when two agencies of the so-called intelligence community fundamentally disagreed over what they felt was an important issue. The State man and I both thought the issue was important. If Tshombe became premier, we agreed, black Africa would explode with anger, and the United States would be over a barrel on whether to support him or not.

Dana and I went up to the the seventh floor to tell the top three men of the Office of Current Intelligence—the shop that ran the Bulletin—about State's footnote. The trio were R. Jack Smith, the chief of OCI, and his two main deputies, Richard Lehman and James Graham. One of them, I forget which, telephoned the head of the DDI, Ray Cline. Fine, they all said. If we felt strongly about our prediction and were sure of the facts, they'd back us to the hilt. Go ahead with the article. Screw State.

The piece appeared in the Bulletin the next morning roughly as I'd drafted it. The State Department footnote was underneath. "We've stuck our necks out this time," Dana said. I was worried too.

Over the first half of June the pressures on Kasavubu increased. Simbas grabbed villages all over the eastern Congo, Stanleyville reported that the city's garrison had begun to drift away, and for the first time a cable mentioned Antoine Mandungu. It said that Mandungu was the chief Congolese expediter and bagman for the Soviet KGB, a fact I underlined on his three-by-five. An embassy cable said Kasavubu was near the end of his rope.

Then it happened. On 26 June Moise Tshombe flew from Spain to the Congo, brandishing an invitation from Kasavubu. Two weeks later, to drumrolls and flourishes, the Congolese president swore in the ex-secessionist from Katanga as the Congo's new prime minister.

"Kasavubu's a smart cookie," I beamed at the AP ticker that announced the appointment. It was a great moment. Dana was all smiles, a stream of DDI analysts from other areas stopped by Southern Africa to snigger at State's footnote, and there was even a solemn call of congratulations from the DDI front office. Later that afternoon the State analyst (whom I actually admired because he knew so much about the Congo) telephoned to ask me to dinner. The only person to omit praise was Colleen, deep into the latest issue of *Mademoiselle* magazine.

There was little time to savor my triumph. As expected, cables swarmed in from all over Africa crying bloody murder over Tshombe's appointment. Some claimed it was a CIA plot, which as far as I could tell, it wasn't. Others complained it would only make things worse. For whatever reasons, over a third of the Congo had slipped from Leopoldville's control by late July.

On 5 August the rebellion took another lurch forward. The signal was a rap on my desk by Colleen, looking unaccustomedly worried. Instead of dropping the usual load of paper in my in-box, she shoved a cable under my nose. "You'd better read this, Sam."

It was from Stanleyville. Through a window in the consulate, the chief DDP man had just watched the arrival of Simbas. They were stark naked and waving palm fronds, according to the cable, marching single file down Stanleyville's main street. Congo Army soldiers were firing in their direction, but to no avail. Perhaps black magic was at work, the cable suggested; witch doctors had put out the story that bullets shot at rebels doubled back, and the Congo garrison appeared to be shooting over the Simbas' heads.

That was the message from the city. Stanleyville fell, and with it the consulate, the consulate staff (including the four DDP-ers) and over a thousand white civilians, mostly Belgian plus a few American missionaries. In short order a rebel spokesman got on Stanleyville Radio— which American intelligence monitored from listening posts farther away—to appeal for help from the Russians.

The fifth of August was a busy day. I wrote up two special memos before lunch, and didn't get around to the Bulletin piece until late afternoon. Stanleyville's fall was such big news that I expected it to be the Bulletin's lead item the next morning. To my surprise it was the second. The lead piece was about bombing raids against North Vietnam launched by the U.S. Seventh Fleet. Apparently the raids were in retaliation for some North Vietnamese PT-boat attacks a short while before against the U.S. destroyers *Maddox* and *Turner Joy* in the Gulf of Tonkin. The Southeast Asia Branch had written the article in the cubicle next door.

Despite the rivalry from over the partition, Stanleyville's capture put the Congo on the front burner. Ambassador Godley, in a catatonic fit since Tshombe's swearing-in ceremony, now radioed his judgment that we had no choice but to support the Katangan—after all, Tshombe's appointment was legal—and the time had come to take drastic measures to scotch the rebellion.

The U.S. government ground into action. Additional planeloads of munitions skidded into Leopoldville's municipal airport, Belgium reluctantly agreed to send more advisors to calm the now-horrified Congolese army, and the seventh floor sent down word—which it seldom did about covert operations—that the DDP had added to its small contingent of pilots in the Congo. The pilots were Miami Cubans who flew converted training planes called T-28s. The T-28s' wings were mounted with machine guns and painted with the colors of the Congolese air force.

At about this point, Prime Minister Tshombe decided to set off his first big bomb. It detonated in the form of a want ad carried in several Rhodesian and South African newspapers, including the *Johannesburg Star:*

Any fit young man looking for employment with a difference at a salary well in excess of 100 pounds a month should telephone 838-5202 during business hours. Employment initially offered for 6 months. Immediate start.

"White mercenaries," Dana explained, "same as in Katanga." Black Africa erupted like a volcano. Foggy Bottom was aghast. A Department spokesman tried to explain that since Tshombe was now the Congo's legitimate premier, his taking on "soldiers of fortune" was an "internal

Congolese affair." Nobody heard him for the din. To add to State's problems, the newspapers began calling the head mercenary, Michael Hoare, "Mad Mike." Even worse, Hoare held a South African passport.

A short while later, Dana called me to his desk to say that the director wanted a Congo wrap-up every morning by eight. That meant I'd have to show up for work by 3:00 A.M. "Sorry," he said, "but you have to include overnight cables, and there's no other way to get it done by eight." The wrap-up would be called the Congo Situation Report, he explained. Situation reports were SOP during times of crisis. Everybody called them "Sitreps."

"But don't feel bad," Dana added. "The Southeast Asians are in the same fix. Ed Hauck told me they're cranking up a Sitrep on Vietnam. It's because of the PT boats." Ed Hauck was the chief of the Southeast Asian Branch over the partition.

The Congo Sitrep was only a few days old when one morning at about ten Colleen shouted in from her desk in the hall: "Hey, Dana. Phone. Front office." He was out. I picked up the telephone instead.

"We need a Congo analyst at the director's right away," the caller said. "Get somebody there pronto."

"Yes, sir," I said. I tried to find Dana, couldn't, then grabbed a stack of my latest three-by-fives and tore up to the seventh floor. Moments later I was in the director's conference room.

Some thirty people were there, seated in leather chairs around a large mahogany table. From photographs I recognized most of the agency's higher-ups: Ray Cline, chief of the DDI, roly-poly, with crinkly red hair; Richard Helms, head of the DDP, looking, I thought, like a Mississippi riverboat gambler dressed in a business suit; and at the head of the table, John McCone, the director. He had white hair, steel-rimmed glasses, and piercing eyes. Next to McCone was a big map of the Congo on an easel.

I didn't sit at the table, already full, but on a chair near the door. The meeting was underway. They were talking about Laos rather than the Congo, so I studied my index cards, waiting for my country to be mentioned. A few minutes passed before I heard someone say "Congo." I looked up. It was the director.

"Now who are the rebels here," McCone asked, pointing to a spot just above Lake Tanganyika, "and where are they getting their guns?" Papers shuffled around the room. Then there was silence.

Good God, I said to myself; I know the answer to that one. I raised my hand slightly and cleared my throat. Ray Cline saw me and wagged his head in encouragement.

"The Bafulero, sir," I said, directly to McCone.

"The who?" McCone replied, looking at me for the first time.

"The Bafulero, sir. They're a small tribe in Kivu Province just north of Uvira, that town right next to your finger at the head of the lake, and they're getting their guns from the Burundi secret police. Who the secret police are getting them from, I'm not sure, although it's probably the communist Chinese. As you know, sir, Burundi's king, Mwami Mwambutsa IV, is a Tutsi—same tribe as in the movie "King Solomon's Mines"—and Peking is backing the monarchy against Burundi's other main tribe, the Hutus, who say they're republicans. Maybe Mwambutsa's running guns to the Bafulero in return for Chinese support. Maybe he wants to do it anyway. In any case, the linchpin of the operations, who's in touch with the Chinese, the rebels, and the secret police, all three, is Doctor Pie Masumbuko, Burundi's minister of health, and also its only doctor. Right now the DDP's trying to get a handle on Masumbuko to determine the extent of Chinese involvement. It's a complex situation."

"I gather. In other words, our immediate concern here is the Bafulero," said McCone.

"Yes, sir," I replied. "As of now, the Bafulero. But the real problem, the potential one, is the Bashi. They're a much bigger tribe to the Bafulero's north, and as of now the Bashi are split in two. One group, led by a chief called Kabare, leans toward the Simbas. The other, led by a Queen Mwami Astrida, is holding out for Leopoldville. It's partly a personal feud between Kabare and Astrida, and Tshombe, who knows what's going on, is trying to sweet-talk Kabare into staying on the reservation."

"I see," said McCone, who had been listening intently, as was everyone else. Pointing to Stanleyville, McCone asked, "And what about the rebels here?"

I ticked off three or four local tribes, explaining that the rebels were about to announce a so-called People's Republic of the Congo. The republic's president would be Christophe Gbenye; the minister of defense, Gaston Soumialot, Gbenye's chief rival; the foreign minister, Thomas Kanza, now in Nairobi talking to Jomo Kenyatta; the head of the Simba army (such as it was), General Olenga, who commanded it from a white Mercedes. They were a rum lot, I went on, a hodgepodge of tribes, often at each other's throats, with very few interests in common. Although the communists supported the rebels, the only rebel who remotely approached being one himself was the KGB bagman, Antoine Mandungu. At the moment Mandungu was in Cairo. The questions continued for almost fifteen minutes. At last McCone turned from me to Richard Helms.

"Dick, what was it you said you wanted?" asked the director.

"The B-26s," said Helms, explaining that the gas tanks on the Cuban T-28s weren't big enough to get them to Stanleyville. Fortunately, however, the Air Branch of the DDP's Special Operations Division had just souped up some old World War II B-26 twin-engine bombers, and he thought these would do the trick. There were still some supply problems; these were being looked into. When Helms was done, McCone asked, "How much will it cost?"

Helms named a sum of over a million dollars. McCone turned from Helms to a man across the table, apparently a finance officer.

"Have we got that in the kitty?" McCone asked.

"Yes, sir," said the man across the table.

"Good," said McCone, turning back to Helms. "Go ahead on the B-26s."

At that, the meeting broke up. I left the conference room amid a pack of Ray Cline's deputies. "First-rate job," one of them told me. "The director's a glutton for detail. He particularly liked your knowing about the tribes, I could tell."

"Money in the bank," said another deputy.

As August proceeded, so did plans to quell the revolt. Some half dozen B-26s, bearing the scarcely dry insignias of the Congolese air force, landed in southern Katanga. Belgian sergeants and captains reported for duty with the Congo army. And the first contingent of white mercenaries joined a unit that Michael Hoare called Commando 5. During World War II, Hoare had been a major in the British army.

With the arrival of these reinforcements, Leopoldville launched its first attack on the rebels. Called Operation Watch Chain, its goal was to retake Albertville. A Congo army battalion moved on the city by land and some two dozen mercenaries approached it from Lake Tanganyika by motorboat while a couple of Cuban-piloted B-26s flew cover. Beset by mechanical problems, the white soldiers of fortune spent most of Watch Chain paddling around the lake. The black battalion took the city. The rebels had fled, scared off by the B-26s.

Albertville's fall brought the first cables describing what life had been like under the Simbas. I read them avidly. They explained that the city folk, hoping for a change for the better, had initially welcomed the rebels, but that disillusion had set in quickly. Most Simbas were teenagers, with neither organization nor discipline. Their sacking of government offices had soon turned into wholesale looting; their execution of government officials into large-scale and random killings. In short order most people had come to think of the pre-Simba era as the good old days. Shortly after its capture, Tshombe toured Albertville in an open jeep. The crowds cheered themselves hoarse.

Despite this first government success, reports were multiplying about potential arms shipments to the rebels. So far, actual deliveries were few—rifles to the Bafulero, but little else. However, I had marked on a map the itinerary of Thomas Kanza, the rebel "foreign minister," and by correlating his stops with local DDP reports of gun-running plots, compiled an alphabetical list of the countries most likely involved. There was a folder for each, some twenty-six in all, "Albania" to "Zanzibar," the thickest being the Soviet Union's. Clearly the Russians were up to no good.

Although they must have known as much as we did about the impending shipments, the rebels' nerves in Stanleyville began to fray. Both mercenary and Congo army units were on the move, Tshombe was stumping the backwoods like a Louisiana politician, and witch doctors were spreading the word that the black magic that had once protected the Simbas no longer worked. One morning Stanleyville Radio announced that on the previous day a crowd had broken into the Simbas's central headquarters and made off with the office furniture. "Whoever stole the furniture must return it at once," the broadcast decreed. "This is a people's revolutionary government, and it can't function without typewriters and chairs." In early October, an intercepted rebel message referred to the whites in Stanleyville as "hostages."

"Hostages!" said Dana. "This has gotten serious."

Others thought so too. For the rest of the month and into November, tense meetings convened, both at the director's office and at State, to discuss what to do. Despite my low rank, I went to several of these, having acquired the reputation—eagerly spread by the front office—as Washington's leading authority on the Congolese rebels.

The last meeting I attended took place just outside the director's inner office. John McCone, Richard Helms, Ray Cline and I hunched in a tight circle in cushioned swivel chairs, listening to Helms describe what the DDP Special Operations Division had in mind to save the five men of the consulate. There were plans for parachute drops, helicopter raids, even something involving speedboats (not as odd as it sounds, because Stanleyville is on the Congo River, which flows past Leopoldville, over a thousand miles downstream, before emptying into the Atlantic.) When Helms had finished his descriptions, McCone asked him what he thought the chances were of success.

"Lousy," Helms said, "because we really don't know where those men are." Several reports put them at the Sabena Airways guesthouse on the edge of the city airport's main runway, "but the information is weeks old at best, and I wouldn't put money on it in the first place. What if we piled into that guesthouse and no one was home. Stand around with egg on our face?"

"What do you advise?" McCone asked.

"Wait," Helms said. "If we play gangbusters, we might get not only our own people killed, but everyone else in the bargain." More to the point, Belgium and the Pentagon had worked up a joint plan to save all the hostages at once. It called for dropping a Belgian parachute battalion on the airfield while a Congo army column, led by Hoare's mercenaries, pushed up from the south.

"Agreed," said McCone, ending the meeting. I went back down to the sixth floor.

The Congo in-box was even fuller than usual. I read through the paper quickly, taking notes and cross-referencing. Towards the bottom was a message from an A-1 source saying that the KGB bagman, Antoine Mandungu, had just shown up at the Sudanese frontier. I called to Dana, "The Russians are coming!"

The Sudan borders the Congo's northeast, which the rebels held, and a spate of recent reports claimed that the Russians were about to run guns from that direction. Dana and I debated how seriously to take them. Mandungu was the clincher. I wrote a quick piece saying that Soviet arms were about to arrive via the Sudan.

It was in the nick of time. A day or so later, an urgent cable came in from Egypt reporting that five Russian-made AN-12 transport planes—their Soviet markings painted over with those of Algeria—had just taken off from Cairo for Khartoum, the capital of the Sudan. A second message, sourced to an agent at the Khartoum airport, said that the planes' wheels bulged out as if they were heavily loaded. A third one, from an intercept station in Ethiopia, placed the AN-12s in Juba, a Sudanese town only a hundred miles from the Congo frontier. A final cable, whose source was a contact in Juba, said the planes had dumped cargo of heavy boxes onto trucks, and that the trucks, covered with tarpaulins, had headed for Aba, a village on the Congo side of the border. I had no doubt that those boxes contained guns. But if they were meant to save Stanleyville, they were too late.

The Belgian paratroopers jumped into the city at 6:30 in the morning (Stanleyville time) of 24 November. The mercenaries arrived from the south a few hours later.[6] I spent the night at the Watch, the seventh-floor office where the cables come in. Speed was essential. The main question was the fate of the hostages.

In fact it wasn't until well after the Sitrep's deadline that I found the answer. It seems that in the confusion of the landing the Simbas had herded most hostages into a city street some two miles away. When the paratroopers finally arrived, the rebels opened fire. In the ensuing melee, hostages dropped to the ground, ducked into doorways, and jumped over walls. Eighty were killed or wounded. But over a thousand were unhurt. Among the survivors were the five American staffers, including the four from the DDP.

Shortly I discovered why they made it. It was dumb luck. The Simbas had thrown them in with the other hostages well before the parachute drop. On hearing this news, I asked myself what might have happened if Helms hadn't quashed the plans to rescue the Americans separately. I could think of only one answer: as bad as it was, the massacre probably would have been far worse except for Helms's caution and good sense.

The Stanleyville drop marked the high tide of the revolt. Naturally there was a storm of protest, but it lost steam when the first ghastly reports arrived from the interior that the Simbas had killed far more blacks than whites. The black victims ran to the many tens of thousands, mostly killed by torture. Congolese popular opinion began swinging back to the government. Tshombe was cheered wildly wherever he went. By late December, the Simbas' main asset was the Soviet gun-running operation through the Sudan.

We had those AN-12s pegged. I had cards on each airplane, with separate times of arrival and departure, cargoes, even the names of the Russian pilots. In a way I needn't have bothered. Most guns captured from the rebels were too rusty to shoot. The Simbas had neglected to oil them.

By March 1965 the rebellion had almost sputtered to a halt, and the Congo Sitrep had changed from a daily to a weekly. With tribal support for the Simbas drying up, the mercenaries captured Aba, forcing the Russians to stop their AN-12s, and the only part of the Congo left in rebel hands—except Kwilu, where government troops skirmished with Pierre Mulele over the remaining chickens—was the so-called Fizi Pocket. Fizi lay in the mountains off Lake Tanganyika, its dominant tribe the Bahembi, reputed to be fierce and loathed by its neighbors. Therefore it seemed to me that the Pocket was just what it said, a pocket, and I began to lobby with Dana to get the Sitrep killed altogether.

But no, the revolt had one last spasm. A group of Cubans, these from Havana, crossed Lake Tanganyika in Russian-made motorboats, landed in the Congo near Fizi, and began handing out rifles. The group's leader was none other than Che Guevera. Dana and I groaned. Foreign advisors were the one thing the Simbas had so far lacked. We couldn't discount the possibility that Che and his Havanans might re-kindle the fire of revolution under the Bahembi.

It failed to ignite. Acting with unusual speed, Leopoldville sent the Congo air force to shoot up the new arrivals. Its Miami Cuban pilots were delighted at the chance to avenge the Bay of Pigs, and Che's advisory effort rapidly became a grudge fight between the two sets of Cubans. The Havanans soon found the B-26's frequencies, and shouted curses in Spanish at the pilots over their combat radios. Later (it was said), the Miamians got some American-made motorboats, and the angry Latins chased each other at high speeds around Lake Tanganyika.

"Deplorable," said the Congo desk chief, when asked about this turn of events. "This was once a perfectly respectable Cold War confrontation. Now it's the goddamn *West Side Story*." Lost in the commotion were the Bahembi, for whom Che had little but contempt.* In May the

---

*When Hoare's mercenaries eventually invaded the Pocket from Lake Tanganyika, the Bahembi put up a stiff fight. Che had disappeared. He later told a colleague that his experience in Africa was "negative," because the human element failed. "There is no will to fight, the leaders are corrupt; in a word, there is nothing to do."[7]

front office decided the crisis was over. It killed the Sitrep. For the first time in almost a year and a half, I had nothing to do.

In fact all southern Africa was relatively quiet. Rebellions against the Portugese were popping along as usual in Angola and Mozambique, apartheid still ruled in South Africa, and the only country that showed any sign of life was Rhodesia. There, the white prime minister, Ian Smith, was wrestling with the problem of what to do about British demands that he give the Africans majority rule. Dana had taken a new analyst to follow Rhodesia, however, and the newcomer—a black who had written a thesis on Ghana at Boston University—seemed to have settled in for the long haul. That's just what it looked like too: a long haul. The consensus in the branch was that although the white-run regimes in southern Africa were headed for deep trouble, the crunch was several years off.

The inactivity put me to thinking about my future. Should I stay on in the now-sleepy Africa Division, or look for a more exciting job somewhere else? My only certainty was that I wanted to stay on with the agency. I no longer simply liked intelligence; in the last eighteen months I had come to love it. Part of the attraction was the CIA itself, as perhaps the best research facility in the world.

But mostly it was the people. Dana Ball was hardly unique. There were excellent men and women in every agency office, and best of all, the excellence ran clear to the top: First, the director, John McCone, awesome in his lust for obscure facts; then the DDI chief, Ray Cline, resolute in backing his analysts (if he felt they were right); and finally the head of the clandestine services, Richard Helms, calm and clear-thinking in a job demanding just that.

It didn't take me long to make up my mind. Despite my good run on the Congo, I couldn't see waiting around for southern Africa to burn out its slow fuse. The long and the short of it was that I decided to sign up as a spy. At the first opportunity, I handed Dana an application to join the DDP.

"So you want to be a spook?" said Dana. He said he'd be sorry to see me go, but that he understood, since at one time or another most DDI analysts caught the same bug. And he fired my chit up to the seventh floor.

The reaction was immediate. One of the trio in charge of the Bulletin, Richard Lehman, called me to his office. I'd seen Lehman often during the rebellion and liked him a great deal. Short and wiry— "like one of those fast quarterbacks they used to have during the thirties," someone had described him—he spoke with an air of quiet deliberation, rocking back and forth in his leather swivel chair as he did so, his hands in a position of prayer.

"Sam," he told me, "you're going off half-cocked. The other side of the house is no better than ours. Besides, you have a bright future in the DDI. You grasp things quickly, write tolerably well, and most important, you're a generalist."

"A what?"

"A generalist," he repeated. "Someone who can cover many subjects at once. What the DDI has most of is specialists. They're a dime a dozen."

"I'm not sure what you mean," I said.

"Okay," Lehman replied. "Take Molly. (Molly Kreimer was an analyst from the Southeast Asian Branch whom I'd seen off and on in the halls.) Molly's a typical specialist. She's been working on the Vietnamese so long she's beginning to look like one. She's a wonderful woman, but she has limited horizons. Whereas you . . ." And he explained how one day I might land in the front office.

I heard him out. Then, with a tinge of embarrassment, I said that my biggest shortcoming on the Congo was that although I knew plenty about the Simbas, I didn't know much about the country itself. "I've never even been there," I explained. "So you want to travel," said Lehman. "I'll see what I can do."

A week or so later he summoned me back to his office. He had a deal. If I'd give up joining the DDP, I could transfer to the Southeast Asia Branch and become a roving analyst on Vietnam. It was a step up, he said, because Vietnam was far more important than the Congo, and instead of writing for the Vietnam Sitrep, I'd be assigned to special

projects, the first being Vietcong morale.[8] As soon as I exhausted the
subject at CIA headquarters, they'd give me a ticket to Saigon. What did
I think?

Not bad, I had to admit. I said yes, and the next day left on vacation—
my first in a year and a half—to visit my father in the Adirondacks.
He had retired not long before from his job as a broker on the New
York Stock Exchange, and was spending the summer in a cabin on a lake
in the woods.

2 THE SITREP

I GOT BACK FROM VACATION the first week of August, 1965, said hello to everyone in Southern Africa, and walked around the partition to Southeast Asia. As I entered the Southeast Asian cubicle—just like the one I'd left except for the maps—Ed Hauck, the branch chief, sprang to his feet.

"Glad you finally showed up," he said, pumping my hand and smiling broadly. In his early forties, Hauck was somewhat taller than average, with a graying crew cut squared at the top, a deep tan, an athletic build, and exceptionally white teeth.

We sat down at his desk. Molly Kreimer—whom Mr. Lehman had said was a woman "of limited horizons"—was at the next desk over, squinting at her typewriter.

"You don't know how lucky you are, not having to plug the damn Sitrep," Hauck said, gesturing at that morning's edition of the Vietnam Situation Report, still in his in-box. "We've been saddled with that son of a bitch since the Gulf of Tonkin. It's a ravenous monster, and we feed it to keep it at bay."

The Sitrep's insatiable appetite, Hauck went on, was the main reason Dick Lehman had sent me over from Africa. Hauck already had a half dozen of his own analysts throwing fodder at it, and a half dozen more were doing likewise down on the fifth floor in the China-Asian

Satellites Division. For some ancient bureaucratic reason, no doubt clear at the time, China–Asian Satellites covered North Vietnam, while Southeast Asia covered South Vietnam, Cambodia, and Laos. Despite its mob of authors, however, the Sitrep had a flaw. Everybody was so busy writing about the daily coup plots, air raids and ambushes that some of the war's larger issues had disappeared down the Sitrep's crack.

"This is where you come in," Hauck said. "You're supposed to man the crack. Keep the larger issues from sliding through. Most particularly, the Vietcong from sliding through. Now this may surprise you, since we've managed to get ourselves in a war with them, but we don't have anyone working full-time on the VC. As far as I know, you'll be the first person in Washington to give the Vietcong his undivided attention. And as Lehman mentioned, your initial problem is to guess their morale."

"But before you start plumbing the Vietcong mind," Hauck said, "you ought to read up on Vietnam. I don't want to sound condescending, but the Vietnamese are an old people, and they've already beat up on the Chinese, the Chams, and the French. You especially ought to read what they did to the French. That was only ten, eleven years ago. Sometimes I think the cables I read now are from that last war, only somebody's changed the dates."

"Me, too," Molly called from her desk. She was now pounding furiously at her typewriter.

"Anyway, don't break your neck getting a morale paper out," Hauck said, "everyone knows it's a tough subject, and besides, the VC aren't about to fold in the near future. Not even by Christmastime, when McNamara prefers they surrender." Did I have any questions, he asked.

I had one. "Mr. Hauck, how long do you think the war's going to last? I mean, how long before we clean it up?"

Hauck's cheerful expression turned sour. He paused, then, speaking slowly, as if it were a painful and much-gone-over subject, gave this answer:

"The Vietnam war's going to last a long time. In fact, the war's going to last so long we're going to get sick of it. We're an impatient people, we Americans, and you wait and see what happens when our casualties go up, and stay up, for years and years. We'll have riots in the streets, like France had in the fifties. No, we're not going to 'clean it up.' The Vietnamese communists will. Eventually, when we tire of the war, we'll come home. Then they'll take Saigon. I give them ten years to do it, maybe twenty."

"You're kidding," I gasped.

"Wish I was," he said, smiling once again.[1]

At that I walked, maybe staggered is a better word, to my new desk at the other side of the cubicle. Good God, I thought. I'm only ten minutes into my first war, and already the boss says we're going to lose it. I was so surprised that I didn't think to ask why. Instead I went back to Southern Africa to see Dana Ball.

"Hey Dana," I asked in a low voice, "what do you know about Ed Hauck? Is he okay?"

"Who? Ed?" Dana replied. "Sure. One of the best men in the business."

Still shaken, I returned to Southeast Asia. My first reading on Vietnam was from the 1965 *World Almanac:*[2]

Vietnam
Total area (est. 1958): 127,000 sq. mi.
Population (est. 1963): 31,517,00.
Vietnam is split between two hostile governments, the Republic of Vietnam, which controls the southern half, and the Communist regime of North Vietnam.

The Almanac also pointed out that Vietnam's chief products included sweet potatoes, sugarcane and shellac. Huh. It didn't look like much of a country to me.

I read on. First I looked at the CIA's country briefing book and the Pentagon's Southeast Asian Factbook. These were fairly short, about such subjects as North Vietnam's gross national product and the size of the Vietcong army. Then I went through the much longer CIA-produced "National Intelligence Surveys" about Indo-China. These were large paperbound affairs, some two dozen in all, classified "secret," with titles like "Vietnam's Urban Areas," "The Structure of the North Vietnamese Government," and "Cambodia's Inland Waterway." Finally I read some old Sitreps.

This first go-around made one thing clear about the Vietcong. They were in an entirely different ballpark from the Simbas. But what struck me most was the size of North Vietnam's GNP, only $1.6 billion a year. I looked up America's: $650 billion. That was 406 times bigger. Shaking my head at the difference (and wondering at Ed Hauck's gloom in the face of it), I asked his okay to go to the CIA library for the next week or so to do some background reading.

"You're our roving analyst," he said. "Rove on down to the library."

I did so, and, settling into an easy chair, plowed through the standard books on Vietnam. These included Vo Nguyen Giap's *People's War, People's Army,* a Vietnamese communist's account of how they had taken twenty years to defeat the French; Bernard Fall's *Street Without Joy,* a Frenchman's view of the same defeat; and Joseph Buttinger's *Smaller Dragon,* a history of Vietnam, whose main theme was that the Vietnamese had been fighting the Chinese off and on for two millennia.[3] By several days later, I had gained the strong impression that although the Vietnamese hadn't much of a GNP, they were abnormally dogged. Also they seemed to detest foreigners. All very well, I told myself, that doesn't beat four-hundred-and-six-to-one odds.

Back upstairs in mid-August, I started work on VC morale. Not knowing how else to begin, I decided to use the same approach I'd employed on the Simbas. I fetched some three-by-fives and black boxes from supply, and commenced copying VC names from the latest cables. Two hours passed, and the Laotian analyst stopped by my desk. He was six foot four, slender, with slick black hair and a big nose. His name was Jack Ives.

"What are you doing?" he asked.

"I'm making out index cards on the VC," I replied. "It seems to me that you can't dope somebody's morale unless you first find out who he is."

"Cheezil," said Ives. He walked off, chuckling to himself.

A short while later Ed Hauck came by with the same question. I gave him the same answer. "There's something you should know," he said. "Those names are aliases. The VC want to confuse us. Keep that up long enough and you'll have a list as big as the Manhattan phone book with nothing but fake names."

"Maybe I should use another approach," I said.

"It's up to you," he said. But I couldn't think of a fresh one at the moment. I read old Sitreps instead.

A couple of days later—Wednesday, 18 August—I was still at a loss on how to decipher enemy morale when a fuss erupted on the other side of the cubicle. Phones were ringing off their hooks, and the two military analysts were talking loudly, rattling paper, and peering at maps. It had the look of a major flap. I asked what was going on.

"The Marines have landed," one of them said. "At a place called Van Tuong Peninsula, south of Danang. They're after the First Vietcong Regiment."

"One of the VC's finest," I said, displaying my knowledge of old Sitreps.

"That's right," he replied, "only this time the Marines actually seem to have found it. They're pulling an Iwo Jima, John Wayne, the whole bit. No more of this jungle crap."[4]

Well, this seems as good a place as any to dig in, I told myself. For one thing, I knew a lot about amphibious operations. After college I'd spent almost three years in the Pacific as communications officer on a U.S. Navy attack transport, the U.S.S. *George Clymer.* While there, I'd been in on about twenty practice landings. A couple of times I'd led the assault boats into the beach.

The military analysts said their out-box was all mine. I read the first messages, and it was like my good old days in the Navy. The command ship for the operation was none other than the U.S.S. *Bayfield!* I'd visited the *Bayfield* many times, once to inspect its communications division, then run by a young lieutenant, Dale Thorn, now a godfather to my son Clayton. The other ships were familiar too: the *Cabildo,* the *Vernon County,* the *Point Defiance,* the *Talledega.* I could all but hear the shout

"Away all boats!" followed by the squeal of the ship's davits as they low-ered the landing craft into the water.

The Marines called the landing Operation Starlight.[5] Their Seventh Regiment had landed in amphibious tractors, line abreast, on "Green Beach" at 6:30 that morning, Vietnam time, one minute after sunrise, on schedule. A few minutes later, more of them jumped from heli-copters onto "Landing Zone Red" a short way inland. For the rest of the day the Marines poured ashore, three thousand altogether, with eleven tanks, and eight little armored tractors called Ontos. Dozens of helicopters and jets flew overhead, while a cruiser and two destroyers (the *Galveston,* the *Orleck,* and the *Pritchett*—I knew them too) stood offshore, pumping in artillery shells.

The landing was unopposed. The Marines pushed inland, there was an ambush, and fighting became heavy. In 110-degree heat, through rolling countryside, rice paddies, and five-foot bush, the Marines rooted out Vietcong. Prisoners were taken, one belonging to the First VC Regiment. ("By damn, they found it!" one of the military analysts shouted.) Toward the end of the day a message reported that "escape routes were being sealed off." The next morning the *Washington Post* headlined there were "2,000 Trapped VC."

Starlight was the first major American ground battle of the war. I fol-lowed it minutely until its end on 24 August. At the cost of fifty-one dead, the Marines had killed seven hundred Vietcong, according to a body count. More interesting was the capture of one hundred VC prisoners. I went down to the library to compare this figure with the number of Japanese who surrendered in the island battles during World War II. Samuel Eliot Morrison's *History of Naval Operations* reported that at Tarawa, for example, the Marines had killed 4,500 Japanese, but cap-tured only seventeen. The message was clear concerning VC morale. They were much more apt to surrender than the Japanese. I couldn't help but recall that America had taken only three and a half years to get from Pearl Harbor to Tokyo Bay. Why hadn't this occurred to Ed Hauck? I asked him what he thought about Starlight.

"Sure put the whammy on the First Regiment, didn't they?" Hauck said, and smiled. On that ambiguous note, I let the matter drop.

Over the next weeks, I settled into a routine. After coffee, I'd read the *New York Times* and the *Washington Post,* and compare them to the Sitrep. How they stacked up depended on the subject. About the fighting, for example, the Sitrep and the papers said almost exactly the same thing. It didn't take long to figure out why. Their information came from the same source: General William C. Westmoreland's headquarters in Saigon. Westmoreland had run the headquarters—called the Military Assistance Command, Vietnam, or MACV, pronounced "Mac Vee"—since 20 June 1964.

About Saigon politics, the Sitrep's coverage was not only much better, there was a lot more of it. The Sitrep was so obviously superior to the newspapers that I asked Ed Hauck why. "There's a lot of reasons," he told me, "not the least of which is that the CIA station's in bed with half of South Vietnam's legislature. But the main reason is Molly. She's been working on Vietnam off and on since 1951, when she learned Vietnamese down in the Foreign Documents Division. She probably knows more about Saigon politics than anyone else in Washington."

Concerning the Vietcong, the *Times,* the *Post* and the Sitrep were unfortunately alike. They didn't have much on them at all. Occasionally there was a piece about an "invisible government," or the VC's ability to pop up where least expected, but most references to the Vietcong concerned their cadavers. I began to see what Ed Hauck meant when he said they had slipped through a crack.

Now and again I'd zero in on an individual story. On 13 September, for instance, there was a piece called "The Brand New War," by columnist Joseph Alsop on the op-ed page of the *Washington Post.* Alsop said that although the communists had beaten the French in 1954, and had been giving the South Vietnamese a hard time ever since, neither Paris nor Saigon had the resources to do the job. America had plenty. One hundred thousand U.S. soldiers were already in Vietnam, 100,000 more were on the way, and bases were going up all over the country.

Operation Starlight was the kind of thing we could expect a lot of in the future. He concluded:

> The importance of this change that is now going on can hardly be exaggerated. It does not mean, alas, that the war is being won now, or will be won without a great deal of effort and sacrifice. But it does mean that at last there is a light at the end of the tunnel . . .[6]

Knowing what Ed Hauck would say about this, I went over to Southeast Asia's Cambodian analyst to get a different opinion. He was hunched over a sheaf of cables from Phnom Penh like a bookie studying his tout sheets.

"What'd you think of that Alsop piece in the *Post* this morning, Stanley?" I asked politely.

"'Light at the end of the tunnel,' my ass," he growled. And he gave me a look like I was a damn fool even to ask the question. I returned to my desk noting that Ed Hauck's pessimism seemed to have infected other members of the branch. Naturally I didn't tell Stanley that I tended to agree with Alsop.

Not long after that I consulted with Molly. A slight, red-haired woman with a pleasant, angular face, she was so short her feet didn't reach the floor when she sat at her desk, so she propped them up on an old Vietnamese-French dictionary. She had owned the dictionary since 1951, when the Foreign Documents Division hired her to translate captured Vietminh documents from Vietnamese into English. There being no such thing as a Vietnamese-English dictionary in those days, FDD had taken on Molly because she was fluent in French, and therefore could use their only Vietnamese dictionary, the Vietnamese-French one. I was consulting her about some terms she kept using in the Sitrep.

"What's the difference between a 'militant' and a 'moderate' Buddhist?" I asked.

Unrolling a draft from her overworked typewriter, Molly swung her chair toward me (adjusting the dictionary with her toes as she did so), and launched into the most complex discussion of religious factionalism

I'd ever heard. In a flat Ohio accent—her family was from Cincinnati—she first discussed the splits in the Buddhist hierarchy, then the schisms between the various pagodas, then the disagreements within the pagodas, and was well on her way to explaining that even individual bonzes were of two minds when I completely lost track. Also, she hadn't answered my question. I repeated it.

"When you cut all the weeds away," she said, "a moderate Buddhist is one who's on our side, and a militant Buddhist is one who isn't." And she laughed. That first encounter with Molly Kreimer was impressive. She knew one hell of a lot about Vietnamese Buddhists.

By now I was getting a bad conscience about my morale project. My only conclusion so far about VC morale—that they were less fanatical than the Japanese—was hardly spectacular. Besides, I kept runing into the same problem. Just what is morale? If you consider everything that makes a person happy or sad, plucky or craven, the subject is boundless. A related problem was evidence. This had the advantage of being nearby. Evidence was arriving in Southeast Asia by the bushel basket.

In late September I decided to attack the evidence problem head-on. Collecting as many reports as would fit on the top of my desk, I began sorting them out. Within a couple of days I had arranged the paper into three piles, each labeled with an index card. Under the first card, marked "Primary Evidence," was a four-inch stack of reports sourced directly to the Vietcong such as captured documents, POW interrogations, and defector interviews. Under the second card, marked "Statistics," was a similar pile, this one of account sheets from Saigon, counting such things as the weekly number of enemy defectors and POWs, or refugees from communist territory. Under the third card, marked "Everything Else," was all the paper that didn't belong under the first two. The third pile was so big I threw it away.

I began with the captured documents. They were not originals, of course, but translations from the Vietnamese (in English, like everything else arriving in the cubicle, which explained why Molly's dictionary had become a footrest). It took only an hour to read them, the vast majority being routine reports like VC company rosters, ordnance chits, and ID cards, which had little to do with morale. In fact, the only document I came across that clearly bore on the subject was a letter from a North Vietnamese private to his parents in Haiphong. He hated the army, his sergeant picked on him, and someone had stolen his flashlight, he wrote, sounding very much like an American GI. I went on to the POW and defector reports.

It took me a short time to realize their bias. Clearly anyone who's fallen into the hands of his enemies is either feeling bad, or that's what he'll tell whoever asks him. The misfortunes varied. Some VC said that they had malaria, others that they were scared, and still others that they had grown sick of communism. The single exception was a VC lieu-tenant who would only say to his interrogator that he (the interrogator) was a "dirty running-dog imperialist lackey." Hard-core VC. I went on to the statistics.

The first account sheet I looked at was a weekly Chieu Hoi report, *Chieu Hoi* being Vietnamese for "Open Arms," the name of Saigon's defector program. The report listed the number of VC soldiers to have shown up at government defector centers for a week in late August. The number was 211.

WHAT? Two hundred and eleven? Once again my mind raced back to the Japanese experience during World War II. I racked my brain, and couldn't recall a single instance, not one, of a Japanese soldier becoming a turncoat. Well, this had at last become interesting. Right away, I looked at the other Chieu Hoi reports for August. Two hundred and eleven wasn't unique; it was an average! That meant that VC soldiers were defecting at a rate of more than 10,000 a year. The Pentagon's fact-book put the size of the VC army at just under 200,000.* In other words, Vietcong soldiers were turning traitor at an annual rate of 5 per-cent, or one man in twenty. It was absolutely phenomenal!

In a state of high excitement, I ran down to the archives in the agency basement, and pulled every Chieu Hoi report for the last two

---

*Plus 39,175 people whom the factbook called "political cadres."

years. I compared them week by week, month by month, and year by year. Then, to see whether the defector figures simply kept pace with other types of VC losses, I compared them to the number of VC reported killed. An extraordinary story emerged. Not only was the defector rate growing fast, it was growing much faster than the number of Vietcong dead. For example, between August 1964 and August 1965, VC dead had about doubled. But for the same two months, VC defectors had almost quintupled. In other words, the more VC we killed, the more there were, proportionately, who wanted to quit. Therefore, if the war expanded (and the ratios stayed the same), the communists would eventually find themselves with a huge defection rate.

Double-checking the figures, I wrote a memo to this effect. It was carefully worded, with a chart for the numbers. The secretary typed it up, and with some trepidation—knowing his bias—I handed it to Ed Hauck. It was just as I feared.

"Statistics," he smiled. "McNamara dotes on statistics, but I've never been able to make head nor tail of them."

"OK, I know how you feel," I replied. "But look at the trend. Let's grant the numbers are inaccurate, probably even padded. But the increase is too big to be explained away by that. Five times higher than before. Five times. Why?"

It was a good question, and Ed Hauck knew it. He reread the memo, and studied the chart (once even looking at it upside down). "Maybe you've got something," he said, furrowing his brow. "Try it out on Molly."

"I'm not much on numbers," Molly said as I sat down by her desk. Holding it like a dead mouse, she read the memo, saying under her breath, "I don't know about that," "Golly," and "Hmm."

"Now you cut that out, Molly," I told her. "I know they're statistics, but you've got to face up to what they mean. Why has the number quintupled? How do you explain it?"

Molly also knew it was a good question. She thought for a while and said, "The communist army used to be all volunteers. Now they're using the draft. Maybe the draftees are taking off as soon as they're out of basic."

"It's a good point, Molly," I said. "I'll put it in my memo."

"Maybe you've got something," Molly replied. "Try it out on Dick Lehman."

I called for an appointment, and went up to the seventh floor. Lehman had the same reaction as Molly and Ed. "But you're right," he acknowledged. "There's a lot more defectors than there used to be." He agreed to publish the memo.

The printers ran it off the next morning. Wednesday, 20 October 1965, under the title, "Vietcong Morale: Possible Indicator of Downward Drift."[7] Filled with caveats about inaccurate statistics and containing Molly's caution about Vietcong draftees, it pointed out (in a very low key) that the upward trend of defectors was simply too big to be overlooked. But there was a disappointing footnote that Lehman had stuck to the bottom of the first page after I'd left the seventh floor. It said the memo was "experimental," that although "comments were invited," it was being circulated "only within the CIA." Slightly annoyed, I asked Ed Hauck why it wouldn't leave the building.

"The military's taken a lot of gas over cheerful numbers," he explained pleasantly. "Lehman doesn't want the agency in the same boat."

I passed Thursday and Friday waiting for comments. None came. A few days later, and for the first time, I actually saw someone reading "Downward Drift." It was the DDI representative, George Allen, back at headquarters for consultation. He was in the cubicle seeing Ed Hauck, whom he'd worked for in 1963.

"This increase in defectors is damn interesting," Allen told me, as he flipped through the paper. "Look me up if you ever get to Saigon."

That was it, the only reaction to my first morale memo. I decided to leave morale for the time being and work on the Sitrep. "A tour of the trenches," Ed Hauck said as he gave his okay. The two military analysts were glad to see me. Now, at last, one of them could go on vacation.

Ed Hauck's gloom on the war may have been misplaced, but not his observation about the Sitrep. Once you started working on it, there was no time for anything else. Skimming the mail (much less reading it) took until one o'clock in the afternoon. It took another three hours to put together a story for the next morning's edition. The best thing to be said for the job was its four-in-the-afternoon deadline. At least we worked something like regular hours.

I plugged at the Sitrep for almost seven weeks. It was a nightmare. In the Congo, the rebellion had been predictable. By watching certain factors—such as the tribes, the B-26s, and the whereabouts of Antoine Mandungu—one could generally guess what was going to happen. But in Vietnam there was no pattern. Everything seemed to be going on everywhere at once. We'd catch the VC in one province one day; they'd catch the South Vietnamese in another the next. Then, every so often, they'd pull a humdinger. On 27 October, for instance, Vietcong commandos outside of Danang blew up eighteen Marine Corps helicopters. (Eighteen! Almost as big as the CIA's entire Congo air force.) And exactly one month later, they wiped out a whole South Vietnamese regiment within fifty miles of Saigon. I quit the Sitrep in mid-December.

Although my "tour of the trenches" had been unpleasant, I'd learned an important lesson. Whatever the VC felt, they certainly didn't act like they had sinking spirits. To underline the dichotomy, I scotch-taped to my desk a *Washington Post* clip quoting an American Special Forces officer in the central highlands: "If those VC are underfed, sick, and have low morale," he was quoted as saying, "I'd hate to have to fight them when they're well."[8]

Clearly, it was time for another stab at VC morale. Because now, it seemed to me, I'd run into two large and conflicting bodies of evidence. On the one hand, there were the defector statistics, which suggested the communists were becoming increasingly downhearted. On the other hand, there were the daily field reports, which seemed to show the VC were in reasonably good shape. Something was wrong. What could it be?

Once again, I began with the captured documents and POW reports. And once again they were little help, for the same reasons as before, only there were a lot more of them. Lacking other inspiration, I decided to take a fresh look at the defector figures, and damnitall, they were running close to the same level they'd reached in August, about two hundred soldiers a week. There had to be an explanation.

I reread "Downward Drift." Its only clear loophole was Molly's suggestion about Vietcong draftees. Maybe, as she had said, most VC defectors took off after boot camp. Well, that was easy enough to check. All I had to do was go to the central defector file—such as the British had had during the Malayan rebellion and we always maintained on the Russians—to see how long the average defector had been with the VC army before throwing in the sponge. The move was so obvious that I kicked myself for not having thought of it before. I asked Molly where the defector file was.

"Never heard of one," she said. "Try R. Sams Smith in China-Asian Satellites. He knows a lot of people over at the Pentagon. Maybe they have one over there."

"You're out of your cotton-pickin' mind," Smith boomed over the phone, so loud everyone in the Southeast Asia cubicle could hear him. "A defector file presupposes organization and good sense, and if there's two characteristics our effort in Vietnam ain't got, it's organization and good sense."

I'd already learned that R. Sams Smith, the chief military analyst for North Vietnam, was a skeptic on the war, and constantly at odds with its chief political analyst, Dean Moor, supposedly an optimist. (Rumor had it that Moor had once predicted that a few Marine regiments would wipe up the VC in less than a year.) Despite his doubts about a defector file, R. Sams Smith gave me some phone numbers to try at the Pentagon.

I called the Army Chief of Staff for Intelligence, the Office of the Assistant Secretary of Defense for Systems Analysis, the Defense Intelligence Agency (its South Vietnam shop), and the Office of the Joint Chiefs of Staff. Nobody had heard of a defector file, or even of a breakdown of defector statistics. A Pentagon analyst told me that I ought to try the Rand Corporation down on Connecticut Avenue in the District, since Rand was doing a study called "Vietcong Motivation and Morale." The man at Rand told me they didn't have a defector file either, but that maybe the Agency for International Development had one, since AID handled the defector program in Vietnam.

"Haven't a clue," an AID man said, "but I bet I know who does."

"Who's that?" I asked.

"Molly," he said. "Molly Kreimer. She's one of yours. She's a walking encyclopedia on Vietnam."

So R. Sams Smith was right! Not only was there no defector file, no one had a clue who the defectors were. It was amazing. The Sitrep published defector statistics each week, the Pentagon fed them into its computers, President Johnson bragged about them to reporters, but not a soul in Washington, not one, knew what these figures represented. I might have worked myself into a lather of righteous indignation but for the fact that I'd used precisely the same numbers, without explanation, in my morale paper.

The beginning of wisdom is finding out what you don't know. I decided to be the first person in Washington to ask Saigon who the defectors were. The branch secretary gave me some cable blanks. I addressed the cable to "AUSTIN J. POLWHELE." c/o the Saigon Station. "POLWHELE" was the code name for George Allen, the DDI representative, "Downward Drift's" sole reader. I asked Allen everything I could think of concerning VC defectors: names, dates of birth, religion, length of service with the VC, jobs held, reasons for quitting, and so forth. Then I asked about Chieu Hoi reporting procedures. Where did the numbers come from? Who compiled them? Were they ever checked for accuracy? Were they padded? I warmed to the possibility of fraud. Had POLWHELE heard of any made-up numbers? If so, who did it? How? Why? It even occurred to me—although I didn't include it in the cable—that the entire system was faked. Maybe there were no defectors. God almighty.

I was filling out my fourth cable blank when Ed Hauck interrupted. "Hey, Sam," he called from his desk. "Good news. Lehman just called about your trip. You're going to Vietnam in January. Three months TDY." TDY meant temporary duty.

That was good news. At last I was on the track of something big. I stuffed the draft cable to George Allen into my safe drawer—its questions could wait until Saigon—and asked Ed Hauck for the afternoon off. It was almost Christmastime, and I hadn't done my Christmas shopping. I drove down to Sullivan's Toy Store on Connecticut Avenue in the District and bought my son Clayton a yellow Tonka-Toy steam shovel with a caterpillar tread and a crank handle.

3 THE PUZZLE OF VIETCONG MORALE

AT FIRST LIGHT ON SATURDAY, 15 January 1966, I was lying in bed on the second floor of a two-story villa at 189/2A Vo Tanh Street, a thoroughfare that led to Tan Son Nhut, Saigon's municipal airport, less than a mile off. The only sounds were the whir of the air conditioner and the distant roar of helicopters taking off on their first missions of the day. I looked sleepily at the wind-up clock on the table next to the bed. It was 5:18.

KABOOM!!! A huge explosion and a crash of glass. I dove under the bed.

"GET THAT SONOFABITCH!!" somebody shouted from downstairs.

POW-POW! Two gunshots, running in the alley below, sirens, more shots, and the squeal of a car tearing down an empty street.

I spent a while under the bed. The noise subsided in due course, after which I went back under the covers and fell asleep.

Getting up about two hours later, I asked a villa guard (an American MP from Winnetka, Illinois) what had happened. He said a VC terrorist had leaned a bicycle packed with plastique against a house used by Americans, and the ensuing explosion had knocked down a wall, killing a sergeant. "It was ten blocks away," he added.

"Then who were you shooting at?" I asked.

"You got me on that one," he said. Whoever it was, he'd missed. That was my baptism of fire in Vietnam. It wasn't much, but I wrote home about it anyway.[1]

By nine o'clock I was wondering what to do with the rest of the day. I had landed at Tan Son Nhut on Wednesday to find that the Vietnamese Tet holidays were about to begin. "Saigon shuts down for Tet," the CIA man who met me at the airport had explained. The holidays were still going strong. With the whole weekend to kill, I caught a ride to Saigon's main PX, bought some cheap binoculars and khaki pants, returned to the villa to put them away, and then walked slowly down the now-crowded Vo Tanh Street about two miles to the center of town. On Nguyen Hue Street, I bought some orange marigolds at a flower stall, and on Tu Do a Vietnamese phrasebook and a map of Saigon at an Indian bookstore. The map showed Saigon had a zoo. I like zoos. I reached Saigon's at midday.

I spent the afternoon under the zoo's vast broccoli-shaped trees, the only American among thousands of locals. It was an unexpected experience. The New York Times and the Sitrep had described Saigon crowds as "sullen" or "anti-American," but these people, families mostly, didn't fit the description. Many smiled and said hello. A small girl in a straw hat with a bright red ribbon gave me a blue flower (her parents beaming approval), and I gave her an orange marigold in exchange. Two couples used me as a photographic prop. I drank some foul-tasting beer pronounced "bah-me-bah." The zoo was so nice that I went back there the next day. By Sunday evening I had almost forgotten about my dive under the bed. When I headed for work at the American Embassy at 7:00 A.M. Monday, the war seemed far away.

The sight of the embassy brought me back to earth. It was a large fortresslike structure surrounded by white concrete barrels, sandbags, and gun-toting guards, both American MPs and white-clad Saigon police. There were more guards in the lobby, including a Marine behind the front desk who said I was in the wrong place, I belonged in the embassy annex. "Turn left as you go out the door," he told me, "it's about a hundred yards down the street." I walked down the street—traf-fickless, having been closed off ten months before when a Vietcong sapper exploded a 250-pound bomb[2]—past a low-slung bar called the Cosmos Club, to a four-story concrete building with a pile of sandbags out front. "You want the top floor," a guard said from behind the sand-bags. I climbed four flights, went down a short hall, and opened a door. Inside it was pitch black.

"Electricity's out," a voice said.

"Third time in two weeks," another voice said.

"Betcha the VC got the power plant again," said a third.

"Hey, you, shut the door. You're letting in the heat." I closed the door and stood in the dark stuffy air. Minutes later, the lights flickered on, along with the air conditioners. A ragged cheer went up. I found myself standing in a hallway with doors on either side, from which peered several squinting faces.

"Welcome to the Collation Branch," said a man with a hawk nose and a blond crew cut. "This is the DDI's penal colony. Name's Howard Beaubien."

Beaubien led me around the Collation Branch's five rooms, intro-ducing me to about twenty people. They were already back at their desks, reading newspapers, gossipping, or staring at the walls. One wall had a Vietcong flag on it, another a VC pamphlet that read in English: "Why die in Vietnam? Your Girl's Going Out With Your Best Friend." There were also filing cabinets, in-and-out boxes, piles of paper, and typewriters—all the trappings of a busy office except activity. Beaubien explained why.

Apparently in 1964, someone had gotten the brainstorm to send out some DDI researchers to help the Saigon Station analyze the VC. The DDI front office had reluctantly agreed, using the opportunity to unload what it thought were malcontents or deadwood. When the spe-cially selected analysts arrived in Saigon, the station couldn't figure out what to do with them, finally sticking them on the annex's fourth floor, where they'd languished for over a year. "Don't pay attention to these meatballs," Beaubien told me. "Man you want in George Allen. He's off at MACV. Be back later this morning."

George Allen arrived at half past ten. He was short, forty years old, with thick glasses and youthful gray eyes. Recalling my morale paper from Langley, he asked me into his office. I produced the cable I'd almost sent him from headquarters before Christmas about defectors, and ran through its questions. Allen answered them quickly. No, there was no master list of defectors in Saigon, so far as he knew. Yes, some Chieu Hoi statistics were doubtless faked, it would depend on the province. Yes, there were defectors, lots of them (answering the question I'd left out of the cable). However, the person I should talk to on the subject was Leon Goure, head of Rand's VC Motivation and Morale project, run out of a villa at 176 Pasteur Street in Saigon.

"But don't get too bogged down with defectors," Allen went on. "An even bigger problem for the Vietcong is *deserters*. Those are VC who get fed up with the war, and instead of turning themselves in to the local Chieu Hoi center, either go home or hide out in the big cities. Half the bartenders in Saigon are ex-Vietcong." He gave me a list of people to contact besides Goure. I left Allen's office to look for a place to sit.

"Here, take Joe Hovey's desk," Beaubien told me; "he's on midtour leave in the States," adding that Hovey had been with Collation for a year now, and was therefore entitled to a month off. I sat down at Hovey's desk and began to collect paper.

South Vietnam had forty-four provinces, and, honoring a cliché that they were all different, I decided to tackle them one by one. Luckily, I found a bundle of papers called the USAID Year-end Reports, less than three weeks old, one for each province, prepared by the provincial USAID reps about what had gone on locally during 1965. I condensed the reports onto five-by-eight index cards, one per province. Sure enough, they were different. "Characteristically, time is on our side," said the one from Bien Hoa. On the other hand, Vinh Long's noted that its anti-VC efforts "had largely failed." Long An's was in between. There was an increase in "roadblocking and mining activity on Highway

Four," it said, but the local Chieu Hoi program "was going well."[3] I made a note to look into the Long An defector program. By eleven o'clock on Saturday, I'd filled out forty-four cards. It was weekend quitting time and everyone was taking off.

"Come on down to the Cosmos," somebody said on the way out the door. "It's the Saturday morning staff meeting." The Cosmos Club was the bar—also, I'd found, the CIA hangout—halfway between the embassy and the embassy annex. I'd had a hot dog for lunch there several times during the week, and had heard that on Saturdays many CIA province officers flew in from the field for its so-called staff meeting to swill drinks and exchange information. Hoping to do likewise, I walked down to the Cosmos and pushed open the door.

The din was terrific. Crammed into its dimly lit thirty-five-foot-long space must have been fifty agency employees, all shouting at the top of their lungs. Recognizing an acquaintance from Langley, I asked him in as low a voice as I could what he had going against the Vietcong. "You mean *spying?*" he shouted. "Zilch! Don't know Vietnamese! Nobody does! Any VC wants to spy for us better damn well learn English." I asked him what he thought about enemy morale. "Helluva lot better than mine!" he shouted. It was so noisy I gave up, just as some customers began to sing from a mimeographed songbook entitled *Songs of Saigon: Songs that Pacify.* Despite the time of year the songs were Christmas carols, the first to the tune of "God Rest Ye Merry Gentlemen:"[4]

> *God rest you Gen'ral West-more-land*
> *May nothing you dismay.*
> *You know the First Air Cav-al-ry*
> *Was wiped out yesterday.*

And so on, more verses and songs, each louder and more raucous. A glass shattered against a wall, and I left, patting my trouser pocket to make sure that George Allen's list of people to see about defectors was still there.

The list was propped on the steering wheel of an old gray jeep (arranged by Beaubien, who had connections in the motor pool), when on Monday morning I drove slowly down Pasteur Street, looking for 176. The Rand villa turned out to be standard design, its front door opening into a big room with fans on the ceiling and tiles on the floor. Leon Goure—maybe six feet tall, graying temples combed into a continental flare—issued from a side office. "Delighted to meet you," he said in a nondescript foreign-sounding accent.

We sat down on a sofa as he described Rand's Motivation and Morale project. It seemed that Rand had formed teams of Americans with Vietnamese interpreters to go around the countryside and interview VC prisoners and defectors. Using standard questionnaires, they had already collected a considerable body of evidence. The questions concerned everything you could think of about enemy morale.

"Are there any questions about deserters?" I asked, recalling George Allen's admonition about VC quitters who went home rather than defect.

"Of course," Goure replied, "we ask everyone about desertion. It's the Vietcong's biggest morale problem. There are *many* more deserters than defectors."

"This may sound dumb," I said, "but have you ever figured out how many more there are? I mean, a ratio?"

"Indeed we have," he answered. "It's based on the interviews. Seven. Seven deserters for each defector."

"Seven!" I exclaimed, and did some quick math; if 10,000 VC soldiers a year defected, then 70,000 deserted, for a total of 80,000 leave-takers per year. "My God!" I said, "that's on top of all their other losses, too—and from a quarter-million-man army."

"You're right," Goure said gravely. "Think of the consequences." We discussed the consequences for half an hour. No doubt about it, they were bad for the VC. Goure then introduced me to Rand's expert on VC defection, Joe Carrier. Carrier and I spent the rest of the morning exchanging stories about the inscrutability of Chieu Hoi statistics. "But maybe things are looking up," he said. He'd made a promising contact at the Ministry of Psychological Warfare. We agreed to trade notes.

My mind still boggled by Goure's seven-to-one ratio, I drove around Saigon in my gray jeep for the rest of the week, checking off names from George Allen's list. My last stop was the main office building of USAID, which administered the VC defector program. On its third floor I cornered USAID's chief for III Corps—the territory surrounding Saigon—to see what he knew about Long An Province's Chieu Hoi program, the one I'd made a note about back at the Collation Branch.

"You're in luck," he told me. "Our Long An rep, Mr. King, just happens to be in the building. He's up for the day from Tan An." Tan An was Long An's province capital, about twenty-five miles southwest of Saigon.

Travis King walked into the office a few minutes later. He was a tall, smiling Texan in his late forties, with cowboy boots, a farmer's straw hat, and the beginnings of a paunch. "I got a nice little Chieu Hoi center," he told me. "You should come down and see it." How about next week? "Anytime," he said, "Just give a day's notice so I can meet you at the airport. But you be careful out there. Somebody got sniped at the other day."

It wasn't until late Tuesday that I was ready for the trip, and the next morning, 2 February, I checked into the Air America terminal at Tan Son Nhut. A pretty Vietnamese girl with bobbed hair and a white sweater stamped my boarding pass, and the pilot, the copilot, three other passengers and I climbed onto a Pilatus Porter, a Swiss-made airplane with a single turboprop engine and huge wings. The pilot pushed the starter button, the Porter belched and gave off a high-pitched whine. The copilot turned in his seat to say: "This is one crazy-ass flying machine. It stops on a dime." The airplane took its place behind a line of camouflaged jet fighters waiting to take off from the main runway. Minutes later we were aloft.

The ground below was soon typical Delta—shining rivers and rice paddies, with thick clusters of houses perched in between. We followed a causewaylike road—I guessed it was Route Four—spotted with tiny busses and trucks. After a short while the copilot, reading from a manifest, shouted: "First stop, Tan An. Mr. Adams, this is you." Below was a small city, through which passed a river in one direction and Route Four in another. The airstrip looked to be a mile out of town.

The Pilatus Porter rapidly lost altitude and speed, and shortly we were approaching the grass strip, about one hundred yards above it, but off to one side. Instead of landing, we shot beyond, then made a sharp U-turn toward the runway. "Whooppee!" the copilot yelled. The Porter went into a stall, drifted gently downward, gave a mild lurch as it hit the grass, and after no more than fifty feet, rolled to a halt. I jumped out, clutching an overnight bag. "Good luck!" the pilot bellowed. The plane took off. I looked around. The airstrip was deserted.

"Jesus, the sniper," I said to myself, and plunged toward a nearby bunker. From inside I saw the airstrip was ringed by puddle-covered fields, beyond which, about two hundred yards off, were some woods. Wishing I'd brought a gun, I wondered how long the sniper might take to wade from the woods to the bunker.

Fifteen minutes later there was a squeal of brakes. It was a USAID pickup truck driven by Travis King. "Sorry to keep you waiting," he said. "I got held up at the bridge." I tossed my overnight bag into the back of the truck and we sped off for Tan An. Long An's province capital was a hot, dusty market town filled with people, oxcarts, bicycles, and busses. We weaved our way through the traffic to a small two-story rowhouse on a side street just off the main square. "This is it," King said, "USAID headquarters."

We went inside, walking through the standard big room with the obligatory ceiling fans, upstairs to a second-floor back porch where King filled me in on the Vietnamese I'd have to deal with: Colonel Anh, Long An's province chief, who was forthright and cooperative; Lieutenant Chat, who ran the Chieu Hoi center ("Chat takes some getting use to"); and Co Yung,* who would be my interpreter. He'd recently hired Co Yung to work for Doctor Lowe, a volunteer from Utah, in bed at the

---

* *Co* means "Miss."

moment with dengue fever. "You can have Co Yung until Doctor Lowe gets better."

I met Co Yung after lunch. She was about thirty-five, short, neatly dressed in white, her black hair in a permanent wave, and her face pock-marked, evidently from an old case of smallpox. King, Co Yung, and I left the rowhouse, strode down the side street (noisy with children, merchants, and blaring radios), and crossed the town's main square (dusty, policed by chickens), detouring past a row of sun-baked armored red cars to a small boxlike structure at one corner. "This is the Chieu Hoi center," said King as we entered the building, "those are the defectors," he went on, pointing at eight to ten dozing Vietnamese in black pajamas, "and this is Lieutenant Chat." A Vietnamese army officer bowed and smiled, revealing numerous gold teeth. "You're in business," King concluded; "Call me if you need me." He made for the door, leaving me with Co Yung, Lieutenant Chat, and the somnolent defectors.

Right away there was a problem. Despite her title as "interpreter," Co Yung knew little English. She was fluent in French, however, of which I had the high school variety, and we spoke haltingly in that language. Realizing that mine wasn't good enough to interview defectors through Co Yung, I decided to work from the files. The center's walls were lined with boxes, apparently containing dossiers. I said to Co Yung in French: "Ask Lieutenant Chat if we can look at those boxes." She did so. Chat shook his head: No. She tongue-lashed him in Vietnamese. He shook his head again: Yes. Led by Co Yung, two VC defectors and I carried four boxes each back to the USAID rowhouse, thence to a small cottage in back. The defectors put the twelve boxes on a big wooden table in the cottage's main room, then left. Yanking the string of the ceiling fan, Co Yung said: "Commençons."

We commenced. She emptied the first box on the table, and skimmed through the papers. They were in Vietnamese, of course, which she translated into French. I wrote what she said onto a legal-size pad of yellow paper, translating as much as I understood into English. Soon she began to ask what such-and-such a word was in English. I'd tell her, and henceforth—to my amazement—she used English. Sometimes I'd ask her what something was in Vietnamese. She'd tell me, and I'd write it down in a notebook.

The first box took almost an hour to get through. Like the other boxes, as I was to find, it concerned one person. For all the time we spent on him, he didn't amount to much: a part-time VC courier, apparently a civilian. However, the other boxes were about soldiers. Co Yung and I sorted out the military terms as we went along. For example:

YUNG: This one belongs to the auto-defense.

ADAMS: That's self-defense in English. What's the Vietnamese?

YUNG: *Tu ve.* (And she wrote it down for me with the proper accent marks.)

A second example:

YUNG: This one's a guerrilla.

ADAMS: Same word in English.

YUNG: *Du kich* in Vietnamese.

The examples were typical. Most of the first twelve defectors were either "guerrillas" or "self-defense" militiamen, belonging to a sort of VC home guard, whose job, it seems, was to defend VC territory. After much passing back and forth of notes—in French, Vietnamese, and increasingly in English—we finished the twelfth box at 6:00 P.M., quitting time. Lieutenant Chat's defectors fetched the boxes back to the Chieu Hoi center. *"La même chose demain,"* I said to Co Yung. "It shall be my pleasure," she replied in English. We parted, me going to the rowhouse for an early supper and bed.

As I lay in the dark, listening to the nightly skirmish start up a mile or two out of town, I thought with satisfaction that at long last I was finding out who the defectors were. Okay, my data base was only twelve, but that was twelve more than anyone else's. I went to sleep not knowing that I had taken the first step on a path that eventually led to the most far-reaching intelligence discovery of the Vietnam War.

Publisher's note: After the CBS-Westmoreland trial Adams intended to rewrite his book to include some of the new information which had emerged during the three-year legal struggle. The following passage, a kind of author's aside, was intended as part of this effort, but it remains unique—no others had been completed when Adams died.

[Until this point, what I have written has been entirely autobiographical, describing what I heard or saw at the time. The following five paragraphs deal with events that took place simultaneously out of my hearing and sight. I found out about them after resigning from the CIA.]

Oblivious to the doings in Tan An, the main overseers of the war were gathering at United States' Pacific headquarters at Camp Smith, Hawaii. It was President Lyndon Johnson's first meeting with General William Westmoreland in the general's role as America's commander in the field.

"I have a lot riding on you," the president told the general. Westmoreland thought Johnson looked worried and intense, uncertain exactly what course to take in Vietnam. That was why they were there: to make basic decisions on the war. Among those present were Robert McNamara of Defense; Dean Rusk of State; Earl Wheeler, chairman of the Joint Chiefs of Staff; Walt Rostow, soon to head the National Security Council; and President Thieu and Prime Minister Ky of South Vietnam.[5]

There was a series of formal briefings, one by Westmoreland's chief of intelligence, the J-2, Brigadier General Joseph McChristian. Yes, McChristian said, things are better than they were a year ago; but don't get your hopes up any time soon. His briefing had so few bright spots that another of Westmoreland's generals—William DePuy, the J-3, chief of operations—interrupted to say that surely McChristian was over-looking many signs of near-term progress. The high-level audience listened raptly as the two staffers had it out. Although their dispute might have seemed the usual one between operations (traditionally upbeat), and intelligence (often glum), Westmoreland was far from dis-agreeing with McChristian.[6] When Johnson asked him in private how long he thought the war might last, Westmoreland answered: "Several years."[7]

Nonetheless the conference had a solid result. Until then, Westmoreland had fought the war in Vietnam without formal orders on strategy. He got them at Camp Smith. Drafted by a deputy to McNamara, dated 8 February 1966, stamped "Top Secret," and approved by President Johnson, the orders concluded: "Attrite, by year's end, [the communist] forces at a rate as high as their ability to put men in the field."[8]

Westmoreland was to fight a war of attrition, its object to grind down the enemy until he gave up. America had fought, and won, earlier wars of attrition: the Civil War for one, World War I for another. General Westmoreland took the orders back with him to Vietnam. He was to carry them even into retirement at Charleston, South Carolina. There, many years later, when a researcher asked him what his wartime strategy had been, Westmoreland referred him to the February 1966 "instructions," the ones he received at Camp Smith.

My next session with Co Yung was just like the first one. She dictated from one side of the wooden table, I wrote notes from the other, while the overhead fan continued its slow revolutions. As the hours passed, our pace quickened. Safaris of box-bearing Chieu Hois came and went. I gave each box its own number: no. 16 for Private Liem's, 261st Infantry Battalion, twelve months with the VC; no. 21 for Assistant Squad Leader Ut's, village guerrilla, thirty-three months with the VC; no. 60 for Recruit Mam's, six days with the VC (he'd previously deserted Saigon's army, having cut off a finger).[9] With Co Yung's English improving rapidly, we kept at it until Doctor Lowe got better from dengue fever. After that I caught her at odd moments, using most of my spare time to rewrite notes and travel around the province.

My first trip was with Travis King. He was doing his "daily rounds," he said, in this case trying to persuade the Vietnamese to put up a school house at Thu Thua District's seat, about five miles to the north by crow, perhaps twice that by USAID pickup. We careened over the narrow, winding dirt track to Thu Thua at about sixty miles an hour. ("Doesn't give the VC time to set up an ambush," he said.) When we got there, he went off to talk to the district senior advisor, while I asked another advisor, a potbellied black sergeant called McCrae, what he thought about VC morale.

"Don't know about your end of the province," he said, "but up at my end they're feeling pretty good." McCrae said that local guerrillas had the run of the hamlets thereabouts, that they collected taxes even in Thu Thua itself ("about fifty feet from where we're standing"), and that they had little trouble keeping their province units up to strength. "Like last month we heard that the VC Long An Province Battalion, that's the 506th, had five hundred men in it. Hell, that's damn near T, O and E." (T, O and E stands for "table of organization and equipment," military jargon for full complement.) When King was done talking about the school, we drove back to Tan An just in time for Doctor Lowe's daily swing through the province hospital. The doctor invited me to come along. I thanked him and went.

The hospital was a two-story stuccoed building with high ceilings, stinking pissoirs, huge cauldrons of steaming rice, and many beds, all taken. I followed Doctor Lowe, Co Yung, and two Vietnamese interns from bed to bed as they read fever charts and checked dressings. Seeing that many patients had leg wounds—some legs were gone altogether—I asked the doctor why. "Land mines," he told me. "The whole goshdarn province is seeded with land mines and booby traps. Mines and booby traps are our biggest medical problems around here, except maybe malaria."

Not long after my visit to the hospital I had a seemingly unrelated experience, this one involving the VC Long An Battalion, the 506th, the same one that Sergeant McCrae had said was near T, O and E. It took place while I was waiting for lunch on the rowhouse's back porch. One of Travis King's sidekicks—Mr. Graessle, an ex–Los Angeles cop who advised the South Vietnamese police—burst upstairs shouting: "They just caught the VC in the Right Testicle." He explained excitedly that the Right Testicle was the nickname of the easternmost of two big loops in the river ten miles south of Tan An, in Tan Tru District, and that the South Vietnamese army had trapped the VC Long An Battalion by blocking the neck of the loop. "Now we can clobber the bastards by air!" Graessle exclaimed. As if to underline his statement, six U.S. Army helicopters roared over the porch traveling south. Higher up I could see some Air Force jets going the same direction.

Just then King arrived, and we went inside for a lunch of crabmeat salad. "The 506th is in deep trouble," he said, to a series of distant bangs. "Those sound like five-hundred-pound bombs." I spent the rest of the afternoon working on notes and listening to explosions. The next morning a U.S. Army advisor from the small MACV compound down the street told me that 156 VC soldiers had died in the fight. "A damn good count," he said. "I eyeballed most of the bodies myself, and if you throw in the wounded, the 506th ought to be sidelined for quite a while." I found out afterward that the South Vietnamese had dubbed the battle "Operation An Dan 14/66."[10]

A day or so later my notes were more or less in order, the Chieu Hoi sample being 146, Long An's entire defection take for the last four months. I decided that rather than do more of Lieutenant Chat's boxes, I'd try to make sense with what I had. This meant putting together a profile of the average VC defector—describing such things as how long he'd been with the Vietcong and where he stood in the organization. The defectors' standing seemed to me particularly important (were we getting honest-to-goodness VC, or just the hangers-on?), so I'd picked up from Saigon several intelligence studies on the VC in order to bone up on their organization. These included MACV's "Glossary of Viet Cong Terminology," and its "Enemy Order of Battle," or OB for short. The OB listed the number of enemy troops by province and by type, but most interesting for my purposes, it said who they were and what they did. By reading the OB and other studies, I began to get a fair idea of what the communist army looked like.

They showed that the VC army was organized like a pyramid with three layers. The top layer consisted of the so-called main forces, heavily armed soldiers formed into big units such as divisions and regiments.

The middle layer consisted of the so-called local forces, well-armed battalions and companies run by the provinces and districts. (The Long An 506th was a typical local force outfit.) The bottom layer consisted of the so-called guerrilla-militia, which acted as a home guard for VC villages and hamlets. I had a lot of notes on the bottom layer types from the Chieu Hoi files.

My notes showed the guerrillas—most of them armed with rifles—were of two types; village guerrillas (du kich xa), who defended entire villages, a village being made up of several hamlets; and hamlet guerrillas (du kich ap), who defended the hamlets themselves.* The hamlet guerrillas were backed up by the self-defense militia (tu ve)—usually equipped with grenades—whose main jobs were to stand guard, dig trenches and tunnels, and lay mines and booby traps. (I guessed it was the militia who filled Doctor Lowe's hospital with leg wounds.)

Then, having sorted out the organization, I began on my VC defector profile. Here's what I found: Of the 146 defectors, just short of 90 were VC soldiers, the rest were part of the communists' civilian structure. Of the almost 90 soldiers, only 6 had belonged to the VC main and local forces, the rest being evenly divided between guerrillas and self-defense militiamen. The average VC defector was young (around twenty), low-ranking (normally a private), and had been in the Vietcong organization for a little less than a year.

So there it was—the result of almost two weeks' work. Not much on its surface, but quite a lot when looked at from a distance. It showed first—what I'd expected—that most VC defectors were low-level and relatively inexperienced. But most important it showed that there *were*

---

*Long An's administrative structure is much like that of the state I was born in, Connecticut. My father's house was in Redding Ridge, part of the township of Redding, which is part of Fairfield County. Here are the rough equivalents:[11]

Connecticut	Long An
state	province
county	district
township	village
town	hamlet

defectors, honest-to-God ones, bona fide members of the communist army as defined by the official United States order of battle. I was particularly struck that during this one four-month period, Long An—one of forty-four provinces—had more than 80 guerrillas and militiamen defect to the government. If Long An's experience was valid countrywide, it was one hell of a drain on the VC army.

At this point I asked myself the next obvious question. OK, 80-plus guerrilla-militia had defected in the last four months in Long An. How big a dent did this put in Long An's VC home guard? This was something I could check. The MACV Order of Battle listed the guerrilla-militia by province. I flipped to the back of the OB to look up Long An. I found it, and my finger tracing along the page, read these numbers: 100 guerrillas, 60 self-defense militia for a grand provincewide total of 160 guerrilla-militia.

"*Cut it out!*" I said to myself; "*that means four months from now there won't be any left. Besides the whole damn province is swarming with guerrillas.*" Clearly something was wrong. I made a note to ask the province chief, Colonel Anh, about it the next day. By luck I had an appointment to see him at nine o'clock in the morning. The appointment had been arranged by the newly assigned CIA province officer, Paul Anderson, whom I'd only just met.

Anderson shook me awake at dawn. "Travis King told me you wouldn't mind," he said with a wide grin. He had a blond pompadour, blue eyes, and enormous shoulders—a Norwegian version of 'Lil Abner. At just before nine, we were climbing the steps of Long An's province headquarters, a handsome French-built structure shaded by trees. Anderson remarked that Colonel Anh was universally well thought-of, having fought with the Vietminh against the French in the earlier go-around.

The colonel proved to be well built, stocky, and fluent in English. "How do you do, Mr. Adams," he said. I stood by as he and Paul Anderson discussed Long An's counter-terror team, a CIA-financed elite unit to fight the VC. A half hour passed before Anh turned to me. "Is there something I can do for you?"

"Yes, sir," I replied. "Could you tell me how many VC guerrillas and militiamen your intelligence people carry for Long An?" To avoid mistranslation, I repeated the question, using the terms du kich and tu ve. The colonel asked a nearby captain, who answered in Vietnamese. Colonel Anh translated: "Two thousand."

"Holy mackerel!" Anderson exclaimed. (I'd told him on the way over about the MACV order of battle holding of 160.) Colonel Anh asked me what the matter was. He shrugged when I told him. "As is so often the case, Saigon is in error. Mr. Adams, the next time you visit MACV, would you please tell them to correct their mistake?" Proud to have spotted the discrepancy, I said I would be happy to do so.

For the rest of my time in Long An, I tagged behind Paul Anderson and his Vietnamese deputy, Lieutenant Lam. They showed me the "counter-terror team," some fifty boyish-looking men, armed to the teeth; we visited the nearby village of Khanh Hau, the collection of hamlets described in Gerald Hickey's classic study of Vietnamese rural life, *Village in Vietnam;*[12] and we dined at a restaurant next to the river. I spent many hours talking to Lieutenant Lam. Gradually, he opened up. Late one evening over supper, Lam told me how much he hated the VC. They had killed his brother, he said.[13]

My last swing through the province was in a silver-colored Air America helicopter, down for the day from Tan Son Nhut. Anderson and Lam were touring Long An's district seats, and on the way to the last stop, Tan Tru, the pilot veered off course so we could inspect the big loop in the river, the so-called Right Testicle. Shouting over the chopper blades, Lam pointed out how the blocking force had trapped the VC in battle. There were bomb and artillery craters all over the loop. My only surprise was how anyone from the 506th could have survived.

A few minutes later, we landed on a concrete slab next to a cemetery just outside the district seat. A black Army major named Foote, olive drab baseball hat set squarely on his head, marched us to Tan Tru, a Verdun-like enclosure of barbed wire, bunkers, and trenches set around a collection of dingy houses. Foote said that VC guerrillas infested the nearby countryside, and that Tan Tru often got hit by mortars. He showed us the district's newly acquired television set, hidden beneath an immense pile of sandbags. ("Best-fortified TV set in the province," he said proudly.) I asked him about the battle of the Right Testicle, just four miles off.

"Helluva fight," he said. "The 506th took it on the nose." I guessed the battalion would be out of action for some time to come.

"You didn't get the message?" the major laughed. "I heard it this morning. The 506th's up in the northern part of the province, up near Hau Nghia. It's back up to T, O and E." Back in Saigon the next morning, I told George Allen about the Long An Battalion's quick comeback. "It's not all that surprising," he said, explaining that the communist army, often described as a pyramid, was more like an upward-pointing funnel. In a process called "upgrading," the main forces drew men from the local forces, the local forces from the guerrilla-militia. There was a constant upflow of replacements, the villages and hamlets acting as a sort of giant boot camp for the higher levels. After the fight at the loop, VC headquarters in Long An had no doubt ordered the local villages to upgrade enough guerrillas and self-defense militiamen to make up the 506th's losses. It probably reached T, O and E within a week. I told Allen about the MACV Order of Battle holding for Long An of 160, as against Colonel Anh's of 2,000. That wasn't surprising either, he said, since the OB had neglected the guerrilla-militia for years. Reminded of my promise to Colonel Anh, I left Allen's office to telephone MACV's Order of Battle Branch about the Long An miscount. Whoever answered the phone said that the new OB chief, Colonel Gains Hawkins, was away, but thanks for the information, he'd pass it on.

Feeling slightly uneasy still about Long An, I returned to my morale project. My first step was to call Rand's defector specialist, Joe Carrier, to tell him about my Chieu Hoi profile. He had good news too, he said; his contact at the Ministry of Psychological Warfare had come through. Apparently the provinces sent a bio sheet on each defector to the ministry, but all that it had done with them so far was file them in a safe. The contact had agreed to smuggle the sheets to Joe. Pretty soon, Carrier

THE PUZZLE OF VIETCONG MORALE / 59

said, he'd have a Chieu Hoi sample of several thousand, representing all forty-four provinces. I was happy to hear it. With a countrywide sample on the way, I could go on to something else.

The most important "something else," it seemed to me, was Leon Goure's ratio of seven VC deserters for each VC defector. If it was anywhere near correct, the communists were already in hot water. I took the question of how to check Goure's ratio to Joe Hovey, back now from his midtour vacation in the States. I'd been talking to Hovey a good deal lately and had found that like half a dozen others in the Collation Branch, Hovey knew quite a bit about the Vietcong. Their main problem was that no one had found a way to make use of their knowledge. Hovey had a red crew cut, baggy pants, and a row of ballpoint pens sticking from his shirt pocket.

"Look at the captured documents," he said. "Sooner or later you'll find anything you want to know in the documents." I borrowed a stack, and going to the next desk, started from the top. Frankly I didn't expect all that much.

I was dead wrong. Virtually the first one hit the nail right on the head. A VC directive entitled "Countermeasures Against Defectors, Deserters, and Traitors," it stated that "desertion for the specific purpose of defecting to the enemy and betraying the fatherland [is] rare in comparison with desertion from other motives." Rare! Exactly what Goure had been saying all along. The directive was all the more impressive for being from the so-called Central Office of South Vietnam (or COSVN), the communists' headquarters for the bottom two-thirds of the country.[14] That meant the desertion problem was widespread. The directive's missing element was a ratio. Exactly how rare was "rare?" I read more documents.

Another hit, also a directive, unfortunately lower-level, but giving a ratio: "Presently desertion is prevailing in various armed and paramilitary forces in the region. According to incomplete statistics, there were 138 deserters . . . [of whom] 5 defected to the puppet government," meaning Saigon.[15] *Godalmighty,* I thought, *that isn't seven to one, that's twenty-seven to one.* A short while later, still another directive: "During a one-month period, one unit had 47 men desert to go home, and 2 defect to the enemy."[16] Twenty-three to one! The examples had to be atypical—if they weren't, the bottom had dropped out of the VC army—but they suggested Goure was right: there were many more deserters than defectors. I went to George Allen's office to tell him the news. "You're on to something, Sam," he said, "but for Christ's sake be careful with statistics. There's nothing wrong with them per se, but they're only a tool, not an end in themselves. See how they stack up against other evidence. If they don't fit, something's the matter."

I said OK, and read documents steadily for several days. There were no more ratios, but many references to desertion. The clearest came from VC unit rosters, the most extreme case telling of a VC weapons company (from the 269th Battalion of the Dong Thap 2nd Regiment in the Delta) which had had 20 men take off in just three months in late 1965.[17] Since a weapons company T, O and E was 87, it was a staggering loss.

By late February, I'd gone through every VC document in the Collation Branch. Tired of reading, I decided to hit the road. On Friday, 4 March, I caught the CIA's morning courier flight to Danang, located in the northern coastal province of Quang Nam, then rated as among the least secure areas in the country.

It was easy to see why, because that Sunday I accompanied the CIA's local province officer on his helicopter rounds of Quang Nam's western districts. The trip was the most exciting I've ever taken, partly because of the pilot's novel way of avoiding anti-aircraft fire. First he'd hover at five thousand feet, then plummet to his destination, revving the blades to full speed at the last moment in order not to smash into the ground. Stomachs in our throats, we'd jump off the chopper and scramble for the nearest tree, and he'd zoom back up to wait for us. At one district, mortar shells were landing in the middle distance. At another a skirmish was in progress. Everywhere there was the sound of gunfire. As the helicopter bobbed and weaved back to Danang that afternoon, I realized I'd forgotten to ask anyone about VC morale.

My rounds through Danang City during the week were tamer. At a U.S. Marine interrogation facility, a Captain Floyd Plowman showed me some statistics he'd compiled on VC prisoners.[18] And at an old French colonial headquarters building, I fortuitously ran into MACV's Order of Battle chief, Colonel Gains Hawkins—the one who was away when I'd called about the Long An guerrilla miscount. I told him about it now, and he thanked me profusely in a Mississippi accent, saying that he'd already talked over the guerrilla-militia problem with George Allen. "Soon as I get settled in we're going to take a fresh look at the entire OB," he explained, cheerfully flicking a cigar. "Right now, for example, we're sweating some new North Vietnamese regiments supposed to have come down the Ho Chi Minh Trail." He'd be back in Saigon shortly, he said; I should look him up.

Early on 10 March I flew north once again, this time to the city of Hue. It was an eventful day. That morning the communists had overrun the nearby Special Forces camp at A Shau, and the Hue citadel was a beehive of activity, the various intelligence agencies trying to find out exactly which units had done it. (By coincidence, I encountered Colonel Hawkins again in the citadel.) And that evening something called the Buddhist Struggle Movement broke out. Apparently Saigon had fired the local South Vietnamese corps commander, General Thi, upsetting the local bonzes so much that they began to riot. Wishing Molly Kreimer were around to explain what it was all about, I returned to Saigon a few days later.

The rest of my TDY was a mix of tear gas and captured documents. The tear gas blew in from street riots, the Saigon bonzes having decided to emulate the ones up north. The documents were those I read at MACV's Combined Document Exploitation Center (or CDEC), which processed and translated them. I reviewed every one in the center, gathering several more enemy rosters. They had the same message as before: the VC army was losing lots of men to desertion. Eventually I flew with a satchel of documents back to CIA headquarters at Langley, reporting to its sixth floor on 2 May 1966.

The Southeast Asian Branch was now completely immersed in the Buddhist Struggle Movement. Hue and Danang had fallen to the Buddhist clergy, and Molly's typewriter was a blur of keys. (She nonetheless took time to tell me what was going on.) Strangely, Ed Hauck seemed listless. The rumor was that the branch was due for reshuffling, with him coming out on the short end. Concerning Vietnam there was a deep air of pessimism, not only in the branch but in the entire CIA.

In the general gloom, I shone as a ray of hope. No one at CIA headquarters had paid attention before to VC deserters, because the main source on them, the documents, were almost entirely neglected. The good news traveled fast. Admiral William F. Raborn—who had taken over from McCone for a year as director—called me in to brief him and his deputies about the enemy's AWOL problem. The briefing was a boffo hit. Right after it, I was told that R. Jack Smith (new head of DDI, having replaced Ray Cline) had called me "*the* outstanding analyst" of the research directorate.

But as usual, there were skeptics—particularly Molly Kreimer and Ed Hauck—who had learned over the years that good news was often illusory. So to be on the safe side, Admiral Raborn decided to send a "Vietcong morale team" to Saigon to see if my news was really true. The team consisted of myself, acting as "consultant," and four agency psychiatrists, who presumably understood things like morale. The morale team landed at Tan Son Nhut in June.

The psychiatrists had no better idea than I'd had, when I started, on how to parse the Vietcong mind. One of the psychiatrists said, "We'll never get Ho Chi Minh to lie still on a leather couch, so we better think up something else quick." They decided to ask the CIA men from the provinces what they thought about enemy morale. After a month or so of doing this, the psychiatrists went back to Washington convinced that, by and large, Vietcong spirits were in good shape. I went back with a new batch of rosters showing a high desertion rate.

Back at Langley, I finished writing my memo on VC morale. Since the White House and Pentagon liked statistics, I had long since decided to express my message numerically. Taking my now-respectable collection of rosters—some from big units—I made an equation. It went like this: if A, B, and C units (the ones for which I had rosters) had so many deserters in such and such a period of time, then the number of deserters per year for the whole VC army was x. No matter how I arranged the equation, x turned out to be a very high number. I could never get it below 50,000. Once it even rose above 100,000. In other words, I had arrived by a different route at the same ballpark as Leon Goure with his ratio of seven deserters for each defector.

The significance of my finding and Goure's was immense. The latest MACV Order of Battle (June 1966) put enemy strength at approaching 280,000. Other reports indicated that we were killing, capturing, and wounding VC at the rate of 150,000 a year. If to these you added 50,000, 80,000, or even 100,000 deserters—well, it was hard to see how a 280,000-man army could last much longer.

There were two main problems with my finding. The first problem was the usual one; the old hands didn't believe it. The second problem was relatively new; I didn't believe it myself. To begin with, I'd seen or heard the war raging unabated from one end of Vietnam to the other. Furthermore, I trusted the opinion of the CIA men in the field who had told the psychiatrists of the Vietcong's resilience. And finally with the Saigon government in a state of near-collapse from the Struggle Movement, it somehow appeared unlikely that the VC were falling apart at the same time. I decided to reexamine the logic that had led me to think that the VC were headed for imminent trouble.

I saw my logic had three main premises. Premise number one was that the Vietcong were suffering very heavy casualties. Although I'd heard all the stories about exaggerated reporting, I tended now to discount them, because the heavy losses were also reflected in the documents. Premise two was my finding that the enemy army had a high desertion rate. Again, I believed the documents. Premise three was that both the casualties and the deserters came from an enemy force approaching 280,000. Perhaps this was the problem. The Long An discrepancy came immediately to mind, as well as the quick recovery of that province's 506th Battalion after the battle of the Right Testicle.

While I was weighing these thoughts, the rumored reorganization had occurred for the CIA's Southeast Asia Branch. The branch had combined with China-Asian Satellites into a new "Indo-China Division" on the fifth floor. Ed Hauck had been whisked to a post overseas, the boisterous R. Sams Smith to a job outside the building. The only old hand left was Molly. The new Indo-China Division chief was the supposed optimist, Dean Moor.

I told Dean Moor about the Long An miscount and the 506th, and asked if I could look into enemy manpower. He said it was OK with him as long as I turned in an occasional item for the Sitrep. "Fine," I said, and decided to have another look at the captured documents. At this time the documents—the same ones put out by MACV's Combined Document Exploitation Center in Saigon—were collected in so-called bulletins. I went down to the agency archives, xeroxed their entire stock, came back upstairs, and began reading. By 17 August 1966, I had reached bulletin number 688.

4 BULLETIN 689

MID-MORNING OF THURSDAY 18 August 1966 was quiet. The dozen or so analysts of the newly formed Indo-China Division were in the first stages of pounding out the daily Sitrep. The division chief, Dean Moor, was away. Molly was less busy than usual, the Buddhist Struggle Movement having lost steam with the arrest of General Thi, the I Corps chief. Likewise the military analysts had slim pickings; the VC had set off a routine bomb in Hue, killing twenty-six civilians, and the Australians had just launched a search-and-destroy mission in Phuoc Tuy Province called Operation Smithfield. I read the *Washington Post,* waiting for Lorrie, the division secretary, to deliver my mail. As main recipient of captured documents, I was her last stop—and for good reason. The documents were at best several weeks old, and therefore unsuited to the current Situation Report.

Lorrie made her delivery at about ten o'clock. I put aside the *Post* and transferred the thin sheaf of papers she had dropped in my in-box to the center of my desk. I read them slowly, hoping to solve the puzzle of how long the VC could bear the drain of deserters from their 280,000-man force. At approximately ten-thirty, I came to Bulletin 689.[1]

It was only three pages long, and unlike most MACV bulletins—which normally dealt with several VC documents—Bulletin 689 concerned only one. Entitled the "Recapitulated Report on the People's

Warfare Movement from Binh Dinh Province," it had been picked up (according to "capture data" on its right-hand margin) by a trooper from the U.S. First Air Calvary Division in the northern part of the province on 30 May 1966. The document itself was undated, but since it concerned the first quarter of the year, it had to have been written some time after 31 March.

Whoever wrote the report first described the "general situation" in Binh Dinh, observing an "increase in American and satellite strength" there, and noting that the communist guerrillas, in addition to their military tasks, "performed civilian labor, evacuated dead and wounded . . ." and so forth, I pushed on to some statistics. These listed the number of guerrilla-militia in the province by type. I copied them down on a separate piece of paper, jotting in Vietnamese terms I'd learned from Co Yung earlier in the year: 3,194 village guerrillas (du kich xa); 11,887 hamlet guerrillas (du kich ap); 719 secret guerrillas (du kich mat); and 34,441 self-defense militiamen (tu ve). I added them up: 50,244.

What? That seemed awfully damn high. I was familiar enough now with the MACV Order of Battle to know that of the 280,000-odd VC it listed, only 100,000 or so were guerrilla-militia. Why should Binh Dinh—one of forty-four provinces—have half of them? The obvious thing to do was to check the OB. I fished my copy (the 31 March edition, which I'd brought back from Vietnam) from my desk drawer, turned to its province listings, and looked up Binh Dinh: 1,446 guerrillas—no breakdown by type—and 3,222 self-defense militia, for a total of 4,668. Dumbfounded, I looked again at the VC total: 50,244. *It was eleven times higher than the OB! Forty-five thousand extra VC in a single province! Good God!!!*

"Molly! Molly!" I shouted. "Look at this!"

"What've you got?" she asked mildly. I vaulted to her desk, slammed down the OB and the bulletin side by side, and with my finger stabbed at the two sets of numbers.

"Holy cow," she said, "MACV sure missed the boat on that one. I wonder if it's true for the rest of the country?"

"Long An!" I cried. Shaking with excitement, I told her about Colonel Anh's local estimate, 2,000, compared to the order-of-battle figure, still 160. "Christ, I've known that for six months," I moaned. "Why didn't I check the OB before?"

"Maybe you better write something up," Molly said. But I was already on my way out the door to the director's special staff on Vietnam on the sixth floor. The person I wanted to see was George Allen, assigned to the staff after his tour in Vietnam had ended a month or two before. I barged into Allen's office, and shoved the bulletin and the OB under his nose.

"Christalmighty!" he exclaimed, adjusting his glasses as if in disbelief. "I knew the OB was screwed up, but I didn't realize it was this bad." It ought to be written up, he said, reminding me that the CIA was about to publish a big study on the war for Secretary of Defense McNamara. I should be sure and get the Binh Dinh document mentioned in the study.

For the rest of the day I galloped around CIA headquarters like Paul Revere, hallooing about Vietcong guerrillas. The reaction was uniform: astonishment, and the realization that this was a terribly important finding that cried for further research. My last visit was to Dean Moor, back from wherever he'd been that morning. He was relatively calm, having been told about the document by Molly. Yes, I should write it up, he said, "but there's no use doing it right away. We couldn't get it out before tomorrow afternoon at the latest—and tomorrow's a Friday. Nobody in Washington ever reads anything on weekends. Have it to me by close-of-business Monday."

At home that evening, I could scarcely eat or sleep, I was so busy thinking about Bulletin 689. Its ramifications were enormous. For obvious starters, it suggested that Vietnam was a much bigger war than we thought it was. Furthermore, there were all kinds of analytical side effects. At this time, all our other intelligence estimates about the VC were tied to the number in MACV's Order of Battle: how much rice the Vietcong ate, how much ammunition they shot off, and so forth. If the OB collapsed, our whole statistical system would go along with it.

My first act on Friday was to check in with Bobby Layton. He gave me a draft of "Will to Persist" so I could jigger around with its morale section. I did so, suggesting that the drain of deserters might not hurt the VC as much as I had originally believed because they had a much bigger army to draw from.[2]

Also I asked Carver if I could highlight the implications of Bulletin 689 in the first part of "Will to Persist"'s summary, since McNamara was more likely to read that than anything else. Carver said no, the study was about to go to print, and besides my findings were only tentative; however, I could stick some caveats about Vietcong guerrillas in the body of the text.[3] This seemed fair enough on such short notice. Layton footnoted the right passages, and I went downstairs to the Indo-China Division.

Molly was waiting there for me with a wad of papers she had squirreled away from previous years. The first was an unpublished memo written by George Allen in October 1963, when George had worked for Ed Hauck. George's memo complained that the guerrilla-militia estimate was too low even back then. The second was a Vietcong document dated 30 November 1965, which claimed they controlled six million people in South Vietnam (about *double* our own estimate for the same date!).[4] This helped explain where the communists recruited the additional soldiers, and was an extraordinary piece of news in its own right. A third was another VC report, this one from COSVN headquarters, which suggested the communists had tried "to increase the guerrilla-militia strength . . . to 250,000–300,000 men" by the end of 1965.[5] This last document gave me a rough idea of the kind of total we were dealing with. It was good to have a lid. In some of my wilder fancies the night before, I had gone much higher.

For the rest of Friday and over the weekend, I tore through my document file. Among the first ones I read applied to Phu Yen, the province on Binh Dinh's southern border.[6] The MACV number for Phu Yen was almost as bad as its number for Binh Dinh.* There were several other

---

*MACV Order of Battle listing for Phu Yen: 916 guerrillas and 2,294 self-defense militia, totaling 3,210. The VC document's: 3,398 guerrillas, and 17,009

provinces with estimates askew. I even came across one, Phuoc Long, where the order of battle was slightly too high.†

The initial draft took shape on early Monday afternoon. As usual, I wrote the text first—carefully referencing the VC documents that had emerged from the files—and then the summary. Its wording was clear, but cautious. It said that enemy reports "strongly suggested" that MACV's guerrilla-militia estimate of some 100,000 was "too low," and that it should "probably be at least doubled." Observing that the higher numbers "would help explain why the southern communists have been able to field an increasingly large regular army despite heavy casualties and a high desertion rate," it suggested dumping the matter in MACV's lap.[7] (I had in mind its Order of Battle section chief, Colonel Hawkins.) Lorrie typed up the draft, and I gave it to Dean Moor, saying: "That phrase 'at least doubled' means it could be a hell of a lot more than double."

"Hold on a sec," he told me. I stood by as he finished editing Tuesday's Sitrep. Ten minutes later, he took up my draft, and (looking bored, I thought) read it. He made a couple of minor changes, and spun it in to his out-box). He said, "The front office'll get it first thing tomorrow morning."

The next day I arrived at work in a fever of suspense. Surely the discovery of "at least" one hundred thousand extra Vietcong would cause a major convulsion. I imagined all kinds of sudden and dramatic telephone calls. "Mr. Adams, come brief the director." "The president's got to be told about this and you'd better be able to defend your paper." I wasn't certain what would happen, but I was sure it would be significant because I knew this was the biggest intelligence find of the war so far. *At least a hundred thousand extra Vietcong.* Surely President Johnson would have to send a lot more soldiers to fight them. I envisaged him calling

---

self-defense militia, totaling 20,407. Thus the VC had 17,197 more people in their home guard in Phu Yen than the OB listed.

† MACV Order of Battle listing for Phuoc Long: 387 guerrillas and 146 self-defense militia, totaling 533. The VC documents' figures: 174 guerrillas, and 141 militia, totaling 315. The OB overshot by 218 men.

the director on the carpet, asking him why this information hadn't been uncovered before.

Nothing happened. No phone calls from anybody. At the end of the day, I approached Dean Moor about the memo. "It's kicking around the front office," he told me. My agitation grew as the scene repeated itself on Wednesday and Thursday. On Friday morning, Lorrie dropped a memo on my desk. It wasn't a carbon but the original, with no comments on it at all—no request for amplification, no questions about evidence, just a routine buckslip attached showing the entire DDI hierarchy had read it.

I boiled into Dean Moor's office. "What the hell's going on here?" I asked. "Don't those people upstairs know what this means?"

He said: "If I were you, I'd make another stab at it. But not today. Remember about weekends. Have it to me close-of-business Monday."

Once again I spent the weekend at CIA headquarters. On the theory that the numbers were covered well enough for the time being, I concentrated on describing exactly who these "guerrillas" and "militiamen" were. After looking at my notes from the Long An Chieu Hoi center, I wrote that guerrillas served in the villages or hamlets, that most carried rifles, and that they often acted as replacements for "regular Vietcong formations." (This last thought stemmed from my recollection of the fast comeback of the VC 506th Battalion after the battle of the Right Testicle.) As for the militia, I wrote, they "dug trenches, burrowed tunnels" and "were expected to defend their hamlets as best they could when the enemy arrived." "This is sometimes hard to do," I explained, "because they are at the bottom of the logistical ladder," and therefore poorly armed. I left intact the memo's opening that the guerrilla-militia strength "should be at least doubled."

New draft in hand, I reported back to Dean Moor, as requested, on late Monday afternoon. This time he took the draft right away, and edited it with a pencil. The first casualty was "at least doubled." He replaced it with the phrase that the guerrilla-militia strength "should probably now be placed at around 200,000 . . ."[8]

"Damnitall, Dean," I said, "how do you know it's around '200,000'? I already told you 'at least' could mean a hell of a lot more than that. If you ask me, it *is* a hell of a lot more than that."

He said: "They didn't accept the first draft. Let's try it this way."

"But that's crazy," I complained. "This isn't a numbers game. There's a war on. These people are shooting at us."

"I want this memo to get out," he replied; "I think it's important." Lorrie typed it with "around 200,000," and the memo winged back to the front office.

By now, I was getting mad. The Sitrep normally made a fuss each time MACV found a new regiment, and here I'd discovered the numerical equivalent of *at least* fourteen VC divisions, and the only mention of it to leave the building so far was in the rear pages of "Will to Persist." My spleen flew mostly at the DDI front office, but also now toward Dean Moor. I might mention here that he was none too popular with the other analysts, most of whom clearly preferred their ex-bosses, Ed Hauck and R. Sams Smith. In fact one such analyst wanted to quit the agency,* and a couple of others were casting about for ways to leave the division.

For the rest of the week, I worked on the numbers. No new documents had come to light, so I constructed a simple equation. It went like this. If there were so many guerrillas and militiamen in the provinces on which we had documents (such as Binh Dinh, Phu Yen, and Phuoc Long), then their strength in the provinces for which we lacked documents must be x. I got some astronomical x's before deciding to shoot for the minimum. That is, I concluded that the Vietcong had reached their minimum goal for 1965 of 250,000 guerrilla-militia.

There were two other events on Friday. One was really a nonevent. It was the nonreturn of my memo by the front office. Which is to say, five

*He did. He was Patrick McGarvey, who later wrote a book about his experiences *CIA: The Myth and the Madness* (New York: Penguin Books, 1973). McGarvey was a classmate of mine at the Farm. He cleared his book, before its publication, with the CIA.

more days had passed without a word from upstairs as to its disposition. The second event was in my eyes more important. An announcement circulated in the Indo-China Division that the following week Dean Moor was going on vacation. That meant my acting boss was Molly.

On Monday I stomped up to the seventh floor to look for my memo. Nobody seemed to know where it was. At length a front office secretary meekly suggested that I ought to check with Elaine Delaney. Elaine Delaney was the workhorse of the production staff, and could generally be depended upon to know where any piece of paper was at a given moment. I asked her about my memo.

"You mean the one that's been driving every one around here nuts?" Elaine Delaney asked.

"I think that's it," I said.

She led me over to a safe, and pulled from it a manila folder marked "Indefinite Hold." Inside the folder was my memo. I took it out and went back downstairs.

I sat down to edit. The first thing to go was the vacationing Dean Moor's "around 200,000." Back came the old wording, "at least doubled." Then, on the supposition that if I had to pull a fast one on the division chief it was dumb to go by halves, toward the end I inserted my real conviction: "It would appear from the foregoing analysis that the Vietcong (guerrilla-militia) strength should be carried at least as high as 250,000. It may, in fact, be even higher." In other words, I upped Dean by 50,000, and gave notice of possible raises to come. Confident in the evidence, I went to Molly for permission to go forward.

"Why not," she said, with an air of amusement. "I'll worry about Dean." (Molly wasn't being disloyal to Dean Moor. She was simply telling me that if there was a rap to be hung over the memo, she'd take it.)

On Tuesday morning I stomped back upstairs, jaw set, and tilted forward, like Ulysses S. Grant entering the Wilderness. My first encounter was with the Asia-Africa area chief, Waldo Duberstein. Normally affable, Waldo had big ears sticking straight out from a billiard ball head, and a booming voice. He boomed: "It's that goddamn memo again. Adams, stop being such a prima donna." In the next office, an official said that the order of battle was General Westmoreland's concern, and we had no business intruding. This set me off. "We're all in the same government," I said, "if there's a discrepancy this big, it doesn't matter who points it out. We're at war." Altogether I made a half dozen stops. The DDI chief, R. Jack Smith, was too busy to see me.

On Thursday, 8 September 1966, eighteen days after I'd written the first draft, the DDI agreed to let a version of it out of the building.[9] Elaine Delaney called me to the seventh floor to explain some peculiar restrictions. It was to be called a Draft Working Paper, meaning that it lacked official status; it was issued in only twenty-five copies, instead of the usual run of over two hundred; it could go to "working-level types" only—analysts and staff people—but not to anyone in a policy-making position (to no one, for example, on the National Security Council) and only one copy could go to Saigon, care of the MACV Order of Battle Section. At this last restriction, I breathed a sigh of relief. Colonel Hawkins would get it. The official selected to carry the memo to Saigon was George Fowler who worked for the Defense Intelligence Agency at the Pentagon.

If on Tuesday morning I had resembled General Grant entering the fray, by Thursday afternoon, I felt worked over by Lee's lieutenants. The next morning I asked Molly for a vacation to recuperate. "You deserve one," she said.

My wife Eleanor, my son Clayton, and I went to West Tisbury on the island of Martha's Vineyard, where we were able to rent a house at the last minute. For two weeks I paced the sands, pondering the order of battle. I returned to Langley on Monday, 26 September and asked Dean Moor, also back from vacation, if I could write a major paper on the guerrilla-militia. He said OK. If he was mad at me for changing the strength memo behind his back, he didn't say so.

I had more good news a couple of days later. A Lieutenant Colonel Robert Montague, military aide to a Mr. Komer of the White House, had seen Bobby Layton's cautionary footnotes about more guerrillas in

"Will to Persist" and had called George Carver asking what they were all about. Carver sent Montague a copy of my strength paper, explaining that the DIA courier George Fowler was already back from Saigon with the message that MACV had started a top-to-bottom review of all its order-of-battle holdings, including those for the guerrilla-militia. This meant not only that Colonel Hawkins was in gear, but that at last the White House had a copy of my paper. I made a mental note that it was George Carver who had sent the memo to the White House, *not* anyone from the DDI front office.

Straightaway I laid into the Vietcong home guard. Determined to find everything available about it, I screened the CIA archives, and even went down to the Washington office of the Rand Corporation on Connecticut Avenue to reread Rand's stock of interviews with the VC. However, my first big step forward came from an article in the rear pages of the 7 October edition of the *New York Times*.[10] It compared American casualties in World War II with those in Vietnam. In the former conflict most GIs had fallen to shards from artillery shells, and very few to grenades, mines, and booby traps. In the latter, artillery wounds were much rarer, while those from grenades, mines, and booby traps were commonplace.*

Right away I thought of my trip with Doctor Lowe through Tan An's hospital, and its many patients with feet blown off or legs missing. Asked about them, the doctor had replied: "Land mines. The whole goshdarn province is seeded with land mines. Those and booby traps." Then I recalled Co Yung's research into the Chieu Hoi dossiers. They had told her that among the militia's main duties was to lay mines and booby traps. My own notes showed most militiamen carried a couple of grenades. I put two and two together. They came to this: despite its lack of sophisticated weapons, the self-defense caused many of our casualties.

---

*U.S. casualties by "causative agent" as taken from the *New York Times* article:

	World War II	Vietnam
artillery	61%	19%
grenades	2%	16%
mines/booby traps	3%	21%

Casualties from small arms and other causes are omitted.

So far, so good. What I needed now was someone who could tell me about mines. No one in 5G44 had served with the military in Vietnam but I remembered somebody who had. He was in George Carver's office, a Special Forces major named Donald Blascik. I went to the sixth floor to talk to Major Blascik. In Vietnam he had run an outfit of South Vietnamese irregulars in the Delta. He was about six feet tall, had a close crew cut, and smoked a pipe.

He said: "Don't talk to me about booby traps. That was the story of my life down there. They were all over the place, in all shapes and sizes. For instance, the Malayan gate—a bent sapling with a spike that could skewer you if you sprung it; punji sticks—sharpened bamboo sticks tempered with fire and smeared with cow dung to give you an infection; grenades with trip wires, spike traps, and so on. Mines and booby traps caused half my casualties near the Cai Cai River." I asked Major Blascik what effect they had on his operations.

He replied: "We call it the 'pucker factor.' The 'pucker factor' means you spend most of your time on tiptoes, trying not to step on mines. Believe me it's difficult to do your job well—pursuing the foe and such-like—if you always have to watch your feet."[11] I asked him whether some mines were worse than others.

He said: "That's a hard one to answer. They're all bad. Let me tell you about the 'toe-popper.' The toe-popper is a fifty-caliber machine-gun shell filled with gunpowder and rusty nails with a primitive priming device sticking out of the top. It won't kill you, it'll mangle your foot, enough to take you out of the war. A lot of my men were setting off toe-poppers, so I decided to do something about it. I put out the word that I'd pay fifty piasters [official rate 118 to the dollar, black market somewhat higher] apiece for them. The first couple of days I got only a few; then people saw I was serious, I was actually laying out the money. From then on the toe-poppers arrived by the basketload. There were so many they became a storage problem. Finally I took one of the later ones apart. It was filled with sand. Subsequently I found out that when the VC discovered toe-poppers were worth fifty p's each, their finance section set up a cottage industry to make them for me. Dozens of little old ladies pouring spoonfuls of sand into machine-gun shells for my personal benefit. I hate to think how much money I spent for those dud toe-poppers."

My research into Allied wounds ended at Marine Corps headquarters, at the Naval Annex to the Pentagon. An old gunnery sergeant just back form Vietnam told me: "How you lose your personnel depends on your location. Up on the DMZ [the Demilitarized Zone, bordering North Vietnam], why it's like it was in the Pacific. Nobody lives there, you're fighting regulars, so you don't lose many men to mines and booby traps. But in populated areas, Danang for instance, you're up against the ankle-biters. Mines are their main weapon, and that's what chews us up. Hold on a minute. I got figures to prove it." He showed me an official Marine Corps report for June 1966.[12] The report indicated that most Leatherneck casualties occurred around Danang, and that 60 percent of them came from mines and booby traps. Two and two still made four. The guerrillas and militiamen (the gunnery sergeant's so-called ankle-biters) were doing us a lot of harm.

Meanwhile my estimate for the Vietcong home guard continued to grow. Since the only other CIA man who knew anything about it was George Allen, I asked his opinion. He said: "More than two hundred fifty thousand? It wouldn't surprise me a bit. MACV's been jacking around that number for almost four years." I asked George what he meant.

"For all practical purposes, the order of battle started up in February 1962," he told me. "That's when an Army lieutenant colonel named Bill Benedict and I went to Saigon to help come up with the numbers. The one we arrived at for the guerrilla-militia was just over one hundred thousand. It was based on good evidence, too, a document from Nam Bo (the VC term for the "Southern Department," or southern half of South Vietnam), and our figure was accepted. Well, Bill and I came home in March, and by November, America was officially winning the war. The trouble with the OB began early the next year. The head of MACV intelligence, the J-2, went in to Westy's predecessor, General

Harkins, and said 'General, we've been finding a lot more VC regulars in the form of regiments and battalions, and we're going to have to raise the order of battle.' Harkins said 'Godammit, you can't do that; we've been killing the bastards right and left. We should lower the OB, not raise it.' They settled on a compromise. The J-2 got his extra regulars. Harkins got a lower OB. They did it by deducting guerrillas as they added battalions. This happened twice—once in early 1963 and once again later in the year. By October, the guerrilla-militia were down to seventy thousand. In my view, they were growing as fast as the VC regular army."[13]

"How did MACV get away with it?" I asked.

He said: "Because we couldn't prove otherwise. Our last document was the one from Nam Bo, and it was dated 1961. Ironically, the hero of the story is Westmoreland. The first thing he did when he took over from Harkins in '64 was kick the number back up to one hundred thousand. Obviously he didn't kick it far enough, nobody's looked at it ever since, and now Westy's in the same bind as Harkins, only worse. But there's a big difference between then and now. Now we have documents coming out of our ears." At about this point Don Blascik dropped by George's office to tell me he was about to visit Saigon. Was there anything I wanted? "See how Colonel Hawkins is coming along," I said.

The first clue to Hawkins' progress hit my desk about a week later—Monday, 7 November. It wasn't from Blascik (who had reached Saigon), but from MACV's advisory detachment in Quang Tin Province, the one south of Danang. Apparently on receiving my strength memo from George Fowler, the colonel had sent a flier to all forty-four provinces asking for their estimate of the VC home guard. Quang Tin's was the first response. The response was detailed, breaking out the guerrilla-militia both by district and by type. I added up the numbers: 17,027.[14] Then I looked at the OB for Quang Tin: 1,760—one-tenth the local estimate!

"The genie's out of the bottle," Molly said; "You better tell the front office." I wrote a short paper, for the first time speculating—on the strength of what George Allen had told me about the strength manipulations in 1963—that General Westmoreland might try "to prevent a mass influx of new bodies" from entering the lists. One way to do it, I said, was to drop the self-defense militia from the order of battle. This was inadvisable, I warned, since the militia's main job was to sow mines, which caused a fifth of our casualties.[15] Dean Moor sent the paper to the seventh floor without change, and a short while later it returned with a buckslip showing that everyone upstairs had read it. Again there were no substantive comments. I was getting madder.

Two days later Don Blascik chimed in from Saigon. According to his cable, he hadn't seen Hawkins, who was away, but he had talked to Hawkins' deputy, a Lieutenant Colonel Clark. Clark had said that the OB Branch had sent a team around the provinces to see what was known about the guerrilla-militia. The answer was not much. (Quang Tin being an exception.) Most provinces didn't even know what the home guard was, and furthermore, they were not getting from Saigon the VC captured documents that might have told them. Clark said that Hawkins had also asked each of South Vietnam's four corps headquarters to come up with a "fast-and-dirty estimate" of guerrilla-militia. Blascik described their answers: "IV Corps caveated its report with the statement that its estimate was not even a speculative guess. II Corps reluctantly gave a figure five times higher than the existing II Corps . . . estimate. [The Marines] refused to reply. Other results were not in. At this juncture and after great inward reflection, Clark indicated that the CIA estimate of at least 250,000 'probably represented a low figure.'"[16] I ran over to Molly to show her Blascik's cable.

I slammed in to Dean Moor's office to berate him about "back burners." He told me to calm down, official Washington was becoming aware of the problem (no thanks to the DDI, I thought), and the way I could help most was to finish my big study on the home guard.

Angrier than ever, I returned to work. By now I had gathered some two thousand reports—VC documents, POW and defector interviews, and so forth. My main problem was sorting them out. The Vietcong organization had begun to emerge as a vast bureaucracy with elaborate chains of command, categories, and subcategories that had to be kept apart. I split the organization into two pieces, assigning each one its own safe drawer. One drawer was for the home guard, the second was for everything that wasn't. The second drawer contained dozens of manila folders with such labels as "Ordnance," "Quartermasters," "Assault Youths," "Armed Public Security Forces," "Couriers," and "Sappers." The home guard drawer had folders for each kind of guerrilla and militiamen. Most folder labels came from my notes from the Long An Chieu Hoi center. They were in both English and Vietnamese: "Village Guerrillas—Du Kich Xa"; "Hamlet Guerrillas—Du Kich Ap"; "Secret Guerrillas—Du Kich Mat"; "Self-Defense—Tu Ve"; and "Secret Self-Defense—Tu Ve Mat." The lines between different types of Vietcong were often blurred, and I found myself continually shifting reports from one folder to another.

In mid-November, Lorrie brought me our latest official estimate for the VC. It wasn't the MACV Order of Battle (which the CIA still didn't get) but a page-long précis issued by the DDI Watch. I glanced it over to see if MACV had added any guerrillas and militiamen. I noted with disgust that it hadn't. Then I glanced at the other numbers, this time jotting them down. They were:

Regulars	108,585
Service troops	17,553
Guerrilla-militia	103,573
Political cadres	39,175
Total	268,886

Somehow they looked familiar: not just the guerrilla-militia, but one or two of the others. Well, it was easy enough to check. I pulled out my copy of MACV's Order of Battle—still dated 31 March 1966, and still (as far as I knew) the agency's sole copy. I turned to the OB's summary, and compared the old numbers there with the new ones from the DDI Watch. This is what I found. The "regulars" had increased by about

30,000. (*Fine,* I thought.) The "service troops" had gone up by some 600. (*Not much of a change,* I thought.) And the "political cadres" were *exactly* the same for November as they had been in March. I ticked off the months that had passed on my fingers: seven. A cartoonist would have drawn a light bulb igniting over my head. I asked myself: Could it be that the political cadres are in the same boat as the guerrilla-militia? I answered: *Yes.*

I beat a path to Molly. She laughed: "This is getting repetitive." I went to the sixth floor to find out from George Allen who the political cadres were.

He said: "They're party members, armed police, and people like that. It's what we call the 'infrastructure.' They're the center of the VC organization; they run the thing, including the army. As for that number, '39,175,' it comes from a study the South Vietnamese army did in mid-1965. It was a lousy estimate back then: it's probably even worse now."

"What about the 'service troops,'" I asked.

"Medics, quartermasters, engineers, the same as in our own military," he said. "Where the OB got its number for them I couldn't tell you, but it's been around for a long, long time. I think it's safe to assume that no one's looked at it for at least two years."

I said: "It looks to me like the entire order of battle is worthless."

"Except maybe the regulars," he corrected. And he confided in me some of the details of his earlier career. He told me that he had started on Vietnam as a civilian in the Pentagon in 1951, that he watched the Vietminh grow steadily until the collapse of the French in 1954, and that he had followed Indo-China more or less steadily ever since. "We've fallen gradually into the same pattern of mistakes as the French," he told me. "They didn't begin by faking intelligence; they merely assumed success in the absence of clear proof of failure. We've been doing that for some time. Take that example I gave you about General Harkins deducting guerrillas from the OB, because, as he put it, 'we've been killing the bastards right and left.' He wasn't really lying. But since there was no document around which showed that guerrillas should be added to the estimate, he felt it was OK to subtract them. The danger in that kind of thinking is that it's only a short step to outright fabrication. It's a frame of mind that drove me to quit the Pentagon for the CIA. That was July 1963. I took a pay cut to come here, but I have no regrets at all. The agency's pretty square. And here in Carver's office, we work for the director, and the chances are good that if we have something to say with reasonable evidence to back it up, it'll leave the building."[17]

George went on like this for almost fifteen minutes before I asked him for a job. He said that he'd be happy to take me on, but that first he'd have to check with Carver. They'd let me know in a week or two. I went downstairs feeling a good deal better than when I'd come up.

There was still plenty to do in Room 5G44. And since the political cadres looked too complex to tackle right away, I decided to zero in on service troops. Question A was where the OB number had come from. But despite repeated phone calls to U.S. Army headquarters, to the office of the Joint Chiefs of Staff, and to DIA, I couldn't find anyone who knew. Shortly I gave up the search, and commenced going through my own files, especially the ones in my Non–Home Guard drawer. Within two weeks I had concluded that a more realistic estimate of service troops was in the neighborhood of 100,000, or about six times higher than the OB's. It was no more than a semi-educated guess, but I felt it was conservative, since it stemmed from the theory that the Vietcong needed only one service soldier for each regular combatant. Our own army—admittedly far more sophisticated than the VC's—had *six* service troops for every one who carried a gun.

As I was putting my findings on paper on Thursday, 1 December, Lorrie interrupted me with the morning mail. One of its reports brought me up short. It was about my old stamping ground, Long An Province, and was apparently responding to Colonel Hawkins' request for a local estimate of guerrilla-militia. I recalled that the province chief, Colonel Anh, had told me there were "two thousand," and sure enough, the report came up with virtually the same number.[18] Then I looked at the fine print. The two thousand were all *village* guerrillas; the report omitted entirely hamlet guerrillas and self-defense militiamen. Well, in every province I'd looked at so far (for example, Binh Dinh) the two latter categories had way outnumbered the former. Therefore two thousand was only a fraction of Long An's real number, and Colonel Anh—whether he had realized it or not—had been talking through his hat. I stuck a codicil on my service memo noting the OB number for Long An's home guard, 160, was probably out of whack by several thousand percent.* Lorrie typed it all up, and I gave it to Dean Moor. Leaving intact the service soldier part, he crossed out the codicil.

He said: "The front office already knows the guerrilla-militia estimate is suspect. No need to rub their noses in it. Besides you oughtn't to bother them with all these details."

"Details!" I exploded. "Maybe if we'd paid more attention to details, we wouldn't be in such a god-awful mess."

Just then Lorrie poked her head in the door to hand me a message. It was from the front office. Richard Lehman wanted to discuss my application for a job with George Carver. I was to go right away. I excused myself from Dean Moor, and stormed up to the seventh floor, muttering to myself about nonattention to details.

Mr. Lehman was rocking back and forth in his leather swivel chair, his hands in a praying position, just like the time I'd seen him about changing jobs from the Congo to Vietnam. He said: "What's this I hear about you wanting to leave the Indo-China Division?"

"I want to work for George Carver, sir," I replied pointedly. "He listens to details. Furthermore, he seems to be having more success than the DDI is in getting the message out about the size of the VC army."

He said: "George Carver is an upstart."

---

*The U.S. Ninth Division later captured a Vietcong report that gave the size of the Long An home guard in 1966. The report listed 1,321 village guerrillas, 2,029 hamlet guerrillas, 198 secret guerrillas, and 3,363 self-defense militiamen for a total of 6,911. You will recall the equivalent numbers in the MACV Order of Battle were 100 guerrillas and 60 militiamen for a total of 160. You may also remember my puzzlement in Long An on 9 February on noting that almost as many guerrilla-militia had defected as were in the official estimate. (See Chapter 3) Obviously my confusion stemmed from the fact that the MACV Order of Battle listing for the province home guard was forty-three times too low.[19]

It was an odd beginning to our half-hour long conversation. The only time I'd heard "upstart" was in an old English movie, and Lehman had aroused my curiosity. I asked him: "Why is Mr. Carver an upstart?"

Lehman was discursive. From what I could gather, Carver had stolen the editorship of McNamara's "Will to Persist" from under the DDI's nose, and that since then he had sent numerous memos about Vietnam to the White House without so much as a by-your-leave. "The CIA ought not to speak with two voices," said Mr. Lehman. I also got the impression that the DDI was annoyed at Carver for having commandeered George Allen, the agency's foremost expert on the Vietcong. Finally Lehman asked me: "Now really, Sam, why do you want to go?"

Feeling slightly unreal—and that I wasn't answering his question—I made the following points: that the Vietnam War was probably more than twice as big as American intelligence said it was; that our estimates of enemy logistics, recruitment, and population control were almost certainly dead wrong; that the Sitrep, which was the DDI's main publication on the war, inadequately covered the Vietcong; that the best source on the VC, captured documents, were almost entirely neglected; that as far as I could tell I was the only analyst in Washington who worked on our southern enemies full time; and that worst of all, the MACV Order of Battle—the bedrock estimate on which all other estimates depended—was still unchanged despite a growing pile of evidence that it ought to be much higher.[20]

"Sam," said Lehman with a kind voice, "we're now aware of the problems with the order of battle, and we're grateful to you for pointing them out. But you're asking too much in too short a period of time. The change you want is enormous. You've got to allow the government machinery enough time to absorb it."

"It's had three months, sir," I said.

"Deserting the Indo-China Division won't help your career," he said, still with a kind voice.

"I want to go to Carver's," I replied.

Lehman told me that the head of the DDI, R. Jack Smith, had said I could go if I insisted, but only under certain conditions. The main one

was that anything I wrote for Carver would have to have a DDI impri-
matur. He repeated: "The agency ought not to speak with two voices."

"With all respect, sir," I said, "it's high time that it did." And I went
below to see my prospective boss, George Carver.

Carver was lounging behind his polished wooden desk on the sixth
floor, hair disheveled like an English don's. In fact he had attended
Oxford as a Rhodes Scholar, and had written there a dissertation on
Thomas Hobbes. A copy of the dissertation was in a nearby bookcase. I
asked him about Mr. Smith's demand that my papers appear under the
DDI label.

He said: "Don't worry about R. Jack. His nose has been out of joint
ever since 'Will to Persist.' Here you work for the director." I was to start
after the first of the year, he told me. The director, of course, was
Richard Helms, of whom I highly approved, recalling the sensible way
he had acted during the Congo rebellion. Helms's office was on the seventh floor.

Freedom imminent, I finished up several memos for the Indo-China
Division. On the following day, 2 December, the service-troop paper
went upstairs, minus the Long An codicil.[21] A few days later, I sent up
my latest guess on the number of VC.[22] It was 600,000,* or more than
double the order of battle. To make sure the military knew what was
going on, I cabled the Saigon Station, telling it to "alert the appropriate
MACV officials, particularly Colonel Hawkins."[23]

My swan song with the Indo-China Division was the home-guard
study. When I gave it to Dean Moor, it was some sixty pages long, with
a hundred or so footnotes—the most detailed paper about the Vietcong
written to that date. One of its features was a map that used VC
province names and VC province boundaries, often markedly different
from those of the Saigon government's. (In part, because there were
then only thirty-eight VC provinces, in contrast to Saigon's forty-four.)

---

*The 600,000 was broken down as follows: Regulars, about 100,000; guerrilla-
militia, about 300,000; service troops, about 100,000; political cadres, about
100,000.

It was the first time an agency paper had ever used a VC map, and to me it symbolized everything that was wrong with the DDI's approach to the war. As I had complained three weeks before to Mr. Lehman, our best source in those days was captured documents, which of course employed VC names. But since the DDI seldom used enemy documents, it felt no need for an enemy map. A cartographer who helped me on the map said: "It looks like we want them to fight the war our way, not theirs."[24]

The last days of December went quietly. The front office sent back my "Service Troop" and "600,000" papers without comment or request for amplification. My home-guard study went below to be looked at by somebody downstairs. And a Collation Branch analyst named John T. Moore—back from Vietnam on midtour vacation—stopped by to tell me that he'd also written a guerrilla paper in Saigon, but that it had been "suppressed."[25] The year-end MACV Order of Battle arrived on schedule. Except for the "regulars," its numbers were unchanged.[26]

New Year's came and went, and on Tuesday, 3 January 1967, I moved— together with my files—from Room 5G44 on the fifth floor to Room 6F19 on the sixth. Room 6F19 was Carver's. It wasn't a single room, as the name implied, but a row of them, connected by a long carpeted corridor where the secretaries sat. I had one room all to myself, overlooking some trees, and I shared a secretary with only two other people. Her name was Theresa Wilson, a tall girl from Texas with beautiful eyes. My first problem was finding room for my files. It had taken three trips with a shopping cart to bring them from Indo-China. Theresa solved the problem in short order by ordering a brand new safe. This was first indication of the advantages of working on the director's staff.

More indications followed. Carver gave me about four papers to write, all for recipients either in the White House or on McNamara's staff. The subjects were unimposing (such as the "Percentage of Allied Wounded Returned to Duty in Vietnam") but I felt that at least the papers would be read. Then on my own hook I arranged to brief the Board of National Estimates on the VC home guard. On the strength of the briefing, the board issued a paper, drafted by Bobby Layton, suggesting the number of guerrilla-militia was "250,000 to 300,000."[27] This was the first time the number had appeared under the official agency eagle, and since the board was independent, there was nothing the DDI could do about it.

By the end of the first week, I knew I was sitting in the catbird seat.[28] I thought: *Why not exercise my new-found power?* So on Tuesday, 10 January, I drafted a decree. Entitled "Revising the Vietcong Order of Battle," it ordered the DDI "to take on the task of researching with all deliberate speed the neglected areas of the OB." These of course included the service troops and political cadres, including such types as "armed public security forces," the subject of one of my manila folders. I also gave my opinion that MACV's strength estimate (the whole thing, not just the guerrilla-militia) "should be at least doubled." The reason for this, I pointed out, was to allow American intelligence to make "a better informed appraisal of what we're up against."[29] Theresa typed up my fiat, and on Wednesday morning I went into Carver's office—a big one with many windows at the end of the corridor—to persuade him to put his signature on it.

He read it and said: "I'd love to see R. Jack Smith's face when this lands on his desk. Well, it's a fine memo, long overdue I might add, but it has a flaw."

"What's that?" I asked.

"The phrase 'what we're up against.' In formal prose, never, *never* elide. 'We *are*' is correct here. Not much of a flaw. Have you ever read James Thurber's *Thirteen Clocks?*"

"Yes, sir," I said tentatively.

"In that case, you'll remember the evil duke. 'We all have flaws,' said the duke; 'Mine is being wicked.'" Having made his single correction, Carver signed the order in the director's name, and shortly thereafter, it went by messenger to Mr. Smith's office on the seventh floor.

I was euphoric. My problems were virtually over. Victors are supposed to be magnanimous, but I couldn't help myself. That evening I went to see a friend of mine in Smith's office to find out what the reaction had been. The friend was Jack Ives, one-time analyst on Laos, who had fled Dean Moor to become spear-holder in the DDI front office. Ives said: "Cheezil, they've been mad as hornets up here all day. One week out of the DDI and already you're sending us directives. Smith's gone absolutely berserk." Just then another spear holder shoved his head in the door. He said: "So it's you, Adams, you damn son of a bitch, come to gloat. I hope you're satisfied."

Two days later I felt the time had come to jar loose my home-guard study from whatever pigeon hole the DDI had stuck it in. I composed a note to Carver suggesting he take it away from R. Jack Smith and publish it in the name of the director. The note said: "Haste makes waste and all that, but I suggest we proceed as rapidly as possible. Maybe we can scoop the *Times*. In any case, it would be a good memo to get out before MACV starts an elaborate shell game to hide its enormous goof." I apologized for the home-guard memo's numerous footnotes, but said they were necessary to lend it an "air of authority."[30]

When Carver got my note, he called me into his office. He was laughing. "I agree we ought to get your paper out," he said, "but let's hold on for a bit. Smith's still in a lather over that last missive, and he needs time to cool down. Meanwhile I want you to know that the logjam on strength estimates is about to break. I think you'll be getting good news in the not-too-distant future."

Carver was right. On Friday, 20 January, a day-old memo arrived in the office from the Pentagon. Its author was General Earl G. Wheeler, chairman of the Joint Chiefs of Staff, and second only to President Johnson in the military chain of command. Obviously Wheeler had read (among other things) the Board of National Estimates paper mentioning "250,000–300,000" guerrilla-militia. He said in his memo: "I am becoming increasingly concerned over the contradictory OB ... statistics which are contained in the numerous documents currently being circulated throughout Washington. Recently there have been specific queries by members of Congress, White House representatives, and others calling attention to these discrepancies . . . in view of the forth-coming congressional hearings, these matters must be resolved on an urgent basis."[31] I showed the memo to Carver.

"I've already seen it," he said, "and I think you deserve most of the credit for getting the ball rolling. Furthermore, I want you to stay with it. Wheeler's calling an order-of-battle conference in Honolulu early next month to sort out the numbers. It's going to be a full-dress affair, with CIA, DIA, MACV, and everybody attending. I want you to go as my personal representative."

Feeling slightly awed with myself, I went to George Allen to consult with him about the trip. I told him that in view of what he'd told me about MACV's shenanigans with the numbers back in 1963, my main worry was that Westmoreland might try a repeat performance.

"I wouldn't put it past him," George said. "but if I were you, I'd keep an open mind. Westy's chief of intelligence is Major General Joe McChristian, the best J-2 that MACV's ever had. And McChristian's Order of Battle head is still Gains Hawkins. I told you before, Gains is a good man. He's a country boy from Mississippi, and bone honest. You know the old saying: 'You can take the boy out of the country, but you can't take the country out of the boy.'"*

Toward the end of January, I received horrendous news. Although I was still Carver's "personal representative," the head of the CIA delega-tion would be Dean Moor. In a high state of agitation, I burst into George Allen's office to tell him. He groaned. "I might have known the DDI'd pull a fast one. Damnation, I should have taken the job myself, but now I'm busy with something else. Dean doesn't know squat about the OB, and if MACV cares to, they can wrap him around their little finger. This makes your job all the more important. You've got to keep them honest."

"But George, I'm an eleven," I said (meaning my government pay grade was GS-11, the rough equivalent to captain). "Moor's a fourteen. He'll be my boss."

---

*Allen's exact wording. It predated the Salem cigarette ad.

"I know, I know," he said dejectedly. "Do your best."

The order-of-battle conference gathered shortly before its scheduled opening of 8:30 on the morning of Monday, 6 February, in a theaterlike auditorium at Camp Smith, a military base overlooking Pearl Harbor, not far from Honolulu. There was the normal hubbub of people finding their seats and greeting old acquaintances, until, from a side door, a major general entered the room. There was a hush. It was Joseph A. McChristian, the so-called MACV J-2, head of American military intelligence in Vietnam, and obviously the star of the show. He had close-cropped hair over a roundish face, a chestful of ribbons, and a pair of blue eyes that looked as though they could drill holes through a wall. He took his seat at the center of a long curved table that dominated the room. Dean Moor plopped down to his left. I found a place four or five seats down from Dean. Colonel Gains Hawkins sat to McChristian's right. I caught the colonel's eye. He smiled and waved.

At precisely 8:30 A.M. the meeting came to order. General Grover Brown—chief of intelligence at CINCPAC (Commander in Chief, Pacific, headed by Admiral Sharp, nominally Westmoreland's superior) made some opening remarks. Another General Brown seconded the first one's. A certain Major Williams from DIA made a plea for "better understanding." Then it was McChristian's turn. As he rose the clock stood at 8:55 A.M.

McChristian said roughly the following: "Gentlemen, I heard some loose remarks earlier in the day that we are here assembled to arrive at a new number for the order of battle. I would like to use this opportunity to inform anyone who harbors this notion to drop it, and to drop it *at once*. The Vietcong order of battle is MACV's business, which is to say, *my* business. *Don't tread on me.*" He glared around the room to spot potential treaders. I had already sunk down in my chair, thinking: "*Here we go.*"

He continued: "In the last few months, certain individuals in certain organizations have raised questions about three of the four categories of the MACV order of battle." (I sunk further into my seat.) "Colonel Hawkins of my OB Branch has made a preliminary investigation into these categories. This investigation shows that each of them will need drastic upward revision." (I sat up.)

Publisher's note: Here ends Adams's finished text for this chapter. What follows is his précis for the remainder, after which Adams's narrative continues as before. This is the only section of Adams's book left in an incomplete form.

The balance of this chapter includes my conversations with Colonel Hawkins, whom I found both knowledgeable and candid. We discussed at length the various documents, including Bulletin 689, on which the "upward revisions" were likely to be based. Thus reassured, I returned to Langley. There, George Allen told me that the conference was a "sellout." Dumbfounded, I asked why. He showed me a copy of the conference report, signed by General McChristian and by Dean Moor, the first time I'd seen it. The report assigned the MACV the sole custodianship of the numbers. George said: "Now Westy can do any damn thing with them that he wants." MACV's end-of-February strength report came in with the VC numbers unchanged, except for the regulars.

The chapter goes on to describe my third trip to Vietnam. The trip's purpose was to investigate the VC's Armed Public Security Forces (their secret police), on whom I already had a thick file. In Vietnam, I traveled around the provinces to interview Vietcong prisoners. I also checked in at the MACV's Order of Battle Section. Hawkins was away, and I could find no sign that MACV intended to revise the numbers. I headed back to CIA headquarters determined to push once again for a higher estimate.

On my return, I discovered that the agency was putting together another big paper for McNamara, this one nicknamed McNamara II. With Carver's permission I inserted in the text all my higher numbers. A copy of the McNamara II went to Westmoreland. He fired back a cable saying: "The CIA has no business challenging our order of battle; it has violated the agreement made at Honolulu." On receipt of the MACV cable, the agency rallied behind the higher strength estimate. It sent a telegram to Westmoreland that said in effect: "It's time to tell the truth."

The cable's author was none other than Dean Moor. On 12 June 1967, Bobby Layton wrote the first draft of "National Intelligence Estimate Fourteen Three"—the annual forecast on Indo-China. Layton's draft used the higher numbers. Since all parts of American intelligence were expected to sign off on Fourteen Three before its issue, the numbers dispute had therefore come to a head, with MACV on one side, and CIA on the other. The first session of Fourteen Three was scheduled for 23 June.

5 FOURTEEN THREE

THE CHIEF HUN opposing the upward revision of the OB turned out to be George Fowler. A gray-haired, heavyset, chain-smoker of Chesterfields, Fowler was the Pentagon factotum who had carried my guerrilla-militia memo to Saigon when the CIA had first published it in September 1966. His battle cry was "Harrumph."

He had arrived with thirty or forty other intelligence people at just before 10:00 A.M. on 23 June 1967 at the Board of National Estimates' seventh-floor conference room, to attend the first session of Fourteen Three.* Windowless, furnished with leather chairs and maps, the room had a large conference table with Bobby Layton, the estimate's drafter, at one end, and General Collins, Fourteen Three's chairman, at the other. The rest—from the State Department, the Defense Intelligence Agency (namely, Fowler), the three services, the National Security Agency, and the CIA—arranged themselves either at the table or along the walls. I sat next to a wall. A board member since his retirement from the Army, General Collins—stocky, bullnecked, with flared eyebrows—opened the proceedings:

"Gentlemen, as you all know, the guts of this year's Fourteen Three is the numbers game, so we might as well face up to it before we do

---

* Fourteen Three's official title was "Special National Intelligence Estimate Number 14.3–67," or, "Capabilities for the Vietnamese Communists For Fighting in South Vietnam"; "14.3" was Indo-China's serial number, "67" the year.

anything else. I want all positions put clearly, so there'll be no misunderstandings. George, you look like you've got ants in your pants, why don't you lead off?" The general was addressing George Fowler.

Fowler said: "Harrumph! DIA cannot agree to this estimate as currently written. What we object to is the numbers. We feel we should continue with the official order of battle." And he read off the OB's four components. As usual, the first one, the regulars, was somewhat higher than a month earlier but the other three—the service troops, the guerrilla-militia, and the political cadres—were the same as ever. When Fowler announced their total, now 296,000, Collins turned to Layton: "Ok, Bobby, it's your turn. Do it succinctly and without vituperation."

Layton said: "The notion that we should use numbers just because they're 'official' simply won't wash. I would like to remind everybody, in case they need reminding, that what we're here for is to decide which numbers *are* official—the ones in MACV's order of battle, which in three of four cases are several years old, or those in the draft, which are based on evidence, some good, some not so good. The nub of the question is *evidence*." And Layton ticked off the draft's four components, the same ones as Fowler's, but three of them much larger. Layton's total came to well over 500,000. Collins scribbled on a pad of paper, and said:

"If my math's correct, you gentlemen are close to a quarter of million apart. That's a heap of folks. George, the ball's in your court. What's wrong with Bobby's numbers?"

The only thing *right* with Layton's numbers, Fowler declared, was the regulars. There the estimate agreed with the OB. However, the draft's service-troop figure is a "wild guess"; its guerrilla-militia number came from a speech by Nguyen Chi Thanh which was "pure propaganda"; and the political cadres were based on "extrapolations from documents." Layton answered Fowler point by point, always admitting where the evidence was weak, but also asking where DIA's component had come from. The response was unvaried: "The OB, harrumph, it's official." An hour and a half later, the onlookers were glassy-eyed, and General Collins interrupted:

"That's enough, George, you've made your point, but Bobby's right. We can't insert numbers in the estimate just because they're official." Collins paused. "Now gentlemen, it seems to me that we have two alternatives. Bearing in mind that counting enemy soldiers is normally a military prerogative, our first alternative is to put the OB numbers in the estimate, but with caveats that they're way too low, and MACV's trying to come up with something better. The second is to use our own numbers, or rather Bobby's—a 'best estimate,' so to speak. I want a round-robin on the choices. OK, what'll it be? The best estimate or the order of battle? George, I'll begin with you. I know what you're going to say, but say it anyway."

Fowler obliged: "The OB."

"Navy?" Collins asked.

"Pass. At last report the VC were still ashore. When they put to sea, the Navy'll count 'em."

"Air Force?"

"Also pass. Same line of reasoning as my colleague in blue."

"Army?"

"Frankly, general, I'd as soon not get involved, but I guess I have to go with the OB."

"NSA? Where do the code-breakers stand?"

"As you know, sir, the National Security Agency doesn't take positions on how to interpret evidence.* We have observed, however, that the communications net serving the communist army has increased severalfold in the last three years. Perhaps this bears on the problem."

"You're damn right it bears on the problem," said Collins. "State Department, what about the diplomats?"

"Best estimate."

Collins then polled a half-dozen CIA-ers, myself included, who all said: "Best estimate."[1]

---

*In theory, NSA is a "collection agency," meaning that it is supposed to "collect" foreign messages rather than analyze what they mean. In practice, it does some of the best analysis in the business, and is all-too-often disregarded.

The meeting broke for lunch, and I went down to the sixth floor to tell Carver about George Fowler's astonishing performance.

Carver laughed. "Don't pay mind to that old curmudgeon. He'll repeat any whopper the Pentagon gives him and do it with a straight face. He's DIA's permanent fixture at the board meetings, but fortunately, he's predictable.[2] It's the unpredictable ones who make all the trouble. Now look, on VC strength, it's time to bite the bullet. You go back up there and do the best you can."

Three more sessions of Fourteen Three occurred in late June. The numbers continued as the main issues, and I took over from Bobby Layton most of the job of defending the agency's position. There was some minor slippage in a couple of categories, but otherwise the CIA held firm. Serenely puffing on Chesterfields, Fowler stuck with the official OB. After each meeting, I reported back to Carver to tell him what had happened. One day in early July, his desk was empty. As was her custom, his secretary, Mary Ellen, wouldn't let on where he'd gone. I found out on 10 July, however, when a "secret" cable arrived from Vietnam signed "Funaro," which was Carver's cover name.[3] Evidently, Helms had sent him to Saigon to break what the message termed "the current Washington impasse" on VC strength. Accordingly, Funaro had met the day before with Gains Hawkins—still MACV's Order of Battle chief—and General Philip Davidson, who not long before had succeeded General McChristian as Westmoreland's head of intelligence.[4]

Carver first relayed Colonel Hawkins' assurances that—George Fowler notwithstanding—the MACV Order of Battle Section basically agreed with the CIA: about 100,000 was OK for the guerrillas, the colonel had said, although our guess of 75,000 service troops was perhaps "a little" too high. General Davidson fingered the real difficulty. "The chief problem," Carver quoted Davidson as saying, "is the political and presentational one of coming out with a brand new set of figures showing a much larger force at a time when the press knows that MACV is seeking more troops."

No doubt the press *was* a problem, a big one, and Carver's message suggested a solution. It was to break the order of battle into two parts: "military," to include regulars, service troops, and guerrillas, totaling about 300,000 (or approximately the number in the old OB); and "nonmilitary," to include self-defense militia and political cadres, coming to around 200,000. The total would be half a million, and then MACV could hold a press conference to explain the transaction. "Some elements in the press would always carp," Carver said, "but the air would be cleared . . . and a valid baseline established for future . . . analysis." Davidson said that it sounded like a good idea to him and that he'd try it out on General Westmoreland. I tried it out on George Allen.

"Balls," said George. "This business of fooling around with the OB for a few dumb reporters makes me sick. God knows what it'll lead to. Maybe stowing the political cadres up on a nonmilitary shelf is legitimate, but not the militia, goddamnit. The militia are part of the VC army, and always have been. That's the reason Bill Benedict and I put them in the OB in 1962, and that's where they damn well belong."

"But George," I said, "Carver's only slicing the pie in a different way. It still adds up to half a million. What difference does it make so long as they show what we're trying to demonstrate: that the war's a lot bigger than we thought it was."

"Balls," he repeated. I left him fuming.

Frankly, the cable was fine by me: I was not necessarily pleased by its "solution," which as far as I could see didn't "solve" Westmoreland's problem of how to explain the higher numbers to the press, but rather by a brief statement in its last paragraph. That said that the next session of Fourteen Three would have to wait until August, at which time Gains Hawkins would come to Langley to take over from George Fowler as champion of the military's numbers. This meant the hankypanky would stop; I shared the general opinion that Colonel Hawkins was scrupulously honest. But there was an even more pressing consideration. On my return from Saigon in May I had promised Bill Johnson of the counterintelligence staff that the study on the Vietcong police would be ready by the end of July. The delay in Fourteen Three would allow me to meet this deadline. A dividend to the postponement was the fact that the VC police were the political cadres, the OB category about which I knew least. I could bone up on them now.

In fact the study was well underway. A chapter on the COSVN Security Section, which Commander Siller and I had started at the Collation Branch, was already in final draft. A second chapter, concerning communist police operation in and around Saigon, had been farmed out to still another helper, Manny Roth, an eager young lieutenant whom Bill Johnson had wangled from the Army. Roth loved the work. "Binh Tanh!" he whooped at my desk one morning: "I got Binh Tanh's!" He had discovered the VC cover designation of Binh Tanh Subregion, one of the six surrounding Saigon. It was "A23," he said, and its police headquarters was "A536." By mid-July he had turned up the cover designation of all six subregions, and for four of their six police headquarters. More important, he had begun to figure out which ones operated where. For example, Binh Tanh's police ran secret agents into Saigon's Second and Fourth precincts.

I was also immersed in cover designations. Having determined through the VC interrogator in Soc Trang that the "83" subsection of their police apparatus was diep bao, (which the Vietnamese sergeant had translated as "espionage") I went through my boxful of VC documents looking for reports marked "83." The policy spy network fell rapidly into place. Subsection 83, it turned out, had three parts: A1, A2, and A3. The first consisted of agent-handlers—who made a special effort to recruit the Vietnamese interpreters working for the Americans. I wondered about that sergeant in Soc Trang. The second section made blacklists of victims targeted for various woes: assassinations (which the VC called "executions"); kidnappings ("arrests"); or other "disciplinary measures" which would surely take place, the documents claimed, when the communists "liberated the south." The third part, A3, were the thugs who actually did the work. Hitmen from A3 wielded silencer pistols, hustled Saigon officials into waiting cars, and set off explosions in city streets. Once again I recalled the *kaboom* that had sent me under the bed on my first Saturday in Vietnam. If the bomber were a VC policeman, I thought, he would have belonged to the A3 component of the B3 sub-section of a local subregion police headquarters. *Which* subregion, I didn't know, because I was unsure which of Saigon's precincts the bomb had gone off in. That was easy to find out. I could look at a map.

When the completed draft landed on Bill Johnson's desk on 28 July, he whistled, saying: "I'd love to see the VC damage assessment when they finally read this thing." It was a high compliment. A damage assessment is what intelligence organizations write after they've been found out. Perhaps "found out" was a little strong. For although the study presented an intricate wiring diagram of the Communist police network from its headquarters at the Ministry of Public Security in Hanoi down to the smallest hamlet in the south, and described at length how the police went about their work, it lacked important details. I mentioned the most prominent of these to Bill Johnson: "Names. There were a thousand documents, but not a true name in the lot. We don't know who these people are."

He replied: "But this gives us a start. If we catch one of the agents, we'll know more about the organization than he does. Maybe he'll think we know everything and tell us the rest. Leastways that's the theory. It doesn't always work out."

The printers ran off the study, its 125 pages bound in a sullen gray cover, on Monday, 31 July 1967, right on schedule.[5] It was in the nick of time. On the same day, George Allen, who was filling in for Carver during one of the latter's unexplained absences, told me that Colonel Hawkins was getting ready to leave Saigon to attend the next session of Fourteen Three, due to convene shortly. I had mixed emotions. On the one hand, Hawkins' honesty was doubtless better than Fowler's harrumphs. On the other, I was daunted by my now having to carry the entire load on the numbers. My main backer at the meetings, Bobby Layton, had a new assignment. Earlier in the month, he had gone to Saigon to join the Collation Branch. Naturally, the DDI would be no help whatsoever. Methodically pumping out Sitreps, it still had no one working full time on the VC —and no one, as usual, who knew anything much about the order of battle. Annoyed at these now-ancient gaps, I wrote a memo to Carver suggesting that the agency form a "Vietcong Study Group." I gave it to Mary Ellen on 2 August.[6] "Thanks," she said, and tossed it in his in-box, where it landed on a paper I'd written in mid-May.[7] The May paper had complained that the DDI still wasn't reading captured documents.

Fourteen Three reassembled a few days later. I climbed to the seventh floor fifteen minutes early in order to say hello to Gains Hawkins. He was already in the conference room. We shook hands. He looked tired, I thought, probably from jet lag. The meeting was called to order by a new chairman, James Graham, a board member who'd recently transferred from the DDI front office. Why he'd taken over from General Collins as Fourteen Three's boss was unclear; perhaps the general was on vacation. In any case, it didn't matter. Graham was one of the front office people who had backed me up in my fight with the State Department over the rise of Tshombe in the Congo. "Screw State," he had said in effect. I supposed he'd take the same attitude towards MACV—assuming it was warranted.

"Gentlemen," said Graham, "we're going to have a slide show. Colonel Hawkins has just completed several new studies for the MACV Order of Battle Section, and he wants to tell us about them. Somebody douse the lights." The room went black. There was a blast of light on one wall. The first slide wobbled to the center. It read:

Headquarters
United States Military Assistance Command, Vietnam
Vietcong Strength Study

As the slide wobbled off, I caught a glimpse of George Fowler. His head was on his chest and his eyes were closed. When the next slide appeared, Colonel Hawkins began to read from an accompanying text. He spoke rapidly and was hard to follow. The slides were a maze of numbers and charts. I couldn't see my pad in the dark, and therefore couldn't take notes. A dozen had come and gone, when something caught my eye. I called out: "Colonel, could you leave that slide on for a minute, please? I'd like to copy it down."

He said: "I figured you'd call me on that one, Sam. Of course you can."

I went to the wall, and in its bright light transcribed the display. The slide show continued for another half hour. The lights went on, and there was a coffee break. I looked at my notes. This is what they showed:

Previous Estimate		Revised Estimate	
Regulars:	120,400	Regulars:	120,400
Service Troops:	24,800	Service Troops:	26,000
Guerrilla-Militia:	112,800	Guerrilla-Militia:	65,000
Political Cadres:	39,200	Political Cadres:	87,500
Total:	297,200	Total:	298,900

Clearly, the two "estimates" were MACV's current order of battle and its proposed new one.[8] I went over the categories one by one. First the regulars: no change. Well, Fourteen Three hadn't argued about regulars, although I was beginning to have doubts. I'd lately come across several small combat units, such as sappers (a kind of commando), which weren't listed in the OB. However, not wanting to pick nits, I decided to leave them alone. Service troops: up 1200. *What?* Less than a month ago, Funaro's cable from Saigon had reported that Colonel Hawkins thought that Fourteen Three's then-current figure of 75,000 service troops was only "a little" too high. Seventy-five thousand is "a little" higher than 26,000? Cut it out. Something funny was going on. Guerrilla-militia: *My God!* Everyone after the hyphen, the self-defense militia—whom Nguyen Chi Thanh* had put at 150,000—had marched out of the OB without so much as a bugle call. And not to Carver's "nonmilitary" shelf, either, but to oblivion. Then there were the pre-hyphen troops, the guerrillas. Only *65,000?* Hawkins had told Funaro 100,000 a month ago, and General Thanh had said 180,000 a year before that. Again, it was *awfully damn peculiar.* I skipped over the

---

*Hanoi Radio had announced General Thanh's death on 6 July 1967. Actually Thanh died in a B-52 raid in late 1966. Thanh's successor at COSVN headquarters was a party official whose cover name was "Muoi Cuc."

political cadres to look at the totals. That was it! They are what had caught my eye! *The totals were virtually the same.*

Immediately I suspected foul play. It looked to me that someone at MACV headquarters had picked the new sum to coincide with the old one, in order to fool outsiders—presumably the press—into thinking the VC strength estimate was the same as ever. And then someone else, most likely from the OB Section, had taken the new total, and jiggering with the components, *worked backwards.* Who was the "someone else?" Colonel Hawkins? At just this point Mr. Graham said: "All right everybody, back to work. Coffee break's over."

I studied the colonel as he resumed his seat at the conference table. I saw my first impression about his being "tired" was wrong. His face was as bleak as I'd ever seen a face. I also saw, for the first time, that he wasn't alone. Sitting to his right was an Air Force brigadier general. I asked a neighbor who it was. The neighbor said: "General Godding. George Godding. He's deputy J-2" That meant he was chief assistant to General Philip Davidson, Westmoreland's new head of intelligence. Aha, I thought: Hawkins is on a short leash.

For the next ten days—or so it seemed to me—Fourteen Three was in almost continuous session. The discussion was now entirely about numbers, with Hawkins and me the main disputants. It was a strange affair from the start. For example:

ADAMS: Colonel, I suppose you remember that General Thanh's speech of April 1966 where he said there were a hundred eighty thousand guerrillas. We talked about it in Honolulu.

HAWKINS: I do seem to recall that, Sam, and I guess you know about Bulletin 4530.

ADAMS: Bulletin what?

HAWKINS: Forty-five thirty. It's not a speech, but an accounting document. Also dated 1966. It lists a hundred seventy thousand guerrillas, at least that's what it says here. Now that seems to pretty much confirm General Thanh, doesn't it?

The colonel handed me the bulletin.[9] I'd seen it before, but had mislaid my copy. It *was* an accounting document (it subdivided the guerrillas by area), and it certainly backed up General Thanh's speech. But hell, I was the one arguing for Thanh's speech, not Hawkins. The discussion continued:

ADAMS: Yet MACV's guerrilla estimate is sixty-five thousand?

HAWKINS: Right.

ADAMS: Well, if you're not using Thanh's speech, what are you using?

HAWKINS: Field reports. Sixty-five thousand is a compilation of field reports. From the provinces. All forty-four of them.

ADAMS: Can I see the field reports?

HAWKINS: Course you can, Sam. (He handed me a thick bundle of paper.) And if I were you, I'd take a close look at them.

That evening I went over the bundle sheet by sheet. It was the biggest mishmash of stuff I'd ever encountered. Some province reports sharply disagreed with enemy documents from the same area; others counted village guerrillas (du kich xa), but not the more numerous hamlet guerrillas (du kich ap); still others showed that the reporting officers didn't know what guerrillas were. Fourteen three resumed the next morning.

ADAMS: Colonel, your Quang Nam Province report put the guerrillas at forty-six hundred. Yet this VC document, only two months old, says there are eleven thousand two hundred. That's sixty-six hundred more than the report. How do you account for the difference?[10]

HAWKINS: We checked up on that one. It turned out the reporting officer didn't know about the document.

ADAMS: Oh. (The colonel had just zapped his own position.)

HAWKINS: By the way, did you see that one from Darlac Province?

ADAMS: The one where the reporting officer thought the local party committee belonged to the guerrillas?

HAWKINS: That's it! Isn't that the damnedest thing you've ever heard of? A committee scampering around the hills with submachine guns. Now that's what I call a *committee*. I tell you, our boy in Darlac doesn't know his ass from his elbow. (Zap!)

At which the colonel lit up a cigar. He still looked unhappy, but not nearly as unhappy as he had in the beginning. I studied General Godding to see if he understood what had happened. It was hard to tell.

A day or two later, the colonel and I were arguing over service troops. He was busy outlining the numerous omissions in his own estimate, when the session broke for lunch. It's nice to know who's missing, I said to myself, but I wish I knew what Hawkins really thought. So far his only indication had been to tell Carver in Saigon that the CIA estimate of 75,000 was "a little" too high. His definition of "a little" came after lunch. At that time an Estimates staffer came barreling up to me and said breathlessly: "Jesus Christ! Guess what Hawkins told me in the cafeteria. He said he thought the communist T, O and E for service troops was 100,000 men."[11] The table of organization and equipment figure represents an ideal rather than actual number. Most armies, including our own, fight at a certain percent of T, O and E. Well, I recalled a study from Saigon which gave the Vietcong percentage. I ran downstairs and got the study from my desk. There it was: 70 percent.[12] In other words, Hawkins thought the VC had 70,000 service troops, only 5,000 fewer than my own guess. Yet up at Fourteen Three—despite his scrupulous honesty over details—he was still upholding MACV's "revised estimate" of 26,000.

Of course the obvious question now was whether to confront the colonel at the conference table with what he'd said in the cafeteria. It was easy to answer: No. If backed to the wall, Hawkins would doubtless blurt out the truth, Godding would report him to Saigon, and a day or two later I'd find myself dealing with Hawkins' replacement, who might not be as candid. That was the last thing I wanted. I'd come to think of the colonel as my most valuable asset at the conference. He was the only other person there who knew the evidence.

Meanwhile I kept my boss, George Carver, abreast of the increasing wackiness of the military's position. Carver was staunch. "Keep it up," he told me. "This is turning into one of the biggest fights the agency's ever had. Fourteen Three's the talk of the executive dining room." Not long after this conversation, Hawkins and I were discussing the proposed exit from the MACV Order of Battle of the Vietcong self-defense militia.

I had mixed feelings on the matter. On one hand, it was clear the militiamen weren't what you'd call ordinary soldiers. Relatively few carried guns, none wore uniforms, and their ranks included a modest share of teenagers, women, and old men. (The argument over shares was particularly frustrating because the only place which adequately described them was my own home guard study, which the DDI had killed in February.)

On the other hand—as was equally clear—Vietnam wasn't what you'd call an ordinary war. As various reports had shown, one-fifth of our casualties came from the militia's favorite weapon, mines and booby traps, the militia made up a good chunk of our Chieu Hoi statistics, and they doubtless showed up regularly as cadavers for MACV's body count. As I said to Hawkins: "Dammit, Colonel, if you count them when they defect, or when they're dead, why can't you count them when they're still alive?" I had in mind a variation of Carver's "solution" in Saigon of taking them out of the military order of battle but leaving them in Fourteen Three as part of its manpower estimate. They were still there, the estimate adding up to about a half a million.

Hawkins said: "There's a lot to what you say. Maybe we can work something out." I figured he'd have to cable Saigon for instructions.

Apparently he did so, because the air was shortly filled with high-level messages from Vietnam denouncing the VC militia. The first one came in on Saturday, 19 August, addressed to George Carver. Its author was Robert Komer, whom earlier in the year President Johnson had sent from the White House to Vietnam to become Westmoreland's chief of pacification. In the message, Komer first noted that Fourteen Three still numbered the militia, mistakenly, he said, since they were "low-level part-timers." Then he came to the point: "MACV is determined to stick to its guns [on getting rid of the self-defense militia], and you can well imagine the ruckus which will be created if it comes out—as everything tends to on Vietnam—that the agency and MACV figures are so widely different. Any explanation as to why will simply lead the press to conclude MACV is deliberately omitting the self-defense in order to downgrade enemy strength. . . . Will you please help straighten out this matter which is of concern to the whole top level here."[13]

More of the top level checked in on Monday morning: first, General Creighton Abrams—Westmoreland's number two—his cable addressed to Earl Wheeler, head of the Joint Chiefs of Staff, who sent it on to the CIA.* Abrams said he wanted to make clear MACV's "command position" over Fourteen Three vis-a-vis the communist militia: drop them. If they stayed in the estimate, he explained, the resulting sum would be "in sharp contrast to the current overall strength figure of about 299,000 given to the press here . . . We have been projecting an image of success over recent months," he went on, and if the higher numbers were to become public "all available caveats and explanations will not prevent the press from drawing an erroneous and gloomy conclusion . . . All those who have an incorrect view of the war will be reinforced and the task will become more difficult."[14]

Shortly thereafter, a cable arrived from Westmoreland himself. He said: "I have just read General Abrams' [message], and I agree . . . No possible explanations could prevent the erroneous conclusions that would result. Warm regards."[15]

I gathered up the three messages (Komer's, Abrams', and Westmoreland's), and went to George Carver's office. Carver said: "I thought I'd be seeing you this morning. Well, don't worry about these. This is the CIA, and we will not, I repeat not, drum the militia out of the estimate just to please the press." Carver began shaking his head. "But what really surprises me about these cables, really astounds me, is not what they say—I've heard variations on the theme for years—but the fact that they have put it in writing. Make sure you keep copies." I said OK, and took the cables to show them to George Allen.

---

*Within the agency, the cable's recipients included Richard Helms, the director; Admiral Rufus Taylor, his deputy; R. Jack Smith, head of DDI; Thomas Karamessines, head of the DDP; William Colby, chief of the DDP's Far Eastern Section; Sherman Kent, head of the Board of National Estimates (where Fourteen Three's chairman, James Graham, would also have seen it); and of course George Carver, Helms' chief assistant on Vietnam. I saw Carver's copy.

Allen hadn't read them yet. He did so now, and began cussing. Between cusses, he quoted from the cables: "*command* position . . . *image* of success . . . *erroneous* conclusions . . . *incorrect* view of the war." The one that annoyed him the most was "command position." He said: "Now who the hell does he think he's commanding? The VC?" George slipped into an imitation of Westmoreland talking to a Vietcong general: "Now I'm sorry, general, but you're only allowed to have two hundred ninety-nine thousand soldiers. That's it. No more'n two ninety-nine. Now go out there and do your best." He became Allen again: "If he can command the *size* of the VC army, why can't he command it to get out of the country? I notice Westy's been having some trouble on that score lately." At which he crumpled one of the messages into a ball and threw it against the wall.

"George," I said, "that's my only copy." I took the message from the floor, where it had bounced, smoothed it out, and went into the hall towards my own office. The secretary, Theresa Wilson, was laughing. "They sure got to him that time," she said. I stuck the three cables into a folder and put the folder in a safe.

Fourteen Three met twice more that week. There were some additional minor slippages in two of the categories. The slippages, which I felt were unnecessary, had begun to mount up. A recent draft put the communists at "between 400,000 and 500,000 men" instead of the usual "around half a million." At the end of the second session Mr. Graham said: "Gentlemen, this estimate's been going on all summer. We're beginning to get stale. Therefore the word's come from up top to knock it off for a couple of weeks, so we can catch up on other work, go on vacations, or whatever else. There's one thing we seem to agree on; the war will still be going when we get back. We'll give you a call as to the time of the next meeting."

It was fine by me. Fourteen Three was already vying for the first place as the longest-lived estimate in agency history, and I'd been working six- and seven-day weeks roughly since Christmas. Eleanor was in Mobile, Alabama, visiting her parents. I straightaway caught the southern flight out of Dulles in order to join her. No sooner had I arrived at her parents' house when the phone rang. It was George Carver. "Sam, come back up. We're going to Saigon to thrash out the numbers."

I had become suspicious. "We won't sell out, will we?"

"No, no, we're going to bite the bullet," he said. I flew back to Washington the next morning to find that our scheduled departure wasn't until the third of September. That gave me a full week to get ready. I could use it. Having been tied up more or less constantly with Fourteen Three sessions, I'd fallen behind on the documents. MACV's Document Exploitation Center had just published its seven thousandth bulletin—a lot of water had gone over the dam since Bulletin 689—and there were several subjects which needed reviewing. Chief among them were the Vietcong service troops.

In a way, "service troops" was the most annoying category in Fourteen Three. In each session, it had lurched slightly downwards, so that the original 75,000 had dwindled to 50,000 in the latest draft. I knew much of the slippage was my own fault. My two main arguments had been too amorphous. The first depended on MACV's omissions. For example, as Colonel Hawkins had observed, his estimate of 26,000 totally excluded the district level. Now the VC had 240-odd districts, each with medics, signalmen, couriers, and so forth; the question was—how many? I couldn't supply an answer. I could only point at holes. My second argument was logic. The communist regular army was a fairly complex outfit. The man from NSA had agreed its communications net was far-flung and efficient. American doctors who had toured captured VC hospitals had found them surprisingly good. And captured weapons were normally in a state of high repair. All this suggested a vast back-up system for the men who did the fighting. Again the questions, how many? My only evidence was a single document. It showed that in one province, VC Can Tho, the communists had about as many service troops as they had combatants. A single low-level document doesn't carry much weight in a forum like Fourteen Three. Hence the cuts.

Knowing what to look for makes research easy. I went through the MACV bulletin collection at the rate of a thousand a day. At the end of the seventh day, I had come up with references to five provinces and twenty-eight districts. They showed beyond doubt that the Can Tho example was a good one. Its ratio of service troops to regular combatants held firm at one to one.* At this time MACV's Order of Battle carried 120,000 "regulars." Thus the *real* service troop number was closer to that than it was to the 50,000 in Fourteen Three. As for MACV's 26,000, why, it was absurd.

And I found something else, potentially more important, which I hadn't been looking for. Most of the "references were actually Vietcong provincial and district rosters, listing so many men in *x* infantry battalion, or so many in *y* ordnance depot. They showed lots of other soldiers, too: "sappers," "special action," "combat engineers," and "scouts," mostly belonging to small units. I'd noticed such units absent from the OB before, so I checked up on each new one. *Not one* was listed in the OB. But these are the communists' elite troops, I said to myself, and went down the hall to see if Major Blascik felt the same way. "Man for man," he said, "they're probably the best soldiers in the world." (High praise from Blascik, who was a Green Beret.) After some simple math, I guessed their countrywide total at around ten thousand. Were there other holes as well? For the first time, I began to suspect that the OB seriously understated the "regulars."

On the afternoon of Saturday, 2 September 1967, I stuffed the documents into a black briefcase, and went home to pack. That night I telephoned my father—routine for such occasions—to warn him that my fourth trip to Vietnam was about to begin. "Don't get yourself shot," he said, "and say hello to Ellsworth." I promised I would. "Ellsworth" was Ellsworth Bunker, our new ambassador to Vietnam. He had once been

---

*In September 1967, there were approximately 480,000 American troops in Vietnam. Well less than 100,000, of these were combat, the rest service. The reason the U.S. Army needed proportionately more service troops than the VC was its greater sophistication. Helicopters and tanks—which at this point in the war the communists didn't have—need lots of men to keep them running.

my father's partner in the small Wall Street brokerage firm of Butler, Herrick and Marshall.[16]

I drove to Dulles airport the next morning, and by the evening of 4 September had reached a tiny room in the Dai-ichi Hotel in Tokyo. There was a knock on the door, which I opened. It was my old boss, Ed Hauck.

"Ed! What are you doing in Tokyo?" I asked.

"It's my place of exile," he said. "They were going to send me to Elba, but maybe they figured I'd find a boat."

Hauck was the DDI's representative to the Tokyo Station, it turned out, and there wasn't all that much for him to do. We talked about the war. I told him that his original forecast that the communists would win it (which he'd made on my first day on Vietnam) didn't look as goofy as I thought at the time. In fact, because of my work on the order of battle, I'd begun to agree. He was full of praise: "Fourteen Three must be a lulu. We've been hearing about it for weeks. Even in Tokyo! You've got the whole damn intelligence community in an uproar." We went down to the bar for a drink. The maitre d' tried to overcharge us for a bowl of peanuts, but Hauck faced him down. He was fluent in Japanese.

A couple of days later I flew to Thailand, bought Eleanor some silk, and on Friday, 8 September, caught Bangkok's morning flight for Saigon. The plane touched down briefly at Pochentong airport outside Cambodia's capital of Phnom Penh—there were some Russian-built MIGs parked at the end of the runway—then it flew over Vietnam's War Zone C (as advertised, "the face of the moon," pockmarked with craters) before finally landing at Tan Son Nhut in the early afternoon. I drove to the embassy, and instead of checking in right away at Collation, asked for an appointment to see Ambassador Bunker. It was granted at once. A receptionist led me to a large air-conditioned office with drawn curtains. Bunker rose from behind his big desk to shake hands.

"I'm Pete Adams' son," I said, by way of introduction. (My father's real name was Pierpont, but everyone, himself included, called him "Pete.")

"A pleasure to see you again," said the ambassador, recalling that we'd met some years back at my father's brokerage house. He was friendly, tall and slender, with white hair, an aquiline nose, and slightly droopy eyes. A white triangle of a handkerchief stuck from the pocket of his dark blue suit. We swapped pleasantries for about five minutes. As I was leaving, he said: "Give my very best to Pete." It was the first time I'd encountered one of the Vietnam war's principal figures—except, of course, those from the CIA.

At ten o'clock the next morning, I arrived at MACV headquarters to attend the order-of-battle conference, scheduled to start at 10:30 A.M. The headquarters was a sprawling structure nicknamed Pentagon East. Colonel Hawkins met me at the front door.

"What you got in that damn briefcase?" he asked.

"Wouldn't you like to know," I said. He laughed. We walked side by side towards the conference room. I told him about the missing sappers, which I'd guessed at ten thousand. "Believe you're a little high," he said; "on the other hand, maybe not." His face regained its bleak look.

The conference room was medium-sized and austere, centered by a big U-shaped table. On one side of the U sat the CIA delegation: George Carver, myself, Dean Moor (now a firm backer, but unfortunately no help on the evidence), and an Estimates staffer named Bill Hyland, who had taken over the job of superintending the various drafts of Fourteen Three from Bobby Layton. Facing us on the U's other side were Colonel Hawkins and several other Army officers, apparently from the Order of Battle Section. From the head of the U pointed Westmoreland's big guns of intelligence. I recognized only one of these: General Godding, Gains Hawkins' escort at Langley. Carver whispered the identity of the rest: "The bald one in the middle is General Davidson, the J-2: that fat colonel over there is Charley Morris, head of Production (that's their DDI); the short one is Danny Graham, chief of MACV Estimates; and the general sitting next to Davidson is Winant Sidle— he's head of MACV's Public Relations."[17]

"Public relations?" I said. I was about to ask what the dickens a PR man was doing at an order-of-battle conference, when the meeting came to order.

"We'd like to open this morning with our latest reading on Vietcong morale," declared General Godding, the first speaker; "this afternoon we'll get to the numbers." For the next hour and a half two MACV officers gave a detailed catalogue of the Vietcong's most recent misfortunes. They were even sicker, hungrier and more frightened than usual and in some areas, running low on ammunition. I kept my mouth shut even though I knew the documents showed the VC desertion rate had lately taken a sharp drop.* We broke for lunch at noon.

The lunch break was unusual. I was asking the whereabouts of the closest cafeteria when Danny Graham—the colonel, really a lieutenant colonel, whom Carver said ran MACV Estimates—came over and said: "The food around here's almost inedible. I know where we can get something decent. It's a South Vietnamese officer's club." It sounded like a good idea. Carver and I accompanied Graham to his jeep, which shortly crunched up to a slope-roofed building with verandahs. A sign over the door showed that it was, in fact, a South Vietnamese officer's club. We went inside. There were no South Vietnamese, only Americans. Graham ushered us to a room whose sole light was a Wurlitzer juke box. We groped our way to a booth, and shortly a woman in a low-cut evening gown appeared from the murk. She sat down beside me, and put her arm around my shoulder. "My name Kim," she said.

"Hello, Kim," I replied. "Where are you from?" (I never know what to say; meanwhile Graham and Carver were in deep conversation.)

"Hanoi. What your name?"

"Pete."

"Where you work, Pete? Betcha CIA."

"No, no, Army Personnel."

---

*So had the Chieu Hoi rate. According to our own statistics, the number of defectors from the VC army had fallen drastically since early spring. Thus: March 1967: 3,155; April: 1,873; May: 1,466; June: 1,412; July: 1,536; August: 1,298; September: 1,047. I had watched these statistics closely. It was clear that something unusual was going on. I couldn't figure what.

"Cut it out, you work CIA."

"Army Personnel!"

"What you do for CIA?"

And so on, this continued for fifteen minutes. She never wormed it out of me. I had a cheeseburger for lunch, and when we got back to MACV headquarters, the first briefer was our mealtime host, Colonel Graham.

Graham's thesis was that the communists were running out of men. Sometime earlier in the year they had reached what he called the crossover point. The crossover point had occurred when the enemy's losses—from killed, died of wounds, defectors, and so on—exceeded his "inputs," either from infiltration down the Ho Chi Minh Trail, or from recruitment in the south. That was the communists' big problem: the inputs. Both had fallen off dramatically. Not only were fewer northerners wending their way down the Trail, but the Vietcong were hard put to keep their boot camps going. MACV had recently done a study that showed the VC recruitment rate had halved—from 7000 men per month a year ago, to 3500 per month now.

"The real significance of all this," Graham went on, "is its effect on the order of battle. The OB is now in a state of substantial decline." Although I agreed the VC army was losing men, I groaned inwardly. Decline, OK, but from what base? Graham launched an attack on the self-defense militia. He gave the standard reasons for their incompetence, ending up with the new one that "furthermore, the majority of the militia are women." Leaving aside the fact that exploding a woman's booby trap can be as harmful as exploding a man's, this statement was untrue, and I damn well knew it. I threw open my briefcase, and grabbed the top document. It was Bulletin 689, the one that had started it all off, about Binh Dinh Province's guerrilla-militia. I looked at the document's statistical section and sure enough: of the Binh Dinh militia's 34,441 members, 6147 were "females." I worked out the percentage, wrote down "18%" on Bulletin 689, and slid it over to Carver, Carver nodded. Graham continued.

"A good example of the crossover's deleterious effect on the order of battle is that we now feel that the number of political cadres is in the neighborhood of fifty thousand."[18] Fifty thousand! Only a month ago Colonel Hawkins' slide show had put them at 87,500. That was a one-month drop of 37,500 men. Incredible! I slid another note to Carter. Once again he nodded. I looked at General Davidson's face. It was blank. I looked at Colonel Hawkins. The bleakness had turned to acute pain.

The order-of-battle conference lasted for three days, and Colonel Graham's presentation proved standard fare. Numbers bobbed, weaved, slithered, and sometimes altogether vanished. The slipperiest of all was the VC service troops. At a late session of Fourteen Three, Colonel Hawkins had pointed out that MACV's slide show estimate entirely omitted the service soldiers of the communists' 240-odd districts. A conference briefer got up to say that MACV had now corrected this oversight, and that five thousand district troops had joined the service estimate. I thought this might be a small step in the right direction until I saw the service estimate's total. Despite the added five thousand it was even lower than before! In disbelief I looked at the total's other components. Each of them (provinces, regions, etc.) had gone down to compensate for the districts' gain. Obviously, MACV had robbed Peter to pay Paul.[19] Well, this seemed a good place to do battle, so I wrote another note to Carver, asking permission to do so. He gave it, scribbling: "Be as emphatic as you want, but be tactful."[20]

How can you tactfully accuse somebody of fraud? I asked myself, as I rose to give the agency's side of the argument. Well, I tried. I called the disappearing troops "an anomaly," and reverted to the evidence. Not only were the province and regional deductions unjustified, I said, but five thousand was nowhere near enough for the districts. I now had a sample of twenty-eight districts, I went on, they averaged out to about seventy-five men apiece, and if this average held countrywide, it would come to eighteen thousand. I briefly reviewed my documents and asked whether there were any questions.

"I have a question," said General Davidson. "You mean to tell me you have only twenty-eight districts?"

"Yes sir," I said, "That's all I could find."

"Well, I've been in the intelligence business for many years, and if you're trying to sell me a number on the basis of that small a sample, you might as well pack up and go home." As I resumed my seat, Davidson's aide, Colonel Morris, turned to me and said, "Adams, you're full of shit."

At which a lieutenant colonel got up from Colonel Hawkins' side of the U to defend MACV's five thousand.[21] He had counted twenty-one service troops per district, he said, and then went on to describe how a district was organized. When he asked for questions, I said, "How many districts are in your sample?"

He looked as if somebody had kicked him in the stomach. Instead of answering the question, he repeated his description of how the VC organized a district.

Then George Carver interrupted him. "Come, come, Colonel," he said. "General Davidson has just taken Mr. Adams to task for having only twenty-eight districts in his sample. It's a perfectly legitimate question. How many have you in yours?"

In a very low voice, the lieutenant colonel said, "One." I looked over at General Davidson and Colonel Morris to see whether they'd denounce the lieutenant colonel for having such a small sample. Both of them were looking at the ceiling.

"Colonel," I continued, "may I see the document on which your sample is based?" He didn't have it, he said, and besides, it wasn't a document, it was a POW report.

Well, I asked, could he please try and remember who the twenty-one service soldiers were? He ticked them off. I kept count. The total was forty.

"Colonel," I said, "you have forty soldiers here, not twenty-one. How did you get from forty to twenty-one?"

"We scaled down the evidence," he replied.

"Scaled down the evidence?"

"Yes," he said. "We cut out the hangers-on."

"And how do you determine what a hanger-on is?"

"Civilians, for example."

Now I knew that civilians sometimes worked alongside VC service troops, but normally the rosters listed them separately. So I waited until the next coffee break to ask Colonel Hawkins how he'd "scale down" the service troops in a document I had. It concerned Long Dat District in the southern half of South Vietnam, and its 103 service troops were broken down by components. We went over each one. Of the 15 in the medical detachment, he'd count 3, of the 15 in the ordnance unit, again 3, until Long Dat's 103 service troops were down to about 40.[22] There was no indication in the document that any of those dropped were civilians. I thanked Colonel Hawkins for his help. As usual, he was laying it on the line.

Not long after that, he did it again. Another lieutenant colonel[23] had been stubbornly defending MACV's guerrilla number, still 65,000, while I was trying for what I felt the documents supported—not quite double that figure. Along came the coffee break. A finger tapped my shoulder. It was Hawkins. He said: "Sam, I want you to know that my *personal* opinion is at variance with MACV's official position. In my *personal* opinion, the real number of guerrillas is between a hundred and a hundred and twenty thousand." Or exactly what I thought. He also handed me a document, published a couple of days earlier, which showed a VC province guerrilla listing far higher than MACV's field report for the same province. I told Carver what Hawkins had said and showed him the document. Carver nodded. The funny thing was the lieutenant colonel wasn't even MACV's regular guerrilla analyst, who was also in the room. During all the arguments this analyst had remained seated. He was a young Army lieutenant, skinny, Irish-looking, by the name of McArthur.

Towards the end of the second day, again after a break, several copies of a mimeographed note appeared around the U-shaped table. I hadn't seen who had put it there, it was unsigned, but the originator was obvious. The note read approximately as follows: "The United States Military Assistance Command Vietnam will agree to add 15,000 to its estimate of Vietcong guerrillas if the Central Intelligence Agency agrees to drop entirely the VC self-defense militia."[24] Carver and I read the note simultaneously. My jaw dropped, he gave out a low whistle and said: "In *writing*. MACV must be crazy. They put it in *writing*." I said something to the effect that this kind of bargaining might be acceptable in a rug bazaar, but goddamnit, it wasn't intelligence. We ought to go home, put what we really think in Fourteen Three, and tell MACV to go jump in the lake. Let'em take a footnote." That was Sunday afternoon.

The CIA's collapse occurred on Monday morning. I wasn't there, and don't know the details. Nor do I know the exact reason why. A friend from the DDI front office later told me that Helms had cabled Carver to throw in the sponge. Another source said that no such cable existed but that Carver had gone to Saigon with the director's bidding to do his best, but above all to come to an agreement. Either way's the same. Helms would go just so far in pursuing a realistic VC strength estimate, but not further. My hero of Stanleyville had taken a dive.

Carver sent Langley word of the collapse on the same day in a cable addressed "Funaro to Knight," "Knight" being Helms' cover name.[25] The cable began: "We have squared the circle." The phrase came from Thomas Hobbes.* I took it to mean: "We have done the seemingly impossible."

The "seemingly impossible" agreement worked out by MACV and CIA in Saigon on that morning of 12 September 1967, was put in writing. To wit:

Regulars:	119,000
Service Troops:	37,500
Guerrillas:	80,000
Military Total:	236,500
Political Cadres:	80,000

---

* Another quote from Hobbes: "What poor geometrician is there, but takes pride to be thought a conjurer? What mountebank would not make a living out of a false opinion that he were a great physician? And when many of them are once engaged in the maintenance of an error, they will join together for the saving of their authority to decry the truth."[26]

In other words, the agency had gone along with MACV's mimeographed bargain—and then some. The militia had marched out of the estimate in exchange for only fifteen thousand guerrillas, not the great many more that Colonel Hawkins and I agreed there were. The service troops, although higher than MACV's earlier number, were still "scaled down" on the order of 50 percent. Even the regulars had dropped a couple of thousand, with no mention whatsoever of the possibility of missing sappers. Finally, the political cadres had flown off to a separate perch.

The agreement paid the political cadres special heed. Under no circumstances, it said, were they to be "included in an aggregate" (meaning, added) to their military colleagues, particularly in "Washington publications" which dealt with the Vietcong, such as Fourteen Three. Furthermore, the cadres' definitions "needed considerable refinement." (something I agreed with), but "when this necessary work is completed, the political figure in its present form will disappear." Poof! Carver's copy of the agreement concluded with the hope that General Westmoreland "would extend to General Davidson and all of his able, most impressive staff, the thanks of the entire Washington delegation for their effective comprehensive briefings and other invaluable contributions to our joint endeavor."[27]

"Thanks of the entire delegation!" I sputtered, and tore off to locate Carver, so he could exclude me from the thank-you note. I couldn't find him. Later in the day I tried to enter the MACV Order of Battle Section to find out what the analysts thought as against the lieutenant colonels. I was stopped at the door. "New policy," a guard said; "No civilians allowed on the premises." Another member of the CIA group, the Estimates staffer Bill Hyland, tried to explain: "Sam, don't take it so hard. You know what the political climate is. If you think they'd accept the higher numbers, you're living in a dream world."

That evening Bobby Layton of the Collation Branch held a party for the CIA delegation (minus Carver), saying: "You people could probably use one—let off steam, that kind of thing." I belched smoke like Old Forty-four. I pounded the table, cursed the military, and drank way too much Scotch. At one point, I announced: "Only officer in the entire U.S. Army's worth a damn is Colonel Hawkins." That was untrue, and I knew it. There were plenty of others, including Major Blascik.

I had a hangover the next morning, but nonetheless felt better. Maybe the party had done some good. After all, I told myself, nothing's in concrete. The numbers won't become official until Helms signs off on Fourteen Three, and that was a bridge we hadn't come to. There would have to be at least one "cleanup session" (as the last one was usually called), probably two, and I could use the occasion to tell the estimates board what had gone on at the conference. I decided to stop by the Collation Branch to apologize to Bobby Layton for the night before.

"Don't give it a second thought," he said. "You were the life of the party." I asked after another Collation member, Joe Hovey. Layton said: "Joe's away at the moment, and it's too bad. He's got a theory that the Vietcong are up to big things, but he can't figure out what. You'd be an interesting person for him to talk to, what with your knowledge of the communist army." I told Layton that the main thing I knew about the order of battle was that it ought to be doubled but that I'd observed another interesting phenomenon; over the last six or seven months the Chieu Hoi rate had fallen off by two-thirds.

"I've noticed that myself," he replied; "why do you suppose they're not coming in? They must know something which makes them hesitate to defect." He suggested that I see another one-time Collation member, Tom Becker, who had taken a job elsewhere in town with a joint Vietnamese-American outfit called CT Four. Begun in late 1966, CT Four was the first serious effort by the Allies to attack the works of the Vietcong's mainspring, the communist party, whose "infrastructure," as we called it, included the enemy's secret police. Aware of my interest in the latter, Layton said: "Maybe Tom could tell you whether CT Four's picked up anyone from the VC security section."

"No VC cops've checked in lately," Becker told me later that day, and CT Four's attack on the infrastructure was having its share of troubles. As usual, the first one was names. They'd collected thousands, he said, but only a handful were real. Worse yet, CT Four had scarcely dented the even more vexing problem of connecting names with faces. The Allies had captured lots of photographs (every other VC owned a Brownie, it seems), but who all the smiling people were was impossible to tell. CT Four had even sent to the States for an Identikit—a device used by American police to draw suspects' faces from composite features (eyebrows, chins, etc.)—but unfortunately the initial portraits all looked like Occidentals. Another problem was fingerprints. Supposedly they appeared on the ID cards of all South Vietnamese citizens, but there was no central fingerprint file to check the ID cards against. "So if we found a bomb under President Thieu's desk, we couldn't trace it, at least not by the prints." Finally there was America's general ignorance of the VC. "We don't know enough about their organization. CIA case officers are showing up all the time who don't even know the difference between the Party and the Front. That's as basic as you can get. You'd think somebody back at headquarters would teach them."

As I was leaving, Becker showed me a study just put out by the South Vietnamese. "It says the Vietcong are reorganizing around Saigon. Apparently they want to 'expedite operations' into the city. They're always saying something like that, but this time they seem more serious than usual. I wonder what they have in mind. Think I'll buy me a helmet."

I reported back to Langley on Monday, 18 September. The Indo-China sections were abuzz with the Saigon conference. George Allen said: "We'll live to regret it." Molly said: 'Squaring the circle,' my foot. I might have known that if Carver sold the plantation, he'd start off with a fancy quote." I defended him: "If it wasn't for Carver, none of this stuff would have come out. I don't think it was his fault. It must have been somebody higher. I put my money on Helms."

"Could be," said Molly. "Maybe even higher than that."

For the next two weeks, much of the paper crossing my desk concerned what we were going to tell the press about the new VC strength estimate. It was a touchy subject, but I didn't pay all that much attention.

What the reporters got was someone else's business. I was waiting for the cleanup session of Fourteen Three.

The meeting, when it convened, wasn't the cleanup after all. It was the pre-cleanup, meaning that only CIA officials were there. The conference room was crowded. Fourteen Three having achieved notoriety, several board members showed up instead of the usual one or two. There were also representatives from all the offices that dealt with Indo-China. The purpose of the pre-cleanup was to settle the Agency's internal quarrels so we could present a more or less untied front when the rest of the intelligence community appeared for the regular meeting. The chairman was the same as before Saigon, James Graham. He said: "It's been a long hard struggle, but I think—to employ a well-known phrase—there's a light at the end of the tunnel. The Saigon agreement may not be perfect, but it seems to have laid to rest the numbers question. Before we start, are there any questions or comments?"

I raised my hand.

Mr. Graham smiled: "OK, Sam, fire away."

I did so. It took almost two hours. First I told them about the difference between Colonel Hawkins' real and official positions (not using his name, since it might leak back, and get him in trouble.) Next I described the bargain that had led to the exit of the Vietcong self-defense militia—MACV's note having unfortunately disappeared, but with Bill Hyland there to vouch for its existence. Finally, at a blackboard, I laid out the affair of Long Dat District, showing how MACV had "scaled down" each of its service detachments. Singling out the ordnance unit, which had dropped from fifteen to three, I described the jobs of each of the twelve soldiers who'd been crossed off the list. They might have belonged to an American ordnance detachment. I concluded: "Gentlemen, if we count them in the United States Army, why can't we count them in the Vietcong's?"

There was a moment of uneasy silence. Mr. Graham broke it: "I guess the numbers aren't settled after all." Bill Hyland—who was tending the draft at one end of the conference table—said: "Christalmighty, this can go on forever."[28] The meeting dispersed. Two board members came up to where I was erasing the blackboard. One, an old southern gentleman named Ludlow Montagu, said: "It makes my blood boil to see the military cooking the books." The other was Sherman Kent, the man who had established the Board of National Estimates at CIA in the agency's early years. He asked: "Sam, have we gone beyond the bounds of reasonable dishonesty?" I replied: "Sir, we passed them in August."

During the next week, the agency's fo'c'stle seethed with rebellion over the terms of the Saigon agreement. George Allen berated Carver twice daily. Major Blascik chomped on his pipe. But the most overt signs of revolt arrived in Carver's office in the form of comments by various CIA officials on MACV's latest proposed briefing meant to explain the Saigon numbers to the press. The average comment was angry, but the most bilious of all came from an official in the Office of Economic Research, Paul Walsh. "As seen from this office," he wrote on 11 October,[29] "I must rank it as one of the greatest snow jobs since Potemkin constructed his village." It was so blatantly misleading, Walsh concluded, that "it gives us all the justification we need to go straight again." The hint was strong that it was Saigon where the agency had gone astray. I called Walsh's office to congratulate him, but he was out.

By Friday the thirteenth, even Carver had begun to waver. Perhaps stung by the ferocity of the attacks on MACV's briefing, he sent his own comments on it to the Pentagon for relay to Saigon. He wrote that one paragraph of the briefing was so bad that it would be "torn apart by the Saigon press corps." Another was "a clumsy piece of dissimulation."[30] These were strong words and when I read them Monday afternoon, I allowed myself to think the Saigon agreement was heading for the brink.

On Tuesday morning a message came from Vietnam that I felt pushed it over the edge. The message relayed the testimony of two midlevel defectors from the Delta. Both had the same story; the communists were reorganizing their army, in part by lumping together the guerrillas and the self-defense militia. I reread the message to make sure I'd gotten it right. I had. Its significance was immense. *If* the two types of soldiers were to consolidate, we could no longer tell them apart, either through captured documents or any way else. Willy nilly the Vietcong were parading the militia back into the MACV's Order of Battle.

I showed the cable to Carver. I hadn't seen much of him lately, not through distaste, but because I'd begun to repeat myself. I said: "Mr. Carver, see if it strikes you the same way it struck me." He read it.[31]

"Lord," he said softly. As I had, he read it again. He said: "Send a message to Saigon, and referencing this cable, have the station send a flier to the provinces asking whether the reorganization is countrywide. If it is, we may have to reopen the bidding on the OB. Meanwhile, I'll tell the director." He sounded almost cheerful.

Theresa Wilson gave me some cable blanks, which I commenced to fill out. As I did so, another thought struck me. This was the *second* big VC reorganization I'd heard of in the last six weeks. The first was the one Tom Becker had pointed out in Saigon; the communists were streamlining their local structure to "expedite operations" into the city. Meanwhile, the Chieu Hoi rate was still falling off. What was going on, anyway? It was interesting to speculate, but my job, as Carver had put it, was to "reopen the bidding" on the VC strength estimate.

I tried. Fourteen Three continued to meet, and at each session I brought in new evidence on the numbers. They wouldn't budge, but Mr. Graham agreed to some changes in wording. The overall estimate became "at least." A sentence was added that it "could be considerably higher." Then there was the exchange between Graham and me over the phrase "we believe their military force is in the range of . . ."

ADAMS: "Sir, how about taking out 'we believe' and putting in 'we estimate?'"

GRAHAM: "You mean on the grounds that we don't really believe it?"

ADAMS: "Yessir."

He did so. But he wouldn't change the numbers. Once again, the Estimates staffer, Bill Hyland, tried to explain: "You're tilting at windmills. Helms has us locked into the military's figures. We can't change them without his permission."

Fourteen Three met for the last time in the board conference room on Friday, 20 October 1967. With the completion of the last draft, resistance to the Saigon agreement ran out of steam. Gloomily I read the comments of the once-incipient rebel, Paul Walsh, on Monday afternoon. On behalf of his office, he wrote: "We share with many others numerous reservations about the estimate. We feel that the OB figures generally understate the strength of the enemy forces but recognize the apparent obligation for the estimate to be consistent with the figures agreed to at Saigon."[32] It was disgusting. Less than two weeks before, Walsh had recommended that the agency "go straight again," and had called MACV's proposed press briefing a "Potemkin's village."

The village was almost up. At the agency's insistence, the Pentagon had reluctantly inserted mention of the militia's exit from the OB into MACV's yet-to-be-given briefing, but this candor disturbed Saigon, including Ambassador Bunker. He cabled the White House ("Eyes Only Rostow") on 28 October that telling the press about the militia's departure "still bothers General Westmoreland, Bob Komer, and myself. Given the overriding need to demonstrate progress in grinding down the enemy, it is essential that we do not drag too many red herrings across the trail." To admit dropping the militia from the OB was "simply to invite trouble . . . Far better in our view is to deal with the matter orally if it arises (in the hopes of) forestalling many confusing and undesirable questions." He concluded: "Sorry to badger you on this, but the credibility gap is such that we don't want to end up conveying the opposite of what we intend."[33] I tried to envisage the white-haired old gentleman whose last words to me in Saigon were to give his best to my father. I couldn't, and stuck his cable in a file marked "self-defense" along with the messages Komer, Abrams, and Westmoreland had sent about the militia in August.*

---

*Unlike the Komer, Abrams, and Westmoreland cables—which received wide distribution within the agency—Bunker's message was closely held from the start. Apparently to keep his own people from seeing it, the ambassador sent it via private CIA channels to Langley for forwarding to Walt Rostow at the White House. Helms did this but kept a copy for himself. He made another for the Board of National Estimates before sending his own (with the notation "BNE has copy") to the agency's deputy director, Admiral Rufus Taylor, Taylor read it, and sent it "by hand" (very unusual) to Carver. That's when I saw it.

My hopes flickered briefly on the morning of 3 November. Helms still hadn't signed Fourteen Three and two big pieces of evidence arrived that I felt might stop him. The first was a cable from the Saigon Station, answering my query about the communists' lumping together the guerrillas and self-defense militia. The station couldn't yet tell whether such a consolidation had taken place, but it had news from the provinces that was equally important. The VC home guard was everywhere in a state of unprecedented flux, with guerrillas joining regular infantry units in some areas, training as sappers in others—a vast roiling about of the entire guerrilla-militia. Although the VC's purpose was unclear, the station recommended a sharp increase in the guerrilla numbers in Fourteen Three. I took the cable to Carver.[34] "A little late," he said, "but I'll send it on to the director."

The other evidence was a captured document. It came from —of all places—the DDI. Its bearer was a young analyst named Douglas Parry from a newly formed office whose main purpose, at last, was to study the Vietcong. Although MACV had published the document in late September, I'd missed it. A staff officer at COSVN headquarters had written the thing in "early 1967," I guessed about April.[35] "Take a look at page ten," said Parry. I did so. There it said that VC guerrillas in South Vietnam numbered 150,000. Assuming April was correct for the date, this figure was only six months old. Yet Fourteen Three's "currently agreed" number was 80,000. Could the guerrillas have dwindled that much in just half a year? It was almost inconceivable.* I thanked Parry, the first DDI-er to have given me a document since Molly had in August 1966. Then I showed it to Carver. "I'll send it on." he said.

It was useless. Late that afternoon Theresa handed me a memo from Helms. It wasn't to me personally, but to everyone who held copies of the final draft of Fourteen Three. His memo was called an "Introductory Note," explaining how American intelligence had managed to

---

*You will recall our previous countrywide reading on guerrillas came from two VC documents, both dated early 1966, one listing 170,000, the other 180,000. This meant that over a year's period—early 1966 to early 1967 —the guerrillas had gone down by about twenty or thirty thousand. This kind of decline was easy to credit.

underestimate the size of the communist army.[36] First, Helms blamed the South Vietnamese, because their information was "unreliable." Then he blamed "a social environment where basic data is incomplete and often untrustworthy." Finally, he condemned "complex methodological approaches which cannot rise above uncertain data inputs." *Baloney!* The reason we'd underestimated the communist army was that no one had looked at a damn thing until August 1966! With growing anger, I read the remaining paragraphs. The last one said that the VC had a "deliberate" policy of "sacrificing" the lower levels of their army in order to maintain the strength of the regulars (which was true), but that the lower level to sacrifice the most was the guerrillas, "now estimated to total some 80,000."[36]

Eighty thousand? So Helms was sticking to the Saigon agreement after all! I quickly reviewed what the "all" consisted of. First, George Allen and me, the only ones at agency headquarters who'd worked on the subject; second, Colonel Hawkins, whose warning I'd passed to George Carver; third, the agency's Saigon Station, its advice for a "sharp increase" in guerrillas only hours old; and fourth—and most important—the latest VC document, which gave a number almost double eighty thousand. Having blithely disregarded the "all," just who was Helms regarding?

I said to myself: *The damn liars at MACV headquarters, that's who!*

At that moment, I happened to be holding a yellow Eberhart Faber no. 2 pencil. I snapped it in half. That was the turning point of my career at the CIA, although I didn't realize it at the time.

I quickly simmered down, and for several minutes looked at the two halves of the yellow pencil, wondering what to do. Gradually the thought formed: Helms *still* hadn't signed the estimate, and by God, I'd make one last try to stop him, this time putting all my thoughts *in writing.* That was important, *in writing.* The maxim had come to mind (I believe it was my old Africa boss, Dana Ball's), "Bureaucrats cringe from written complaints as Dracula does from the cross." Ok, that was funny, but I'd have to be careful.

I reread the Introductory Note. Its one piece of useful information was that the chiefs of the big intelligence agencies were scheduled to gather at 10:30 Thursday morning, 9 November, to review the final draft of Fourteen Three. That gave me six days to write my complaint. I tossed the pencil halves into a wastepaper basket, took out a ballpoint pen, and wrote down the title: "Comments on the Current Drafts of the Introductory Note and Text of National Intelligence Estimate Fourteen Three." Not very pithy, but precise. I chewed on the end of the ball point, and began:

"Having studied the Vietcong manpower problem since early 1966, and discussed various drafts of Fourteen Three for what seems almost as long, I wish to make the following comments as a matter of permanent record. They are my views and not necessarily those of my office." (This last took George Carver off the hook.)

I kept at the comments off and on for five days, using the same documents and arguments I'd used since early summer. By midafternoon of Wednesday, 8 November, I was beating an old hobbyhorse of mine, how the low manpower numbers had skewed all the other estimates, such as logistics, when I lost power. I read the comments over. There was something missing. It hit me what was wrong. Until that point they simply rehashed evidence. There were no conclusions. I chewed some more on the ballpoint pen, and under the heading "General Comments on the Text," wrote as follows:

> I see no reason to dwell at length on why I think the current draft of Fourteen Three is an inadequate piece of analytical work. I will make four points, briefly.
>
> First, the current draft is ill-formed and incoherent. Discussions of logistics, losses, and manpower are largely unrelated.
>
> Second, the draft is less than candid. It conceals rather than edifies, using such devices as the phrase "at least" to obscure the possible existence of tens of thousands of Vietcong soldiers. Too often, it attempts to blame the evidence as inadequate, when the fault is not in information but in analysis.

Third, the draft is timid. Its history is one of attacks by soldiers and politicians, and retreats by intelligence officials. Rather than admit the extent of past underestimates of enemy strength, its authors hide behind disclaimers and refuse to add up numbers, while protesting that it is inadvisable to make sums of apples and oranges.

Finally, it is unwise. Although it intimates that there are "considerable" numbers beside the "at least 223,000 to 248,000" (listed in paragraph 37), it does not come to grips with the probability that the number of Vietcong, as currently defined, is something over half a million. Thus it makes canyons of gaps, and encourages self delusion."[37]

The "gaps" referred to were credibility gaps. Now, I realize by current standards, these conclusions look pretty dry, but for me back in those days, they were high rhetoric. Therefore, I decided to try the comments out on some other people before handing them to George Carver. Theresa Wilson typed it all up—saying "I hope you know what you're doing" when she was done—then I showed them to Don Blascik. "You've hoisted the Jolly Roger," he said. Next was George Allen.

"Chicken thieves," he said. "You're calling the CIA leadership a pack of chicken thieves."

"Is it too strongly worded?" I asked nervously.

"No," he replied. "It's about right. Much weaker, and they wouldn't get the point. Much stronger, and they'd hang you for insubordination. We've got to stop those numbers from getting in concrete." He handed the comments back, saying "When you give this to Carver, tell him it's with my blessing."

Carver read them the following morning with what I took to be horrified disbelief. When he was through, I said: "Sir, I have two requests. The first is that you show these to Mr. Helms before his ten-thirty meeting today. The second is for permission to give copies to the other people around the building, particularly the Board of National Estimates."

Looking me square in the eye, he said: "Permission granted." Under the circumstances, it was an admirable reaction, especially so since he'd had a hand in what I was complaining about. Carver disappeared—I presumed to the director's office—and I went to a Xerox machine. I distributed twenty-five copies by nine-thirty. Among the recipients were Mr. Graham and several other board members: R. Jack Smith, the head of the DDI, and his deputy, Edward Proctor, plus a number of lesser entities, such as Bill Hyland, Paul Walsh, Dean Moor, and Molly. Then I hunkered down to await the arrival of goodness knows what, maybe a posse.

No posse arrived, however, either for the rest of Thursday, or on Friday either. In fact nothing happened at all. On late Friday afternoon, curiosity overcame me, and I went to see my old friend in the DDI front office, the ex–Laotian analyst, Jack Ives. He showed me a note Edward Proctor had sent to R. Jack Smith concerning my comments. The note said: "This is the work of an angry young man. We ought not to allow it in our files without writing an answer." However, no answer was forthcoming.

Helms signed Fourteen-Three on Monday morning, 13 November 1967.[38] Since the first meeting 144 days earlier, the estimate had gone through twenty-two separate drafts, the hardest-fought in agency history. When I saw Helm's signature—"concurred in" by the entire "United States Intelligence Board" (it said just below it)—I went to Carver to say I wanted to quit the director's office. Carver looked embarrassed when I told him why, but he said there was nothing he could do. I thanked him for his help on the order of battle earlier in the year, and asked to transfer to the new DDI office whose job was to follow the Vietcong. He said OK, he'd see what he could do. I returned to my desk.

Well, maybe Helms and the U.S. Intelligence Board thought the numbers problem was laid to rest, but there was one group who didn't: the Vietcong. They were trying to build up their regular army. Several more missing units had turned up lately, and I increasingly suspected that the order of battle might be as low for this type of soldier as it was for the others. There was a problem, however; checking regulars was a prodigious task. Whereas the OB carried guerrillas, for instance, in a lump sum by province, it listed regulars by individual unit. Thus I'd have to snake them out battalion by battalion, platoon by platoon. There seemed no way of accomplishing this except by plodding once more through the VC documents. This I commenced to do.

It was a frustrating experience. On one occasion, for example, I flushed a covey of little rocket units the Vietcong had concealed in the central highlands. Their total complement was less than three hundred men, however, a drop in the bucket. An added indignity was the presence in Washington of Bunker and Westmoreland, who—recalled temporarily from Saigon—were buttonholing reporters to announce the VC were in a bad way. They had their effect. "The Enemy Is Running Out of Men" proclaimed a *Washington Daily News* headline on 16 November (a Jim Lucas exclusive).[39] "Westmoreland Is Sure of Victory," said the *New York Times* on the twenty-third. The *Times* story reported that the general had said at a Pentagon briefing that the Communist Army had dropped from 285,000 men in 1966 to 242,000 at last count.[40] I read the story carefully to see if he'd mentioned the self-defense militia's exit from the OB. He hadn't. George Allen was as disgusted as I was. The day after the *Times* account, he sent a note in to Carver saying Westmoreland's numbers were "phoney" and "contrived," and "controlled by a desire to stay under 300,000."[41] I didn't bother to complain, partly through the conviction that it would do no good, but mostly because I was too busy looking for communist regulars.

I didn't find many that day—Friday, 24 November—but I found something else, perhaps as significant: a VC report about faking South Vietnamese ID cards. It was of a kind I might easily have passed over but for my conversation in Vietnam in September with the CT Four analyst, Tom Becker. Becker had seemed to think that ID cards were an important subject, and in deference to his opinion, I read the report carefully. It laid out the activities of a small Vietcong forging cell on the outskirts of Saigon during a recent nine-month period. During that time the cell claimed to have distributed 145 false ID cards, as well as a number of lesser papers, such as fifty-five draft deferment certificates, and forty sets of discharge papers from a South Vietnamese airborne battalion. That looked to me an awfully big output for a single cell—cells ran normally from three to six people—but there was an even more astonishing claim at the report's end. It said that during the same nine months, the cell had received from "higher authorities" two hundred South Vietnamese civilian ID card blanks, fifty Government National Police ID card blanks, and two seals of Saigon's Seventh Police Precinct, *all genuine.*[42]

It didn't take long to think out some harrowing implications. First, the VC had one or more spies in the government's central ID-card-issuing office (meaning there were plenty more cards where these came from), and probably a spy in the Seventh Precinct's National Police headquarters as well; second, the papers they were "forging"—on genuine blanks, stamped with genuine seals—were probably indistinguishable from the real thing (bearing in mind Tom Becker's observation that the fingerprints on real ID cards were a mere formality since there was no place to check them against); third, the number of people the Vietcong could send into Saigon with legal documentation must be very large indeed. If this one cell could provide papers for 250 people (incidentally, the size of a standard Vietcong sapper battalion), several cells could provide—it was staggering to think. I called up my friend in the counterintelligence staff, Bill Johnson. "Better send me a copy," he groaned. I showed the document to George Carver. "Write it up," he said cheerfully. I think he was pleased not to get harangued again about the order of battle. "But it can wait 'til Monday," he added. "Why don't you take the rest of the afternoon off?" I did so with thanks.

On Monday morning I got back to find that my discovery of Friday had been eclipsed by a long cable that the Saigon Station had sent in over the weekend. Apparently Walt Rostow of the White House had some days earlier asked the station what it thought the VC were going to do in their upcoming winter-spring campaign. Based on documents and POW reports, the station answer was a shocker. George Allen read me some of the significant passages "'The communist strategy is in a state of flux,'" he quoted. The VC were describing their campaign as the "decisive phase of the war." Its goals were to be achieved through "a coordinated and countrywide, political and military offensive utilizing all Vietcong assets."[43] George handed me the cable, saying: "Looks to me like a balls-out attack, even bigger than what's going on now at Loc Ninh and Dak To." (He was referring to unusually large battles then in progress in South Vietnam's interior.) "Now this is the station's first cut at answering Rostow's request. The final one's due in two or three weeks. When it goes to the White House, it'll probably cause a flap. I want you to keep a file on this offensive, and show me any reports—let's call them 'extraordinary documents'—which shed light on it."

I got from Theresa Wilson a new manila folder to which I affixed the label "VC Winter-Spring Campaign." In fact, as I thought about it, the station cable seemed to make sense out of some things I'd seen earlier. *If* the Vietcong were about to launch an attack "utilizing all their assets," it was scarcely a surprise that they would want to shift the assets around to prepare for it. This might explain the reorganization around Saigon (the one Tom Becker had told me about), and the unusual activity among the guerrilla-militia. Christ! the guerrilla-militia. If you added them together, there were three times as many as we allowed in the order of battle.* I thought: This was the last time on earth we should be playing games with the OB. Hurriedly I returned to my document hunt for VC regulars—the type of soldier who would spearhead an attack. On Monday, 4 December, the November Chieu Hoi statistics came in: 553 military defectors, the lowest number I'd ever seen.

Over the next ten days, there was a good deal of back-and-forth over the station cable. Its "last cut" came in, and I reread it for further details. It said that the Winter-Spring campaign's next phase was planned for "January to March 1968"; that the communists had set for themselves

---

* At that time the VC had perhaps 250,000 guerrillas and militiamen in their home guard. Of these, the OB listed only 80,000 guerrillas.

"the task of occupying and holding some urban centers in South Vietnam, and isolating many others"; and that their object was "to inflict unacceptable military and political losses on the Allies regardless of VC casualties during a U.S. election year, in the hopes that the United States will be forced to yield to resulting domestic and international political pressure and withdraw from South Vietnam." "In sum," it concluded "the war is probably nearing a turning point . . . The outcome of the . . . campaign will in all likelihood determine the future direction of the war."[44]

This was heady stuff to let loose on the White House without comment, so Carver sent it around Langley first to solicit opinions. The first to come back was from the Office of Current Intelligence, the one that produced the Sitrep. The station was blowing smoke, it said; "We question whether communist strategy . . . is in a state of flux," and OCI had seen nothing "to suggest that the communists think they can really mount a decisive campaign."[45] Much more likely, the VC would do what they'd been doing all along, which was to wage "protracted warfare." Protracted warfare doesn't include all-out offensives.

The next opinion was mine. At this point my main feeling about such an attack—other than it seemed to make sense—was that if one was coming it would be enormous. Therefore, I used the opportunity to take another swipe at the order of battle. I listed the usual omissions plus a couple of new ones.[46] In the last few days several documents had turned up that mentioned regular VC infantry battalions listed in the order of battle, but with strengths much higher than the OB acknowledged.

Carver sent the station assessment to the White House on 15 December, but with a cover sheet of his own, written on Office-of-the-Director stationery. Doubtless mindful of OCI's pooh-poohing, he pointed out that the station cable was "a field study and should not be read as the considered opinion of the agency."[47] The field—whose assessment was based on captured documents—didn't get all the high-level intelligence available in Washington, he continued, and the VC's "current activity patterns" were not unlike those which prevailed in 1965 and 1966. He didn't mention my comments on the order of battle. When I saw this omission, I felt the CIA was digging itself into a deeper and deeper hole. Only a few days before it had sent another big "Will To Persist" memo to McNamara, using all the numbers from Fourteen Three.[48] I'd tried to change them upwards, but had been told that unfortunately the manpower account had gone downstairs to Paul Walsh, the one who had recognized in late October "the apparent obligation for the estimate to be consistent with the figures agreed to as Saigon." At that time we'd been prisoners of the Saigon agreement; now we were prisoners of Fourteen Three.

Christmas came and went, so did New Year's, and about the only person I talked business to regularly any more was George Allen. From time to time I brought him "extraordinary documents"—which he'd asked for concerning the offensive, and which still pointed to a big one—and we jawboned about the evils of doctoring enemy strength estimates. On the fourth of January, MACV's year-end Order of Battle came in. It had actually *declined,* another 9,600 guerrillas having bitten the dust, and with some additional seepage from the regulars.[49] I looked at the fine print to discover, for example, that the R20 Local Force Battalion near Danang had dropped 50 men, that the 32nd North Vietnamese Regiment had gone from 1,600 to 1,100 men, and so on.[50] The decline was damn peculiar for an enemy that was supposed to be priming for a big attack. On the following morning, Helms' New Year's briefing package for Congress arrived on my desk using Fourteen Three's faked numbers,[51] and that afternoon, Theresa told me that my transfer had come through to leave the director's office. She said I was to report to the DDI's new Vietcong Branch down on the fourth floor at the end of the month.

Meanwhile in Vietnam, VC activity was picking up. The communists were closing in on a U.S. Marine Corps redoubt called Khe Sanh near the DMZ, and there were reports that as many as three North Vietnamese divisions were involved. One was the 304th. "The Fightin' Three Oh Four," George Allen had cried a couple of weeks earlier; "It fought at Dien Bien Phu!" This was the first mention of Dien Bien

Phu I'd heard for some time, but it had since become the main topic of conversation. Its surrender in May 1954 had precipitated the French decision to leave Indo-China, and the theory had developed that the communists wanted to pull a repeat performance on us at Khe Sanh. In discussing the 1954 fracas George knew what he was talking about. He had been a Vietnam analyst for the Army back then and could describe the fall of the French base bastion by bastion. To keep abreast of the latest battle, Major Blascik—who had just opened a large situation room at the other end of the hall from Carver—was negotiating with the Cartography Section for a giant chart of the area around Khe Sanh.

On the morning of 12 January, a Friday, I was watching the installation of the map, which was truly gigantic, when Theresa hollered in from the hall that I was wanted on the telephone. I picked it up and the caller said: "That you, Sam? This is Colonel Hawkins."

"Colonel Hawkins!" I said. "Where are you?"

"Up in Baltimore at Fort Holabird. I run a course in intelligence up here, and this afternoon I'm coming down to visit Langley."

"Can we talk about the OB?"

"That's one of the reasons I'm coming," he said. We made an appointment for 2:00 P.M.

It was the best news I'd had in months. For several weeks now I'd been chipping away at the enemy's regular army, finding companies here, platoons there, never more than a few hundred men a day. Here was the man who probably knew more about VC regulars than anyone else in the United States government. Furthermore I could ask if he still felt as he had earlier about the rest of the OB, particularly the guerrillas. As for MACV's chicanery, it was best left alone, at least for the time being. The colonel was taking a big risk as it was, and my object was not to rake muck, but to find enemy soldiers. When he entered the situation room at two, we must have shaken hands for a solid minute, all that time smiling broadly.

"Those were the worst three months of my entire life," he said, obviously referring to July, August and September.

"They were none too pleasant for me either, Colonel," I replied. "Now let's get down to business." We talked for two hours. He confirmed his earlier opinion that there were as many as 120,000 guerrillas, and identified a number of service units MACV had scaled down. We ended up on regulars. When he'd left Saigon in mid-September, his regular estimate was "conservative," but not outrageously so. Certain types of formations needed work, such as sappers (I knew about these), city units (one for each of the forty-four province capitals), and oddball formations such as *vung* (area) units. A good place to look for missing battalions was among the divisions, he suggested, of which the communists had nine. As for the recent decline in regular strengths in the OB, he couldn't explain it, not having seen any documents since his departure from Vietnam. As we were breaking up, he invited me to Holabird to give some lectures on the VC. I said I'd be delighted to help him out, and meant it.

After the weekend, Theresa typed up my notes in a formal memorandum of conversation,[52] which I sent around the building with the notation "This is completely off-the-record, so please be careful in using it. That is, protect Colonel Hawkins." Among those to get it were George Carver and Paul Walsh, the new manpower chief, but neither of them did anything about it, such as demand a higher strength estimate. Thanks to Helms, we were still tied to Fourteen Three.

Having been pointed in the right direction by Colonel Hawkins, I got to work, starting with the divisions. Now Vietnamese communist divisions are like ours in that they have three infantry regiments, plus a number of support units, such as artillery. So I got out my MACV Order of Battle and looked up the Vietcong Ninth Division, which operated not far from Saigon. The OB listed the three regiments all right (the 271st, the 272nd, and the 273rd), but it had *no support units whatsoever*.[53] Christ! I dove into my files and quickly came up with a VC document about the Ninth.[54] The document listed *ten* support units, including four companies and six battalions, among them an artillery battalion, a mortar battalion, an anti-aircraft battalion, and a battalion of scouts, arguably the best troops in the entire division. I looked up the other eight divisions, and similar omissions, normally including all the divisional artillery.

Next I investigated city units. As a rule, city units didn't operate in the cities themselves, but stayed just beyond the suburbs, waiting for an opening. In urban assaults, like the one forecast by the station cable, such units would be expected to lead the way. I began with Danang. Danang didn't have *one* city unit, it had several, including the T89 and T87 battalions,[55] and a whole mess of commando platoons, none carried in the OB. What surprised me most was the number of VC documents on the T89, maybe twenty. How could the OB Section possibly have missed it? It looked fishy. On the other hand, most things looked fishy to me nowadays, and I telephoned everyone I could think of to tell them about omitted regulars. I might as well have been talking about hot dog buns. By Monday, 22 January, it was clear that the number of unlisted regulars was at least 50,000—the equivalent of seven extra divisions— and conceivably a lot more.

Monday was an active day. Over the weekend, the enemy had loosed a big artillery barrage at Khe Sanh, and the Marines had captured a North Vietnamese lieutenant who claimed that the communists intended to take the place in the not-too-distant future. To prepare for the attack General Westmoreland was plastering the adjacent landscape with B-52 raids, and Major Blascik was marking up his enormous map. Blascik's map was incredible to behold. He had two helpers now, and with red and blue pins and various kinds of stickers they were plotting not only the last-known locations of all friendly and enemy units, but also the precise whereabouts of every skirmish, no matter how small, and even the strike pattern for each stick of B-52 bombs. Word of the map spread quickly through the building, and CIA people began to arrive in the situation room to take a look. George Allen was in his element. "You should have seen what they did to Gabrielle," I heard him tell a caller, "Gabrielle" being the name of a French bastion which fell to the Vietminh in the early stages of Dien Bien Phu. As if taking their cue from George, the communists that afternoon overran a Special Forces camp a few miles west of Khe Sanh.

By Thursday, the map had become a lodestone for official Washington. Dignitaries came from the Pentagon, the State Department, and even the White House to see it.* A Blascik helper had penciled in the trenches, which the visitors eagerly traced with their fingers. Communist divisions in the general vicinity now included the 304th, the 325C, the 324B, and the 320th. As he was leaving the situation room, I heard a dignitary tell George Allen: "My God they've got a lot of troops up there."

When the visitor had gone out the door, I took Allen aside. "George, you know as well as I do, it's not just at Khe Sanh. The VC have troops all over the place. They could launch an attack everywhere in the country and still have plenty of men to spare."

George said: "I know, I know. I tell them that, but they won't listen. They aren't interested in the OB. They want to hear about Khe Sanh." Later in the day I read a newly arrived study from NSA. It was called "Coordinated Vietnamese Communist Offensive Evidenced in South Vietnam," and it noted "an almost unprecedented volume of urgent messages . . . passing among major commands." Most of the messages concerned the northern half of the country, but there was some "possibly related activity" in "Nam Bo." Nam Bo was the south, including Saigon. The study said the precise timing of the offensive was unclear, but that several VC messages referred to it as "N-Day."[56]

I passed the next day, Friday, quietly at work, spent the weekend at home, and returned to Carver's office on Monday morning to pack. It was 29 January and my transfer orders to the DDI's new Vietcong Branch on the fourth floor read "end of the month." I guessed it would take the entire day to ready my files for the big move, since they now occupied the better part of four stand-up safes. The safes held an almost complete set of MACV's nine-thousand-odd bulletins, and a variety of

---

*But not President Johnson. He had a big Khe Sanh chart of his own in the White House basement. An acquaintance who saw both Johnson's and Blascik's maps said Blascik's was much better.

manila folders, including one marked "VC Winter-Spring Campaign." It was funny how little mention there'd been of the station cable since it had gone to the White House in mid-December. I presumed the NSA study that had predicted a "coordinated offensive" was talking about the same thing.

In any case, Vietnam was relatively peaceful. In honor of the Tet holidays, General Westmoreland had declared a cease-fire (except in I Corps, where Khe Sanh was), and the procession to Major Blascik's situation room had considerably abated. The job of tidying files went quicker than expected, and I decided to leave an hour before my customary departure time of six o'clock. On the way to the exit, I stopped by the fifth floor, as I often did, to read an advance copy of the Sitrep. I found one in somebody's out-box, and scanned its front page, the summary, called the "Highlights." It had its usual notation in the upper right-hand corner, "Information as of 1600" meaning four that afternoon. The highlights began: "Military activity in South Vietnam has slackened since the beginning of the modified allied cease-fire. Hanoi had indicated willingness to discuss a new proposal for negotiations with U.N. Secretary General Thant." I skipped to the heading, "*Political Developments,*" which read: "*Reaction in Saigon to President Thieu's 'state of the nation' address has been mixed.*" Thence to "*North Vietnamese Military Developments*": a couple of MIGs had flown toward the DMZ. And finally to "*Other Communist Military Developments*": "There is nothing of significance to report."[57]

I tossed the Sitrep back into the out-box without reading the full text (which went on for seventeen pages), and caught the elevator to the ground floor. On the way to the door leading to the parking lot, I glanced at a clock. The time was exactly 5:00 P.M.

At the same moment in Vietnam it was six o'clock in the morning of 30 January 1968. "N-Day"—the codename for what became the turning point of the war, the Tet offensive—was approximately four hours old.

6 N-DAY

TO ENTER ROOM 6F19, you first had to poke the right buttons. There were ten of them protruding from a small metal box by the outer door, and when on Tuesday morning I chose the appropriate ones— 1–9–5–4, the date of the Geneva Accords, which George Carver felt everyone could remember—I had no idea that unusual events were happening in Vietnam. The buzzer sounded, the door swung open, and immediately I recognized that something was the matter. It was only 8:35, coffee time on normal days, but *all four* secretaries were typing. I walked past them to the situation room at the end of the hall, and opened the door.

The room teemed with officials, gesticulating, reading cables, and squinting at maps. That is, all but Major Blascik, who was talking calmly on the gray phone between puffs on his pipe. In front of one of the maps I saw my friend Tom Becker, whom I'd last seen in Vietnam at CT Four in September. I said:

"Hello, Tom, when did you get back?"

"A few minutes ago. I left Saigon in late November. Been on leave ever since."

"What's going on, anyway?"

"The little beggars seem to have run amok," he said, "But I really don't know. I just got here myself."[1]

I looked at the map before him. It was of I Corps and already measled with red pins. Clearly, Blascik had come in early to stick them there. Just then the major hung up the gray phone. I asked him for a quick rundown.

He said: "They've been at it since early this morning—that's Vietnam time—and they're hitting targets throughout the northern half of the country; first Nha Trang on the coast, fighting's still going on there; then Ban Me Thuct and Kontum in the highlands; next Hoi An in the lowlands; then they tried to get into Danang, but the Marines seem to have kept out the infantry so far—least that's what they claim—but not the rockets; next Qui Nhon and Pleiku; Cam Manh and Tuy Hoa as well; also several district towns, some that we know about, and others, probably, that we don't. Communications have broken down in some spots. The interesting thing about these attacks, what makes them so unusual, is that they're going into the cities. They've never done that before, at least not on this scale. God knows what's happening in the countryside."

"What about Khe Sanh?" I asked.

"Nothing on Khe Sanh. Some shelling, yes, but no major attacks, not yet."

"Any word on which units are committed?"

"A couple of mentions in the cables, but that's it. Everyone's too busy fighting them off to find out who they are. That'll come later. The cables are on one of those clipboards on the wall over there. Help yourself." With typical Blascik efficiency, he had all the traffic in one place. I took down a clipboard and flipped through it. Unable to find the units Blascik had seen, I replaced it and took down another, this one holding the most recent intelligence publications. The top publication was the morning Bulletin, which, like the Sitrep, was put out by the Office of Current Intelligence.

This Bulletin was only two hours old, and had picked up the information the Sitrep had missed the night before.

The Bulletin read: "Communist forces have launched a series of well-coordinated attacks on . . ." and it listed the cities that Blascik had already mentioned. It also noted that Westmoreland had announced cancellation of the Tet cease-fire, and concluded that the assaults were a "blatant violation of the truce period."[2]

At this point, George Allen showed up at my elbow. "This is the one they've been planning," he said excitedly, "and they haven't even started in on the south. That should begin in a few hours." I showed him the bulletin's comment that it was a "blatant violation of the truce period."

"Blatant?" he said; "it's *outrageous!*" And he gave an imitation of General Westmoreland lecturing Ho Chi Minh: "Damnitall, Ho, you should be ashamed. Don't you know *Tet's a religious holiday?* Have you no Christian respect? *Another* sneak attack. You think I forgot your last one? Pearl Harbor? It was on a Sunday, goddamnit, a *Sunday!*"

I asked George if he'd heard which units were involved in the offensive. He said: "No, I haven't, but I imagine they include the elite ones you've been telling Carver about. It's logical. Urban attacks are what they're for."

I left the confusion of the situation room for my desk, in order to draft a cable to the Saigon Station. It began: "Although we are obviously ignorant of what units carried out the city penetration operations . . . we suspect that many . . . were undertaken by units not listed in the MACV Order of Battle." Then I mentioned some types of OB normally omitted (city, sapper, scout, special action, etc.), threw in a few examples, such as the Danang city unit, including the T89 and T87 battalions, and concluded: "We request you draw MACV's attention to this matter, and suggest they address the question of how to add the missing units . . . to the OB. Frankly, we find it something of an anomoly to be taking so much punishment from communist soldiers whose existence is not officially acknowledged."[3]

Fortunately, Carver was alone at the moment and I was able to see him. Stroking his already mussed-up hair, he perused the draft. His main alteration to it was to change anom*o*ly to anom*a*ly. He said: "That's a pertinent question, whether these units are in the OB. Send it on, as is. But come to think of it, you should check it out first with Drex Godfrey." Drexel Godfrey was the head of OCI, the same man who'd complained in May about my using "unofficial" figures. Theresa addressed a buckslip to OCI, stapled it to the draft, and I went to the credit union to cash a twenty-dollar check.[4] Dawdling over some errands, I had a later-than-usual lunch, and didn't get back to the situation room until two o'clock.

If anything, it was more hectic than in the morning. The maps of I and II Corps were now a forest of red pins, and George Allen was expostulating to a visiting dignitary about woes to come. At about 2:15 P.M., a person clutching some AP ticker crashed into the room, shouting: "Christ, they're into the embassy!" The dignitary's face went pale, even George Allen looked surprised, and Major Blascik stuck a red pin into the capital city.[5] It was the first one on the III Corps map. He said to a subordinate: "Better go downstairs and get some additional pins." The subordinate reappeared a few minutes later with several more boxes. Blascik had already mounted on the wall a large-scale map of Saigon.

The rest of the afternoon was a big drain on the pin supply. Only now—as George Allen had predicted—they skewered III and IV Corps. The province capitals checked in one by one from the Delta: Vinh Long, Bac Lieu, Can Tho, My Tho, Vi Thanh, Ben Tre, Moc Hoa, Ca Mau, Soc Trang and so on. Few Americans were in the Delta, so reporting was sketchy about the district seats. I wondered about those I'd visited in Long An. Had Major Foote survived with his sandbagged TV set? The first reports came in of American aircraft losses. They were heavy, mostly on the ground and mostly from rockets and artillery shells. I supposed the guns that shot at them weren't in the OB. I checked Blascik's clipboard for mentions of VC units: a few now, primarily big ones, the easiest to spot. The communist Fifth, Seventh and Ninth divisions were said to be closing on Saigon. With no official duties, I left work at five o'clock. Tomorrow was the last day of January, the date set for my departure for the third floor.

The next morning the situation room had settled into a busy but cheerful routine. Blascik had drafted Tom Becker into the room's staff, and he, with three others, kept up the numerous tote boards and charts. There were frequent entries, sometimes accompanied by whistles of admiration. Becker said: "I thought the VC were supposed to be little people who crept around the jungle in rubber sandals." The cables showed that although the embassy grounds were now clear of Vietcong, the fighting had spread to other parts of Saigon, including its racetrack, and many more infantry assaults and shellings had occurred elsewhere during the night. A preliminary report from Danang said the communists had destroyed or damaged forty-three planes and helicopters at local runways alone. The worst news came from Hue. Enemy soldiers had overrun the citadel, and were roaming the imperial city in captured jeeps. About the only place in the country left quiet was Khe Sanh. By now the attacks had taken on a collective name—the Tet Offensive.

All this was interesting, but the time had come to pack. I began loading my files into a shopping cart. As I did so, the "VC Winter-Spring Campaign" folder caught my eye. I skimmed the station cable that had prompted the folder's start. Its date was 24 November 1967, and out popped the key phrases: *All-out offensive; January to March 1968;* and *urban centers.*[6] My Lord, the message was almost ten weeks old, but whoever'd written it was right on the button. I asked Tom Becker, who'd been in Vietnam in late November, if he knew the author.

"Joe Hovey," said Becker. "He wrote it on Thanksgiving Day. I saw it at Collation right before I left Saigon. The Agency should put his name in lights on top of the headquarters building: *Joseph Hovey, The Man Who Predicted The Tet Offensive.*"

"Fat chance," I replied, recalling that Hovey's cable had gone to the White House in mid-December under a note by Carver which strongly implied—at OCI's behest—that Hovey was crying wolf. I was still annoyed at this thought when Theresa handed me the draft that I'd sent Drexel Godfrey the day before about VC units omitted from the order of battle. Godfrey had scribbled on the buckslip: "To Sam Adams. Suggest you hold this until things quiet down. Also, its validity seems a little dubious—at least as of now."[7]

That buckslip was too damn much. Godfrey had tried to kill realistic numbers nine months before, and he was still at it. Overcome with disgust, I wrote Carver a letter of resignation, something I hadn't intended to do. The letter said that the CIA's failing was to acquiesce to MACV's half-truths, distortions and sometimes outright falsehoods." Furthermore, Westmoreland's order of battle was a "monument of deceit" to which the agency had cravenly bowed in Saigon in September. These were the last sentences I composed for the Office of the Director, and when I slid it in Carver's in-box on my way out the door, it occurred to me that he was the wrong recipient.[8] It wasn't really Carver's fault, not even Drexel Godfrey's. It was Helms's.

I found myself wheeling the shopping cart back and forth all day. The VC Branch secretary, Beverly, was appalled. "Where am I going to put all this crap?" she asked. It turned out not to be a problem. There was room. The VC Branch was so new that it had few files of its own. Unfortunately, it was also on the bottom of the mail room's distribution list, so I spent most of the rest of the week back with Major Blascik, looking for VC unit designations. I searched everything in sight, even the newspapers. In fact, there were a couple of interesting stories. On Thursday, for example, Ward Just of the *Washington Post* wrote that "even the toughest pessimists here had not thought that the communists could mount so many offensives with so many men."[9] When I showed it to George Allen, he looked insulted. And in a later *Post*, Peter Arnett reported from Saigon that Allied soldiers rifling the pockets of dead VC sappers after their attack on the U.S. Embassy had found forged curfew passes. The story said that perhaps five communist battalions were now in Saigon, and that many VC troops had entered the city three days before the attack.[10] Five VC battalions equals two thousand men, likely a fraction of the people involved. I recalled the pre-Tet document which had put the claimed production of a VC forging cell for nine months at 250 fake ID cards, scarcely enough for that big a force. My suspicion heightened that this forging cell was only one of many such cells.

Saturday's Bulletin observed that VC troops were still in Hue, Hoi
An, Phan Thiet, and Dalat, with new assaults on Xuan Loc and Phuoc
Le, and that "the effectiveness of the Saigon government was being
sorely taxed in the current military crisis."[11] Eventually, the situation
room maps showed that the VC attacked forty of South Vietnam's forty-
four province capitals, almost a hundred of its district seats, and four of
the five autonomous cities. In most of these places, they'd broken into
town. Other situation-room records showed the VC destroyed or damaged twelve hundred U.S. aircraft.[12] The offensive was not only a
slam-bang performance, it was a fine piece of evidence. How could the
communists have mounted such a big attack with an army of only
225,346 men, the number carried in MACV's latest Order of Battle?[13]

I put that question on Monday morning to the VC Branch chief,
Ron Smith. A friendly man of ruddy complexion and Maine accent, he
said: "It's obvious they couldn't. They've got double that figure, and
probably a lot more. The main question is whether the higher numbers
are acceptable to the chain of command." I was well aware of the problem with the chain of command. The VC Branch was part of the Office
of Economic Research, whose boss on Vietnam was Paul Walsh, a pre-
Tet supporter of the Saigon agreement. Moreover, as part of the DDI,
Walsh reported to its head, R. Jack Smith, who in turn reported to the
director, Richard Helms. Looked at from this angle the numbers
predicament was the same as ever.

But for two other reasons, it wasn't. I've already mentioned reason
number one—the enormous indisputable fact of the Tet Offensive, over
which the whole United States press was in a grand halloo that showed
few signs of abating. The second reason was less obvious, but in my view
almost as important. Finally I had some help. There were four analysts
beside myself assigned to work on the Vietcong. Two were alumni of
Saigon's Collation Branch, which meant they knew something about
the VC; a third was named Joe Stumpf, who'd already visited Vietnam
briefly to look into enemy recruiting; and the fourth was Doug Parry,
who had given me the enemy document before Tet about the 150,000

VC guerrillas. A tall, clean-cut Mormon from Salt Lake City, Parry was eager to get to work. That was another problem. Having no direction from up top on what to do, the branch was at almost a dead standstill.

In other words, the machinery was in place; all that remained was to turn it on. I made my first pass at this switch on 5 February, with a memo that began: "The events of the last week may well have changed many of the assumptions on which U.S. intelligence has operated in the past." It tossed out some suggestions for research projects, most with an eye to upping the numbers, but some on other important-looking topics, such as VC spies. Its final recommendation was speed, because "big decisions are in the offing, such as whether to stay in or get out of Vietnam."[14] When I gave it to Ron Smith, he said: "I'll see if I can get a decision from upstairs."

Goodness knows how long that would take, so I started to crank out papers by myself. On 7 February, for example, I wrote five: one about VC policy, three on missing regulars, and one about an attack at Tet. The fifth stemmed from new evidence, Vietcong documents having arrived at last concerning the offensive. Among them were the plans for the VC assault on Pleiku, including the formations assigned to do it. They were the Vietcong H-15 Battalion, Unit 90 (part of the VC 407th), and the Pleiku City Unit. Only one of the three, the H-15, was in the MACV Order of Battle.[15] I showed the memo around the building. Ron Smith said: "I'll take it upstairs." George Allen said: "It makes me sick." George Carver said: "If any more of these show up, I want to see them."

Over the next few days, I must have visited Carver a dozen times. The situation room crew joined in and so did George Allen. The situation room came up with the T89 and T87 battalions as having been in on the attack on Danang. Allen was the first to spot that the VC had formed extra units to help in the attack. Apparently, provinces with a single infantry battalion had formed two, districts had doubled up on companies, and so on. The new units were manned by late recruits and upgraded guerrilla militia—which helped explain the pre-Tet ferment in the VC home guard. George Allen told me: "One of the biggest casualties so far is the pacification program. The South Vietnamese have pulled in to protect the cities, and the guerrillas are raising hell in the hamlets."[16] He added that Vietcong local forces had borne the brunt of the attack so far, the communists having held in reserve most of their big divisions and regiments. There were exceptions. At least two enemy regiments were holed up in Hue, and the communists were finally moving in on the Marine Corps base at Khe Sanh. Troops of the North Vietnamese 304th Division had just overrun another Special Forces camp to Khe Sanh's west—Lang Vei—for the first time using tanks.

There was only one type of communist soldier unheard from so far. George Carver brought it up on the afternoon of 11 February, a Sunday. He asked me: "Did you read President Thieu's speech?"

"No, Sir," I replied.

"Well I did just a little while ago, and he said that many of the enemy soldiers active in the cities belong to the VC militia."

"The self-defense militia?"

"Yes," Carver said. "Apparently the Vietcong are using them as support troops for the attack, and to keep order in occupied parts of the cities.* You'll remember that MACV read them out of the order of battle last September."

"I remember."

"It's time to bite the bullet," said Carver. "We plan to send a cable on the quiet to the Saigon Station voicing headquarters' concern about the troops MACV dropped from its OB, such as the militia. This might be a good opportunity to reopen the whole numbers question, since the recent offensive obviously couldn't have happened if MACV's figures were accurate. I don't see how we can start subtracting losses from the communist force structure until we have a handle on how large the structure is."

"Yes, sir," I replied, smiling enigmatically, and went below to write a memo of conversation. This had become habit. To Carver's remarks, I appended these comments: "It appears to me that the last hand has been

---

*A captured VC document showed that fifty self-defense militia units helped occupy Hue, for example.[17]

taken from the brake (at least on the quasi-working level), and that we can now plunge forward toward making a realistic estimate of enemy strength. With the political atmosphere being what it now is—a new willingness to hang the rap on MACV—I think we can push forward many ideas that would have been rejected two weeks ago."[18] For Ron Smith's benefit, I suggested the same research projects as the week before. The front office was still sitting on them.

Not having come in over the weekend, Ron Smith didn't read the memo until Monday morning. "I'll see what I can do," he said and disappeared once again, presumably to tug the chain of command. Smith had no sooner gone out the door than Doug Parry observed, "You realize that in most other trades, these people would be in deep trouble. They lied about the OB before Tet, which caught them by complete surprise as a result, and now they're trying to think up ways to get out of it. There ought to be an investigation. Somebody should be told about this."

Parry had touched a sore point. As if trying to excuse myself, I explained that although an investigation was a good idea, it was unclear how to get one started. Who should I complain to? The CIA Inspector General? He reported to Helms. The White House? The White House had probably put Helms up to it. Congress? The committees supposed to oversee the agency were well-known patsies. A more important problem was timing. "The CIA's about to go straight," I said, "and if I complained now, they'd probably stay crooked." Parry agreed it was a problem.

The next morning Carver at last sent off a cable to Saigon that indicated that headquarters was thinking of reopening the order-of-battle dispute. Among those to sign on it were Drexel Godfrey of OCI, plus a close colleague of OER's Vietnam honcho, Paul Walsh. Helms' name didn't appear on the message, but I guessed he must have given his OK.[19] In any case, Ron Smith was optimistic. "The light is no longer red," he said. "I think it's amber."

Six days later, the Saigon Station sent in a message the effect of which was to turn the light green. It said that, far from repenting, MACV had climbed out even further on its limb. According to the DDI representative in Saigon, a "crash" J-2 study entitled "Cost and Impact on the

Enemy of the Tet Offensive" had concluded—after some intricate math involving VC casualties and recruitment rates—that the communists had suffered a net loss during the offensive to date of 24,000 men. OK so far but in order to reflect this mayhem, MACV had slashed its order of battle from 225,000 (the truncated number before the offensive) to 201,000 men.[20] "You see where they're headed," I said to Ron Smith, "at this rate there won't be any VC left by the end of the year." "Impossible," he replied, and took off to see Paul Walsh.

A short while later, Walsh called me up to his office. I had mixed feelings about him. Although he'd gone along with the fake OB before Tet, he'd done so reluctantly. Furthermore he'd fought the military over enemy logistics, having argued repeatedly that despite the bombing, the Ho Chi Minh Trail provided the VC with all the munitions they needed throughout the country. He was pale, with pouches under his eyes, which looked balefully over plastic-rimmed glasses.

"This is a travesty," he said, pointing at the message. "and I don't think we should let MACV get away with it. I want you to draft a reply to the 'Cost and Impact' paper." I did so, saying we didn't doubt that the Vietcong had suffered a net loss of 24,000 men—if anything, the losses were even higher, what with the carnage—but it came from a force two or three times bigger than MACV would admit. This put the offensive into a different perspective; for example, belying Westmoreland's claim that communist casualties were "disastrous," when actually they were quite reasonable under the circumstance. Walsh signed my cable almost without change, and shortly thereafter the DDI front office gave Ron Smith the go-ahead for the sidelined research projects.[21]

The next seven weeks were among the busiest I ever spent, rehashing and bringing up to date my old papers. There were occasional side trips, however, including a visit to Port Holabird on 27 February to give a lecture on the VC for Colonel Hawkins.[22] He gave a lunch in my honor, toasting me as the "best OB man in the business." From Hawkins this was high praise, and my pleasure in getting it was in sharp contrast to what I felt a couple of days later when the DDI chief, R. Jack Smith, and his deputy, Edward Proctor, visited the VC Branch. They pumped my hand, and told me what a fine analyst I was, with Mr. Smith saying: "You know even more about Vietnam than you did about the Congo." When they left, I said to Doug Parry: "If they thought I was such a fine analyst, why did they cave in before Tet?" He replied: "The wind was blowing from a different direction." Parry had a point.

The press was gloomier than ever,* and not without reason. Although the Marines had finally pushed the last North Vietnamese out of Hue, it was with great loss of life. The communists killed some two thousand U.S. soldiers in February, the highest monthly toll in the war thus far.

On Tuesday, 19 March, I was still scribbling away on the third floor, when Don Blascik called from the situation room to ask me to check a paper he'd put together on VC strength.[23] I went upstairs and did so. He'd used the higher estimate (now "500,000 to 600,000 men"), so it was fine by me. "This is for the director," he explained, "he's about to give a briefing." I asked who for, Blascik said he didn't know but would try to find out. I told him not to bother, and went below to continue what had become a running conversation with Doug Parry. He said: "Now that Helms is using those numbers, the rest of the agency's got to use them too."

Of course Parry was dead right. It also meant my biggest excuse for not seeking an investigation—fear that the agency might back off—was less valid than before. As March wore on, the excuse grew thinner. On 26 March, for example, George Carver cabled the Saigon Station: "We are making a thoroughgoing review of the whole OB problem and hope to get an agreed Washington position prior to broaching the subject frontally with MACV. We will keep you advised of the progress in this exercise, and would appreciate your alerting us to any MACV rumbles possibly related thereto."[24] Already hardening, the agency position set in concrete on 30 March. On that date the CIA issued a joint paper with the

---

* On 23 February, the *Wall Street Journal* commented that "the American people should be getting ready to accept . . . the prospect that the whole Vietnam effort may be doomed." Four days later, Walter Cronkite of CBS said he thought the war might end in a stalemate. According to President Johnson's press secretary, Cronkite's comment sent "shockwaves . . . throughout the government."

Defense Intelligence Agency that announced that the communists had an "insurgency base" (a newly coined euphemism for OB) of "around 500,000 men." The paper concluded that "manpower is not a factor limiting Hanoi's ability to continue the war."[25] There was no way out of it. Now my only excuse for not trying to get an investigation was the problem of finding an investigator who wouldn't end up being its butt.

The next day was Sunday, which I spent at home. Normally the war was an avoided subject on days off, but this one was an exception. President Johnson had scheduled a "major policy address" concerning the war. I had a good deal of sympathy with his predicament, having long since concluded that Kennedy had boxed us into Vietnam. The president came on at 9:30. "Good evening my fellow Americans," he said. "Tonight I want to speak to you of peace in Vietnam." He continued in this vein for some twenty minutes, saying that he planned to stop bombing North Vietnam except near the DMZ, and there'd be no more big troop increases. None of this was new; he'd scheduled bombing pauses before. The bombshell came at the end: "Accordingly, I shall not seek, and will not accept the nomination of my party for another term as your president."

I said to Doug Parry the next morning: "It looks like LBJ is serious. Whoever the next president is, he ought to be warned what's gone on down here. This is a good time to do it." And I took off for the seventh floor to see the CIA Inspector General. According to agency regs, the IG is supposed to handle employee grievances.

A secretary said the chief inspector wasn't in, but one of his assistants was, a Mr. Douglas Andrews. As I entered his office, Mr. Andrews smiled in welcome: "What can I do for you this morning?" I said: "I've come to file a complaint. I feel the conduct of American intelligence on Vietnam has been far less than satisfactory, and that the director and the head of the DDI might well have to be replaced. I want an inquiry started to alert the incoming president . . ."

He gulped slightly, but otherwise kept a straight face. Also, he began to take notes. It took an hour to tell my story. I laid out the problems with the OB, and such DDI failures as its omission to assign anyone to work on the Vietcong. I explained that although my ultimate goal was to reach the White House, I wanted to do so through channels. That's why I'd come to the IG. When I was done, he said: "This isn't what I'd call our usual employee grievance. Normally we get complaints about cafeteria food, or slow promotions. That's not the real problem, is it? Slow promotions?"

"No, sir," I replied.

He looked at me appraisingly. "I guess not. Well, I'll see what I can do. However, if I were you, I wouldn't count on getting Mr. Helms fired in the immediate future." I said I harbored no such expectation, and would supply a written bill of particulars as soon as my work load let up. This might be a while since the rumor was around that another order-of-battle conference was about to occur. Then I went downstairs to tell Ron Smith what had happened.[26]

Amazingly, he already knew. He said: "they warned me you might be trouble. This is a snootful." I said that none of my complaints were about him, and that he'd be the first to know if there were further developments.

The rumor about the OB conference turned out to be true. It was scheduled for 10 April, with a delegation expected from MACV. I turned on the heat to finish up my OB papers. Around 5 April Ron Smith stopped by my desk to say: "The front office just asked me to take you off the numbers business. I told them, 'Over my dead body; without Adams MACV'd knock us apart.'" This took guts, and I was grateful to Ron Smith. I said: "Thank you."

For the first time in the war, the CIA came to an OB conference adequately prepared. We had detailed papers for every category of enemy strength: one on guerrillas by Doug Parry: another on the self-defense militia by George Allen: and others on the regulars, service troops, and political cadres by me. Adequate preparation had never been the real problem, however, it was will. We had that now too. Resembling the English literature professor he'd once been, DDI chief R. Jack Smith laid it out on the opening day: "Since Fourteen Three, we have had a steady succession of problems with the numbers. We had hoped for a surcease of these problems, but it did not happen. The White House said to Mr. Helms: 'Straighten this out.' We will come up with a draft. Footnote it if you wish."[27] In other words he told MACV to go fly a kite.

The MACV delegation listened in stung silence. It had four people in it, headed by Colonel Danny Graham. A lieutenant colonel when he'd taken me to lunch at the South Vietnamese officer's club in Saigon, Graham had gotten his promotion recently. With him were Hawkins' replacement as OB chief, a Marine lieutenant colonel named Paul Weiler; one of Weiler's deputies, Navy Commander James Meacham, and a MACV political analyst, Captain Kelly Robinson.

There's no point in detailing the conference. With Paul Walsh now leading the pack, we ran roughshod over MACV. The most interesting occurrence wasn't the argument, which I'd heard many times before, but something Captain Robinson told me during a coffee break. He said: "Remember that kid called McArthur, our guerrilla analyst at Saigon? They tried to change his numbers, and he blew his stack. Now he's transferred to Gia Dinh." I had a vague recollection of a skinny lieutenant who'd sat quietly on the sidelines during the Saigon go-around, so I jotted down what Robinson said, unfortunately forgetting to ask McArthur's first name. At the end of the conference, the agency's top count of VC was just below 600,000.[28] Among other things, we'd marched the self-defense militia back into the estimate.* As Doug Parry said a short while afterward: "A little late."

I felt the same way as Doug, and thus saw no reason to abandon my quest for an inquiry. It took several weeks to tie up the conference's loose ends, however, so I didn't get around to sending my bill of

---

*The supreme irony of the militia's re-entry into our estimate at this point was that in many areas it had almost ceased to exist as a separate organization. The reasons were manifold. For example, right before the offensive, the VC turned large numbers into guerrillas, and sent others to higher-level units. Furthermore Tet was the first time the Vietcong employed militia formations away from home, partly—as Carver pointed out—as back-up troops in the cities, where they doubtless sustained high casualties. During Tet the toll of southerners recruited locally by the VC was so great that the communists had to rely increasingly thereafter on North Vietnamese replacements. According to a CIA estimate, the number of northerners to march south in 1968 was just short of a quarter million, another indication of the vast scale of the offensive.

complaints to the Inspector General until late May. On the day this happened, the twenty-seventh, Doug volunteered to go in on the project
with me. I declined the offer with thanks, saying: "There's no point in
both of us sticking our necks out. It gives them a bigger target."

Putting the package together had been ticklish business. On the one
hand—since it was meant for the White House—I had to go easy on
accusations of political pressure from on high. On the other—since its
eventual purpose was to inform Johnson's successor of what had gone
wrong—I had to be as specific as possible. With these objectives in mind
I split the package into two parts. The first were the complaints themselves, which dwelt on the shortcomings of the DDI. Detailing the
almost total absence of serious research on the Vietcong, it emphasized
the results. The most obvious, of course, was our underestimation of
"the strength of the enemy and therefore the scale of the Vietnamese
war." A second was closer to home. The CIA's attempts to recruit spies
among the VC had "met with scant success, in part because we knew so
little about what we were operating against." I tossed in a footnote here
that of the five-hundred-odd CIA employees roving Vietnam, the number who spoke Vietnamese was "considerably less than" six.*[29]

Part two of the package was the memo I'd written in November
1967 criticizing Fourteen Three. Outlining my problem with the OB, it
said the "estimate's history was one of attacks by soldiers and politicians,
and retreats by intelligence officials," but I hoped this rhetoric might slip
by to the next administration.[30] In any case, the memo showed that mine
wasn't just a case of twenty-twenty hindsight—that I'd begun complaining before Tet. When I read this package over before sending it to the
seventh floor, it looked to me like a formidable piece of work. "It might
even get results," I told Doug Parry.

---

*At the time of the Tet Offensive, the CIA's sole agent among the Vietcong was
run by a now-retired case officer named Foster Phipps. The spy's warnings allowed
the Marines to repel the VC from Danang, one of the few cities the communists
failed to penetrate. Phipps—who reminded many people of W. C. Fields—received
a letter of commendation from the Marines, but none from the CIA. He retired
from the agency in 1973.

"Well, you've laid the damn thing on the table," the IG said at 12:30
P.M. the next day; "I suppose we've got to do something about it."
Stern-looking, with a patrician accent and a Brooks Brothers suit, the
IG was Gordon Stewart, who already knew what I was up to from his
assistant, Mr. Andrews. Rumor was that Stewart was a close friend of
Helms, and interestingly, his main questions weren't about the complaints' substance, but over some requests I'd made at their end. The first
was for an IG investigation ("Quite possible," he said); the second that
the package be sent to the White House ("That remains to be seen");
and the third for "a modest amount of storage space for the safekeeping
of relevant memoranda which have been collected over the past two
years."

"What's all that about?" Mr. Stewart asked.

"In case I get run over by a Mack truck, sir; I want to be sure my old
memos are in a safe place. Xerox copies, of course."

"Xerox copies?"

"Yes, sir," I said. The clear implication was that the originals would
be stored someplace else, presumably beyond his reach. My main worry
at the time was that the agency might kick me out, and feed all the early
evidence about the low OB into a shredding machine. Incidentally, I
said this in a highly respectful manner. The last thing I wanted was to be
thought of as a wiseacre.[31]

The next week was quiet, as I worked on routine papers. Finally, suspense got the best of me and I visited a friend in the DDI front office to
find out if there'd been any reaction. "Reaction?" he said. "It's like the
day the soap sank at Proctor and Gamble." This is the only word I got
that my complaint had caused a stir.

The next day, 5 June, Mr. Stewart called me back to his office. He
told me that Helms had seen my bill of particulars, but had decided to
"defer" sending it to the White House. Then, looking me straight in the
eye, and with a hint of menace, he said: "We regard this as an internal
matter. It would be a mistake to take it outside the CIA. The only person who can decide that is the director." However, Stewart went on,

Helms had said that an investigation by the Inspector General's office seemed perfectly reasonable, and would be pushed. Thereupon he introduced me to two IG investigators who'd been standing by his desk: "These are Mr. Breckenridge and Mr. Grier. They will try to pin down the various episodes in the case."[32]

I spoke to Breckenridge and Grier many times over the next few days.[33] Their first question was "Are you against the Vietnam war? Is that why you came to the IG?"

It was easy enough to answer. I replied: "No, I'm not. My complaints are about American intelligence, not the war. Intelligence officers aren't supposed to take sides, at least in theory, and partly for that reason, I'm neither a hawk nor a dove. Also it happens to be true. I can see why some people think it was a mistake to have gotten into Vietnam in the first place, but now that we're there, I have no illusions about our enemy, the Vietcong."

And I meant it, even more so at that moment. Only a short while before, I'd seen several VC documents which the Marines had captured while retaking Hue. These showed that during the three weeks the communists had held the city, they had executed almost three thousand Vietnamese[34]—mostly government officials, but also relatives, including women and children. The South Vietnamese had already dug up over a thousand corpses. According to one report, many victims "had been beaten to death, shot, beheaded, or buried alive," while many bodies were found "bound together in groups of ten or fifteen, eyes open, with dirt or cloth stuffed in their mouths."[35]

It was cold-blooded murder, and I was curious to find out who did it. There was no surprise. The Vietcong organization that planned the slaughter was the VC Security Service, about which I'd written the study a year before. The local communist police headquarters had chosen victims from blacklists prepared by the A2 branch of their B3—espionage, or diep bao—subsection. Shorthanded, the secret police had enlisted the help of other VC who had infiltrated the city. Among them were soldiers from the fifty self-defense militia units used by the communists as backup troops—the same ones MACV had expelled from its OB in late 1967.

Breckenridge and Grier continued their investigation through the rest of June and into July. To my surprise, it was straightforward. They talked to my coworkers, to higher-echelon types such as R. Jack Smith and Paul Walsh, and to most of my immediate bosses, including Ron Smith, George Allen, and George Carver. They even consulted Doug Parry. On Thursday, 1 August, Mr. Grier called me on the telephone at nine o'clock to ask if I could come upstairs. I could. Mr. Breckenridge was there too. One of them—I forget which—said: "This is the damnedest investigation I've ever been on. Normally we pull the troublemakers, but everyone we saw said you weren't one. Personally, I think you've fingered some interesting problems. In fact . . ."

"Anyway," the other cut in, "we've finished our investigation, and now it's in the hands of Mr. Stewart. He'll write the final report." At that point, I asked the obvious questions:

"Who writes Mr. Stewart's fitness report?" (A fitness report was the yearly evaluation a superior prepares on his subordinates.)

"The executive director does. That's Colonel White," said Mr. Grier.

"And who writes Colonel White's?"

"Mr. Helms."

"And who appointed Gordon Stewart Inspector General?"

"Mr. Helms."

"Very well," I replied. "Please inform Mr. Stewart that I still want my bill of particulars to go to the White House." Then I thanked them both, saying it seemed to me they'd conducted a fair investigation. As I left, they shook my hand and said "Good luck."[36] Figuring it would take some time for Mr. Stewart to finish the investigation report, I resumed my latest endeavor.

The project had first suggested itself over a year earlier. On my return from Saigon in May 1967, the Office of Training (or OTR) had asked me to give a one-hour lecture about the Vietcong secret police to CIA case officers headed for Vietnam. I said OK, and had done so ever since, maybe once every six weeks. During these lectures—held in Rosslyn, Virginia, in a blue-colored office building run by OTR under the nickname Blue U.—I discovered that the only other person talking on the VC was George Allen. Also an hour long, George's lecture was about the history of the Vietnamese communist movement, starting with Ho Chi Minh in 1919. Therefore agency men got only two lopsided hours on the VC before being sent to the provinces with orders to spy on the enemy. Since none spoke Vietnamese, it was scarcely surprising that the CIA had so far managed to recruit only a single agent. The fault wasn't with the men in the field, who were generally high-caliber, it was other factors, not the least of which was inadequate training. I didn't speak Vietnamese either; but I knew something about the Vietcong. My project was to draw up a lesson plan increasing instruction time on the VC from two hours to twenty-four. On my last trip to Blue U. I'd gotten up to about five.

In fact they were among the most valuable hours I'd ever spent. As anyone knows who's done some teaching, the teacher always learns a lot more than the student. Since my main job at the time was the VC order of battle, naturally I gave the clandestine-service operatives a short talk on the OB. After one of these talks, a grizzled old DDI-er asked me: "Why are the numbers important?"

After three years of working with sums, I was taken aback by the question. I retorted approximately as follows: "The numbers are important because we *think* they're important. The U.S. government seems to live or die over how many VC there are—for example, the size of our troop deployments depends on enemy numbers—and that being the case, we might as well use the right ones."

He said: "OK, I'll buy that. We think they're important. But *are* they important?"

I thought for a minute before making this answer: "Given the size of our underestimate, yes. But the key is the ones we shortchange: the low-level types, the hamlet cadres, the guerrillas, the militia. In overlooking these people, we willfully disregard what the communists do best. They say this is a political war, a war of allegiance, a 'people's war.' That's where they put many of their best cadres—at the bottom of the heap, in the hamlets, to mobilize the people. Not all the people volunteer, you can argue that most of them are coerced, but there are a lot of them, and so far the Vietcong have managed to keep them coming."

The DDP-ers were more interested in statistics about the Vietcong forging cell. At one point I said: "And the number of phoney ID cards that cell turned out in nine months near Saigon was two hundred and fifty."

"*What?*" said someone in the first row: "Would you care to repeat that figure?"

"Two hundred and fifty."

There were about eighteen simultaneous whistles. The man in the front row said: "My God, I once spent the better part of two months equipping an agent with fake papers. One agent. Two months. If a single cell cranks them out at that rate, Saigon must be like Swiss cheese."

I said that the same thought had occurred to me, but I didn't know much about their espionage network, not having looked into the problem. A related question came as I was explaining VC doctrine: "They claim they're fighting the war on three fronts: military, political, and military proselyting."

"What's military proselyting?" somebody asked.

It was the Vietcong effort to subvert the South Vietnamese army, I said, and the documents suggested that it included letter-writing campaigns, appeals to relatives, and suchlike. The proselyters also appeared to run agents.

"Are they having any success?" he asked. I replied that it was hard to tell, but everyone always said how screwed up the Saigon army was. Maybe the proselyter agents had something to do with it. This wasn't much of an answer, but it was an intriguing question, and when I got back to headquarters, I asked Ron Smith if he could put someone to work on the subject. Not long before, two analysts named Bob Klein and Bob Appell had joined the VC Branch. Ron said he could spare Klein.

Bob Klein was fresh out of college, and didn't know anything about the VC. But he was bright, easygoing, and had an open mind. By mid-August, he'd gone through enough evidence to figure out the rudiments of the VC military proselyting organization. Another bash was scheduled at Blue U. for 19 August, and I felt confident enough in Klein's abilities to let him give an hour's speech on what he'd found out. By now I'd upped the training time on the VC to two full days. Klein spoke on the second day. He told them what he knew.

Among other things, he'd uncovered the fact that the military proselyters ran the enemy's prisoner of war cages. This wasn't as odd as it seemed, he told the DDP-ers, since the Vietcong felt they could convert the POWs, and send them back to our side as agents. Naturally the communists were doing better converting South Vietnamese prisoners than they were with ours. To illustrate this point, Klein read from a study the VC had made on U.S. captives. The study pointed out that one American prisoner had spent two whole years doing nothing but computing his back pay. Another had invented a self-cleaning comb, which threw off dandruff as fast as it collected. Yankee captives were hard to fathom, the study remarked; because "they're immune to the class struggle." Klein also told the students which group of proselyters ran these agents once they got back to the South Vietnamese army. "It's the Fifth Columnist Subsection," he said; "the Vietnamese for 'fifth columnist' is *noi tuyen*. Remember that—'noi tuyen.'" I made a note to spend more time on VC agents in later courses on the enemy.

Gordon Stewart brought up my other big concern at ten o'clock the next morning, 21 August. After calling me to his office, he read a statement, solemnly, as if from a marble tombstone: "In view of the seriousness of your charges, the director feels they deserve more consideration. Therefore, he has appointed a review board to go over the charges again and advise him what to do. The review board will consist of Admiral Rufus Taylor, the deputy director; Mr. John Bross, one of Mr. Helms' aides; and Mr. Lawrence Houston, the CIA's general counsel, that is, our chief lawyer." Then Mr. Stewart told me to cooperate with the review board. I said that of course I would.[37]

It was clear what was going on. Helms had thought up another excuse not to send the complaints to the White House. Doubtless he could create review boards forever, but at this moment there seemed no point in raising a fuss. After all, my object was to warn the incoming administration, and although the Republicans in Miami had already chosen Richard Nixon as their presidential candidate, the Democrats— now gathering in Chicago—had yet to choose theirs.

The person whom the review board annoyed most was Doug Parry. By now he'd gotten so fed up with what he called malarky that he'd decided to quit the agency to attend the University of Utah Law School. At the last moment he wanted to charge up to the IG to let off steam, but once again I dissuaded him. Partly I didn't think it would do much good, but mostly he had the idea that he might want to rejoin the CIA after law school. If he had an IG complaint in his jacket, they probably wouldn't let him back in. He was too good to lose.

As Parry took off for Utah, I edited a recently drafted paper by the other new branch analyst, Bob Appell. Assigned by Ron Smith at my suggestion, Appell's paper was an experiment. Hitherto, all our order-of-battle memos, in computing VC numbers, had used MACV definitions of who the enemy was. But this one—which zeroed in on just two provinces, VC Gia Lai and Kontum—employed Vietcong definitions.* Furthermore, Appell made extensive use of circumstantial evidence. For example, he had assumed that ordnance reports of large numbers of ninety-millimeter rockets heading for a certain area in Gia Lai implied the presence there of a ninety-millimeter recoilless rifle unit. On the face of it, this wasn't much of an analytical leap, except that it hadn't been done before, at least not by American intelligence in Vietnam. Actually it was an ancient technique, used by the French in

---

*As already noted, the VC divided their army into three parts: main forces, local forces, and guerrilla-militia, with service troops integral to each part. MACV lumped the first two parts under the heading "regulars," created the separate category "service troops," and counted only the top half of the guerrilla-militia. What this meant in practical terms was that American OB analysts had to shoehorn the numbers appearing in VC documents into MACV's categories. Appell's paper was an attempt to forego this step.

estimating Vietminh in 1954, and no doubt by George Washington in counting the British in 1776.

I finished Appell's paper over the Labor Day weekend, and when Ron Smith got it the day after, he tossed it in his in-box, where it stayed for some time. This isn't to blame Ron, who had higher priorities. The memo wasn't all that important, and the only reason I mention it at all was that it became the basis for another paper, which—using the same analytical methods, and also involving Bob Appell—was to shake the foundations of American policy in Indo-China some two years and nine months later. The second paper was dated 8 June 1971.

Meanwhile, amid tear gas and billy clubs in Chicago, the Democrats nominated Hubert Humphrey as their candidate for president. This might have been a good time to start pushing my IG complaints toward the White House, but I decided not to. As far as I could make out, Helms' three-man review board had yet to meet, and it would have seemed presumptuous for a low-level analyst like myself to demand action right away. So I went on vacation, spending ten days with Eleanor and Clayton at my family's cabin in the Adirondacks. On my return to CIA headquarters on Monday, 16 September, the first thing I did was check my back mail to see if the review board had gotten into gear. It hadn't. However, another piece of mail shed light on the matter. It was a routine notice from the seventh floor announcing the "temporary absence of John A. Bross from 13 September 1968 to 23 October 1968."[38] That was six weeks, and since Bross was one of the review board trio, I telephoned his office to find out where he'd gone.

"Mr. Bross is a canoe enthusiast," his secretary answered. "Every year he takes his holiday exploring the lakes." So that was it. One third of the review board had gone canoeing, with no plans to paddle back to headquarters until right before elections. Obviously, I was getting the runaround. Something had to be done.

Therefore, at nine o'clock on the following morning I went up to the general counsel's office, and talked to an agency lawyer, Mr. James B. Ueberhorst. I said: "Mr. Ueberhorst, I wrote a report for the White House about four months ago complaining about CIA management, and I've been getting the runaround ever since. What I want is some legal advice. Would I be breaking any laws if I took my memo and carried it over to the White House myself?" In a highly agitated voice, Mr. Ueberhorst told me about the "employer-employee relationship" including the prerogatives of each, about the National Security Act of 1947, as amended, but he didn't answer my question. I repeated it, adding that the last thing I wanted was to break the law, and would he please relay our conversation to his boss, the general counsel, Mr. Lawrence Houston, who also happened to be a member of the review board. Mr. Uberhorst said he would, and I went below to await the reaction.[39]

It came on 20 September 1968, a Friday, heralded by a telephone call at 11:30 A.M. from Colonel Lawrence White's secretary, asking me to come back upstairs. Colonel White was the executive director, number three man in the agency after Richard Helms and Rufus Taylor. I entered his office at 11:35. Bald, with a fringe of reddish hair—his nickname on the seventh floor being Red—he motioned me to sit in a large brown leather sofa catty-cornered from his desk. I did so, and commenced taking notes. Standing before the sofa, he said: "Mr. Adams, the director has indicated that he doesn't want your memo to leave the building. We believe that at this moment you're an asset to the agency, and that you have a role to play in its future, but what the role is depends on how you conduct yourself in this matter."

He paused briefly to let this sink in, and continued: "I would like you to know that if you take your complaints independently to the White House—and even if you obtain the results you desire by doing so—your usefulness to the agency will thereafter be nil. Let me repeat that: Nil."

"The director feels that this is an internal affair, and to handle it he has appointed the review board, all that anyone can ask. But if you feel that it isn't, and take this matter outside the agency, you will be doing so *at your own peril,* for *practical* rather than legal reasons. It seems to me, Mr. Adams, that the most serious question at stake is whether you destroy your usefulness to the intelligence business." The colonel went on in this vein for half an hour before asking if I had any questions. I did.

"May I take this, sir, as a direct order not to forward my complaints to the White House?"

"It has the *effect* of a direct order," the colonel replied.

"And you're aware, sir, that Mr. Bross had gone canoeing, and won't be back until 23 October?"

"How John Bross spends his vacation is no concern of yours," said the colonel.

"Of course it isn't, Sir," I replied. "But his going bears on whether the incoming administration receives timely warning of the CIA's failures over the last two years. I think they are far too big to be dealt with by the people who made them. Therefore, please tell the director that I intend to take action no later than the end of the month."[40]

Colonel White dismissed me, and I hotfooted it down to the VC Branch, well aware that he'd handed me a potent weapon—an outright threat, made for "practical" rather than "legal" reasons, obviously designed to prevent a president-elect from discovering CIA malfeasance. All that remained was to put the threat in writing. I did so, transcribing everything White had said in a memorandum of conversation. Beverly typed it up on Monday morning, and straightaway I sent it with a cover sheet to Colonel White. The cover sheet asked the colonel to comment in writing whether the memorandum of conversation was accurate or not. To make sure he couldn't wiggle out of it, I stuck in a final paragraph that said: "Please do not feel you need to inform me in writing if the . . . memorandum accurately reflects the statements you made. If I have not heard from you by the end of the month, I will respectfully assume your silence means assent."[41] Therefore even if he chose to ignore the memo, he was still on the hook.

Colonel White must have realized he was in trouble. Maybe he even envisaged the possibility (which I hoped he would) that I might take my bill of complaints to the White House with a copy of his threats stapled to it, thus making the package look even worse than it did already. For whatever reasons, when he called me back to his office that afternoon, he was profuse in his denials that he'd tried on Friday to "threaten, coverup, or delay. In fact," he said, "I've just talked it over with the director and deputy director, and they agreed you can go forward." I thanked Colonel White, saying that now that the principal of external review was established, I'd be happy to wait until after elections. I tried to hand him an extra copy of the memo of conversation, but he backed away from it, unfortunately tripping on the carpet as he did so. "I'm too busy to read that sort of thing," he said.[42]

"You nailed 'em that time," Ron Smith said delightedly, when I told him what had happened. By now it was clear he had mixed emotions over my battle with the hierarchy. Sometimes he acted as if he were harboring a viper, other times as if he wanted me to succeed. I appreciated his dilemma, and had grown to like Ron a good deal.

Another reason for my thinking him a satisfactory boss was that he allowed me to pick my own research topics. The VC Branch now had the order of battle well in hand, so I decided to help Bob Klein on the military proselyters. I recalled the question the DDP student had asked at Blue U., "Are they having any success?" This led rapidly to a second question—success at what? At this time, the South Vietnamese army was losing about one soldier in four per year to desertion. This seemed as good a place as any to start research. Klein and I tried to figure out how many deserters quit at VC urging. The problem was knotty. As might be expected, the enemy proselyters claimed credit in their reports for the entire desertion rate. This was unlikely. Many government soldiers doubtless went over the hill for other motives, such as fear, detestation of sergeants, and bad food—the same reasons which caused many Vietcong soldiers to desert. The problem went on a shelf on 26 October. On that date Klein got married and went on a honeymoon. Ten days later Nixon beat Humphrey in a squeaker.

After the returns were in, I fulfilled my promise to Colonel White. That is, I sent a request to the seventh floor asking if it was all right now to forward my bill of particulars to the White House. Admiral Taylor, the deputy director, replied at once: Yes, he believed it was, but first I should talk to the director. I called Helms' office and got an appointment to see him at 10:30 on Friday morning, 8 November. Frankly, I didn't know what to expect. Although technically a member of the director's staff while working for George Carver, I hadn't actually laid eyes on Helms since May 1966. At that time he'd been head of the DDP.

I arrived at the director's suite a quarter hour early on Friday. This was necessary in order to check in with the security guards, sign the visitors' sheet, and warn the secretaries. I was familiar with the procedure, having visited John McCone several times in 1964 while I was Congo analyst. At 10:25 I entered Helms's outer office. His secretary said: "Don't bother to knock, Mr. Adams, he's expecting you." I opened the inner door.

And there he was, Richard Helms, CIA director, archvillain, sitting behind his big desk with a half-smile on his face. He didn't look much like a villain. He said: "Hello, Sam. Good to see you. How have you been?" He didn't talk like one either. "Sit down," he went on. "What seems to be the problem?"

As I sat in the chair beside his desk, I took out a pad of paper and a ballpoint pen. Observing this, he said: "I'd rather you didn't take notes." Apparently, he knew of Colonel White's unfortunate experience with the memorandum of conversation. I put them away.

"Now tell me," he reiterated, "what's the matter? Are your supervisors treating you unfairly? Are they being too slow on promotions?"

No, I said. My main problem was that he had caved in on the numbers before Tet. I enlarged on this theme for about ten minutes, repeated others that I'd made in the bill of complaints—such as lack of research on the VC—and added a couple of new ones, including the dearth of training on the enemy for DDP men going to Vietnam. "Thirty thousand Americans have died in the war so far, sir, and I don't think we're taking it seriously enough. The biggest evidence of this, the one thing that's really inexcusable, is our collapse on the order of battle in September last year."

Hitherto Helms had listened without expression. Now he leaned toward me and said intently: "Sam, this may sound strange from where you're sitting. But the CIA is only one voice among many in Washington. And it's not a very big one, either, particularly compared to the Pentagon's. What would you have me do? Take on the entire military?"

I replied: "Under the circumstances, that was the only alternative. The military's numbers were faked."

"You don't know what it's like in this town," Helms said. "I could have told the White House there were a million more Vietcong out there, and it wouldn't have made the slightest difference in our policy."

"We aren't the ones to decide about policy," I said. "Our job is to send up the right numbers and let them worry."

He replied OK, who was it I wanted to see in the White House. I said I didn't know. How about Maxwell Taylor and Walt Rostow, he asked. I told him that was not only acceptable, it was generous, and he said he would arrange the appointments for me. He accompanied me to the door.[43]

At the last moment I remembered a question. By extraordinary coincidence, Helms had spent the previous weekend in Alabama, visiting one of my wife's uncles, Earl McGowin. He'd even slept at Edgefield, a large house with white pillars where Eleanor had grown up. I asked: "By the way, how's Uncle Earl?"

"Uncle Earl?"

"Earl McGowin, sir, he's Eleanor's uncle."

It took a moment to register. His face lit up in a smile. He chuckled. Then he started laughing so hard he had to lean against the wall for support. This lasted maybe fifteen seconds. When he recovered, he said: "Excuse me for laughing. It struck me as funny. Uncle Earl's just fine. He's a nice person, Uncle Earl, and so's Aunt Claudia."*

Later I was talking to my friend in the DDI front office. He said: "Helms is in a difficult position. He's one of the gloomiest men in town on the war, but gloom is seldom what's wanted. He feels if he pushes bad news too hard, he'll get thrown out of the White House,

---

*My notes indicate that this conversation lasted until 11:05 A.M. Some hours later, perhaps as long as a day, President-elect Nixon summoned Helms to the Hotel Pierre in New York City to inform Helms confidentially that he intended to reappoint him as director of the CIA. The source of this information is Thomas Powers, author of Helms' biography, *The Man Who Kept Secrets*.[44] Powers' source was John Bross, the canoeist. Nixon announced the reappointment publicly on 16 December.

thus leaving the field to the military. He thinks he has the agency's best interests at heart."

Over the next few days I went around to see the deputy directors. The head of the DDI, R. Jack Smith, asked me what the matter was, and I told him the same things I had told Helms. Smith said that the Vietnam War was an extraordinarily complex affair, that the size of the enemy army was only a "small but sensitive byway of the problem," and that I had picked up a "bad case of tunnel vision." His deputy, Edward Proctor remarked, "Mr. Adams, the real problem is you. You ought to look into yourself."[45]

On 18 November I wrote letters to Mr. Rostow and General Taylor telling them who I was and asking that they include a member of Nixon's staff in any talks we had about the CIA's shortcomings. I forwarded the letters, through channels, to the director's office, asking permission to send them on.[46] Permission was denied, and that was the last I heard about meeting with Rostow and Taylor.[47]

In early December I did manage to see the chief aide of the President's Foreign Intelligence Advisory Board, J. Patrick Coyne, at the Executive Office Building, next to the White House. He told me that a few days earlier Helms had sent over my bill of complaints, and that some members of PFIAB had read it, and that they were asking me to enlarge on my views and to make any recommendations I thought were in order. Coyne encouraged me to write a full report, and in the following weeks I put together a thirty-five-page paper explaining why I had brought the charges and why, among other things, the Sitrep was a less than adequate publication. My paper was ready for typing on Nixon's inauguration day, 20 January 1969.*[48]

I watched the swearing-in ceremony on television, after which the new president made his way up Pennsylvania Avenue. As he passed Twelfth Street, the cameras pointed at some peace demonstrators, who were chanting: "Ho, Ho, Ho Chi Minh, the NLF is going to win."

---

*When Nixon got up at 6:45 A.M. on the 21st—the first full day of his administration—his initial action (according to his memoirs) was to read the Sitrep. In March, he confidently told his cabinet that he expected the war to be over within a year.

Someone was waving a Vietcong flag. I remember thinking: *Why that damn flag? Maybe the VC are going to win, even probably so, but it will be ghastly when they do.* I had followed the progress of the South Vietnamese in Hue, who had continued to exhume bodies. The government's tally now coincided almost exactly with the VC police report's, three thousand. Captured documents suggested that the communists had executed additional thousands, only in smaller lots, during their rampage through other cities at Tet. What made Hue unusual was that the Vietcong had had access there to more victims. I stopped watching TV when Nixon got to the White House.

Unfortunately, Beverly was busy typing other papers so she didn't get around to mine until Friday, the 24th. I sent it up to Helms's office on the 27th with a request for permission to send it both to Mr. Coyne of PFIAB, and to Walt Rostow's successor as head of the National Security Council, Henry Kissinger. Permission was denied in a letter from the deputy director, Admiral Taylor, who informed me that the CIA was a team, and that if I didn't want to accept the team's decision, then I should resign.[49]

There I was—with nobody from Nixon's staff having heard of any of this. It was far from clear whether Nixon intended to retain the President's Foreign Intelligence Advisory Board. J. Patrick Coyne said he didn't know. He also said he didn't intend to press for the release of the thirty-five-page report. I thought I had been had.

For the first time in my career, I decided to leave official channels. Not long before I had met a man named John Court, a member of Kissinger's incoming NSC staff. I gave Court my memorandum and explained its import—including Westmoreland's deceptions before Tet—and asked him to pass it around so that at least the new administration might know what had gone on at the CIA and could take any action it thought necessary. Some weeks later Court told me that the memo had gotten around all right, but the decision had been made not to do anything about it. So I gave up. If the White House wasn't interested, I'd reached the end of the line. I felt I'd done as much as I possibly could, and that was that.

Obviously, the time had come to take stock in my career at the CIA. It was pretty much in shambles. Not only had the deputy director suggested that I resign, but now I was working under special restrictions. The word had long since arrived that I was no longer permitted to go to Vietnam. After the order-of-battle conference in Saigon in September 1967, Westmoreland's headquarters had informed the Saigon Station that I was *persona non grata,* and that they didn't want me on any military installations throughout the country. Somewhat later, Ron Smith had told me, as tactfully as he could, that I shouldn't expect to attend meetings at which outsiders were present. But the weightiest blow fell on 8 April. On that day, OER's Vietnam boss Paul Walsh called me in to say that I had spent far too much time on "extracurricular activities," and to correct this fault, I should cut back on my lectures at Blue U. This was particularly discouraging since I'd at last gotten instruction on the VC up to twenty-four hours. The dons at Blue U. were as unhappy as I was over the development. Adding to my general discouragement was what had gone on with other people. Fed up with Vietnam, George Allen had asked for reassignment, and in late 1968 had taken off for London to attend the Imperial War College. That meant that one of my closest allies was no longer available. But the sorriest case of all was back at headquarters. It was Joe Hovey, the Collation Branch analyst who in November 1967 had composed the Saigon cable that had predicted the Tet Offensive. After leaving Vietnam in June 1968, he had reported to Langley several weeks later, naturally expecting some kind of recognition for his feat. This failed to occur. If anything, his cable had proved an embarrassment to the DDI for whom the offensive was an almost total surprise. For a while he couldn't even find a job. Eventually, the Office of Current Intelligence picked him up and put him to work on the Sitrep. His boss was Thaxter Goodell, the author of OCI's dismissive claim that Hovey's message was crying wolf.

As usual, there were compensations. In February, for example, I had put together a bilingual chart detailing the communists' provincial organization. It was going like hotcakes, with one customer—the Army's Special Warfare School at Fort Bragg—having ordered five thousand copies. Then a new batch of captured documents came in from the B-3 Front. The B-3 Front was a communist military command in South Vietnam's central highlands made up of the VC provinces of Gia Lai, Kontum, and Daklak. The documents listed the Vietcong soldiers stationed in each province. Using these rosters, Bob Appell and I were able to check the communist troop estimates in his experimental order-of-battle memo, now several months old, about Gia Lai and Kontum. It was incredible. In one province (I forget which), it came within 10 percent of the actual number. In the other, it was within 5 percent. That's about as good as you can get without seeing the daily morning reports. Despite its narrow focus, Appell's memo was clearly one of the best OB papers written in the war so far. As already mentioned, its methods came into play—with a vengeance—in June 1971.

My biggest satisfaction, however, came from the Blue U. lectures, even in their truncated form. In contrast to many higher-ups at headquarters, most Vietnam-bound DDP-ers couldn't give less of a damn about office politics. The majority were headed for the provinces, so that their main interest was what they were up against. As always, their questions concerned not, How many? but Why? And on many subjects I found myself gradually adopting their point of view.

One such subject was the numbers. Granted, the numbers were important as far as they went, but they failed to explain why the communists continued to hang in despite their enormous casualties.* Almost every time we found an enemy unit, we trounced it severely.

---

*At about this time, the *Washington Post* published an interview with North Vietnam's minister of defense Vo Nguyen Giap by the Italian newswoman Oriana Fallacci. In the course of the interview, she said: "General, the Americans say you've lost a million men." He replied: "That's quite exact," with Fallacci adding the comment that Giap "let this drop as casually as if it were quite unimportant, as hurriedly as if, perhaps, the real number was even larger." Giap's answer tended to confirm my belief that the American press's suspicions were ill-founded that MACV was inflating enemy casualties. The real numbers problem was that the entire war, casualties included, was a lot bigger than generally thought. Another quote from Giap, taken from the same interview: "The U.S. has a strategy based on arithmetic. They question the computers, add and subtract, extract square roots, and then go into action. But arithmetical strategy doesn't work here. If it did, they would have already exterminated us." This quote was blown up into large print, and displayed prominently over one of the VC Branch safes.[50]

The trouble was that we didn't find them often enough. This led to the questions: Why was it the Vietcong always seemed to know what we were up to, while we could never find out about them except through captured documents? The DDP-ers kept asking about communist spies. I knew a fair amount about their espionage organization, but not that much about its accomplishments. A related problem was—for the lack of a better word—subversion, particularly of the South Vietnamese army. As we already knew, the group responsible for this was the VC Military Proselyting Section.

Unfortunately, research on the subject had come to a dead halt. The reason was the absence of Bob Klein. After his return from his honeymoon in November, he had made some additional stabs at trying to find out how successful the proselyters had been in encouraging desertion from the Saigon army. His attempts were to no avail. The problem was too complex. In late February, the U.S. Army called Klein to three months active duty in South Carolina. I had plenty to do myself. Proselyting could wait.

Meanwhile, the Sitrep continued to gush facts. Some of them were pretty interesting. On 28 April, for example, an accident occurred at Danang. Some grass had caught fire, leading to explosions that destroyed no less than forty thousand tons of American ammunition. On 14 May, President Nixon announced his "Vietnamization Program." It envisaged our gradual turning over of the war to the South Vietnamese army. On 22 May, Ron Smith stopped by my desk to say: "The military's sprung loose Klein today. He'll be back to work on Monday." Monday was the 26th. I reread the VC policy document that said: "We fight the war on three fronts—military, political, and military proselyting."

Until now, American intelligence had concentrated on the first front, glancing from time to time at the second. Except for Klein's first efforts, it had entirely neglected the third. At this moment I decided to join Klein full-time in investigating the third front.

7 THE THIRD FRONT

"SHE WAS MUTTERING to herself. That's how they caught her. Walking on the runway—well, plenty of Vietnamese do that, you'd think they didn't give a hoot about getting run over—but this old lady was different. Not only was she walking on the runway, incidentally walking straight for a parked United States Air Force F-105 jet fighter, she was muttering as she went. 'Holy mackerel' said an alert young private in the Air Force. 'Bet she's got a bomb. Bet she's gonna blow up that airplane.' So he arrested her on the spot. It turned out she didn't have a bomb. Still, that muttering was suspicious. So they kept asking her why. Finally the old lady confessed. She'd been pacing the distance between the edge of the runway, and the parked jet. The mutters were her counting her steps. That night the Vietcong planned to set up a mortar outside the compound in order to shoot at the jet, and they wanted to know exactly how far the plane was from where they were going to lay down the mortar baseplate. That way they wouldn't have to waste so many rounds finding the range. Now, that's what I call intelligence."

The speaker was a jovial Counterintelligence staffer from Bill Johnson's shop who looked like Burl Ives. His name was Stu Vance. He gave lectures with me at Blue U. about the Vietcong, one of his specialties being communist military intelligence. After relating the story (which he swore was true) he opened it up for discussion. "A Pentagon watchword these days is "cost-effectiveness," he told a class of DDP-ers. "I wonder if you'd care to guess how cost-effective that operation would have been if successful. Compared to, say, the cost-effectiveness of one of our B-52 bomber raids." In bringing up B-52s in such an offhand manner, he was disingenuous. Another of Vance's specialties was how well our B-52 raids did.

I forget what was said, but recall what it came to. Nobody knew the precise weight or cost of anything, so the numbers were all approximations. Say it had taken the VC ten rounds to hit the jet. If an 81-millimeter round cost $25, and weighed maybe 10 pounds, that meant for $250 and 100 pounds of ammunition, the VC had done a job on a $1.5 million airplane. This contrasted to the job done by the B-52's. Often they flew in formations of nine planes, each carrying 25 tons of bombs, for a grand total of 450,000 pounds of high explosive. The average raid cost what, maybe $500,000? "And from what I've been able to find out," Stu Vance said, "the bombers usually don't know what's down there, or if they did, it's probably left, and they're darn lucky to knock apart more than a few ten-dollar huts, and maybe a blick." (*Blick* was the military word for boat. It came from the first letters of MACV's official term for one, Water-Borne Logistics Craft.)

"Now let me put this into perspective," he went on. "Sometimes the VC only put holes in the airplane, and frequently they miss it altogether. Whereas if a B-52 bomb lands on a hut, that hut is demolished, I mean *eradicated,* so you can't find a shingle, only a bent nail or two a couple of hundred yards away. And an occasional bomb even lands on a communist.* But that's not my point. My point is that the VC do things more efficiently than we do. And the reason is that they usually know what

---

* "That's tongue-in-cheek," Vance said later. Some raids hit major targets! Furthermore he was talking about preplanned raids, normally based on day- or week-old reports. These differed from tactical raids, such as the Marines called in on the communists around Khe Sanh. Often based on visual sightings which were hours and sometimes only minutes old, these raids could be devastatingly effective. One is said to have destroyed an entire communist infantry battalion.

they're aiming at, and we usually don't. Another way of putting it is that *they* have good intelligence." He added that Vietcong military intelligence had a lot more going for it than old women who talk to themselves. "They have a radio intercept service with more than 600 listening posts—200 of them manned by people who know English and an espionage organization with agents, secret ink, couriers and microdots. It's not primitive, it's sophisticated, and good as anything we had in World War II. I might underline once again that this is an entirely different outfit from the ones Mr. Adams told you about."

He was referring to two lectures I'd just finished. One concerned the Vietcong Security Service, whose B-3 component also ran spies in the Saigon government. The other was about the VC Military Proselyting Section, which, as Bob Klein had pointed out, had fifth columnists, or noi tuyens, in the South Vietnamese army.

Klein got back from South Carolina on Monday, 26 May 1969. "Maybe we've gone at the proselyters from the wrong direction," I told him. "Perhaps by trying to see how many desertions they cause without first finding out how big their organization is, we've put the cart before the horse." We discussed this thesis off and on for almost a week before deciding that Klein's next job should be to guess the size of the VC's fifth column. "Coming up with a number is pointless," I said. "Probably there's not that much evidence on noi tuyens, so the best we can hope for is to say that the 'network is extensive,' or 'it's little,' something of that nature." We decided the best way to go about it was the one we'd used on the order of battle; start with the latest captured document, and work backwards. MACV's document center had just published bulletin number 22,000.

I'd have helped Klein, but was too busy on my own. With the announcement of the Vietnamization Program on 14 May, the administration was pumping out questions on how well the South Vietnamese army could be expected to do when it took over the war. "Have a look at this one," Ron Smith had told me. It was the draft for the latest Fourteen Three, the annual estimate to judge the "capabilities of the

Vietnamese communists for fighting in South Vietnam." I knew that phrase well, having spent five months on it while arguing the order of battle in Fourteen Three, 'Sixty-Seven.

Fourteen Three, 'Sixty-Nine was somewhat better. For example, the OB paragraphs were satisfactory, since the VC Branch had provided all the numbers. Nonetheless, the draft seemed out of balance. Of its forty-odd pages, twenty-three were about Vietcong supply problems. I'd never thought supplies were very important, and there was little mention of the VC's political prowess, and none at all on such subjects as communist espionage. By now I thought politics and spying were closely related. Ron had already heard the story of the old woman and the F-105 when I said to him: "This is supposed to be a 'political war,' and persuading that old lady to walk on the runway was a political act. It seems to me that the draft spends too much time counting boxes." For good measure, I repeated my old bias on logistics. When the CIA had doubled the order of battle, it had neglected to adjust upwards its estimate of VC supplies. Therefore, the draft's calculations on enemy logistics were based on the needs of a smaller army than actually existed. I didn't want to get into a fight over this, because I didn't think it mattered.

"If you want to write up something on VC spies and politicians," Ron Smith said, "be my guest, but stay away from logistics. That's Paul Walsh's territory, and he doesn't like other people intruding." As already mentioned, Walsh's reputation had come from his studies on the Ho Chi Minh Trail's ability to successfully withstand our bombing.

I started up on Fourteen Three about the same time that Klein launched into the captured documents. He couldn't have been at it for more than a few minutes when he interrupted me with the first reference to a VC fifth columnist. "Wow!" he exclaimed, as he waved the document in front of me. The fifth columnist was a South Vietnamese army lieutenant who ran a DIOCC. "DIOCC" stood for District Intelligence and Operations Coordinating Center, the basic engine at district level for the CIA-designed Phoenix Program. Phoenix's purpose was to root out the VC political infrastructure person by person. It looked as though in this district the program was rooting out the wrong people. Klein and I speculated what the lieutenant could do to sabotage Phoenix:

"He could put the government supporters in jail as 'VC agents.'"

"And let loose the real ones."

"He could shuffle the files."

"Throw them away."

"Switch names."

"Do in the district chief."

And so on. It was a fine start to his project.

Thus encouraged, Klein went off to find more examples. I called the counterintelligence staff's Bill Johnson, who said he'd alert the station about the DIOCC lieutenant. He added: "Meanwhile, you ought to know we just rolled up a net of Cuc Ngien Cuu agents in Saigon. The report'll be coming out shortly. I'll see that you get a copy." By rolled up, he meant arrested. *Cuc Ngien Cuu* is Vietnamese for "Central Research Directorate," the communists' name for their military intelligence head-quarters in Hanoi. It was the same outfit that had recruited the old lady on the runway, and incidentally, was the Saigon Station's main counter-intelligence target since the start of the war.

Not long after this conversation, Doug Parry appeared unexpectedly from the University of Utah Law School in Salt Lake City. "The agency hired me on for my summer vacation," he explained, making me glad that I'd talked him out of going to the Inspector General nine months before. (It was no surprise when I found out Parry was near the top of his law class.) Ron Smith didn't know what to do with him over such a short period of time. I had a brainstorm: "How about putting him on the documentation problem? While Klein's looking for fifth columnists, Parry can find out how hard or easy it is for them to get government ID cards." I already suspected the answer—fairly easy—but thought it was a good idea to be able to prove it. Ron said OK, and Doug disappeared from sight to pursue the research. This was fine, because Parry liked working on his own, and on the basis of past performance I figured he'd do a good job.

Activity was intense over the next three weeks. I doubt an intelligence proposition has fallen into place as quickly as this one. Namely: the Vietcong espionage and subversive network was well-oiled, highly successful, and possessed of vast numbers of agents.

This proposition was scarcely a world-beater for anyone familiar with Vietnam, but it involved two major surprises. The first was the enormous amount of hard evidence available to support it. The second was that nobody paid much attention to the evidence except the Counterintelligence Staff. The CI Staff seemed to have known about it all along. In fact, Bill Johnson gave me my biggest single piece of information. It was the station report he'd promised in early June, the one about the Cuc Ngien Cuu roll-up in Saigon.

The report was a doozie. It said the South Vietnamese National Police had recently arrested *seventy* Cuc Ngien Cuu agents in the capital city. These included the police's own chief dentist—who apparently extracted information as he pulled teeth—a deputy in South Vietnam's lower house, and a South Vietnamese army lieutenant "who regularly provided sensitive documents of strategic value." I crossed over to the DDP side of the building to ask Johnson who the lieutenant was.

"A liaison officer," he said.

"Liaison between what and what?" I inquired.

"Between Abrams's* headquarters and the South Vietnamese Joint Chiefs. He carried paper mostly, such as plans for Allied operations, requests for B-52 raids, including the coordinates thereof, and so forth, Always in three copies—one for Abrams, one for the Joint Chiefs, and one for the Cuc Ngien Cuu."

"Is that as bad as it sounds?" I asked.

"Let me put it this way," Johnson replied. "If we had his equivalent in Hanoi, we'd have probably won the damn war three years ago." This may have been counterintelligence hyperbole over the danger of spies, but the news was doleful; but not as doleful, however, as the report's

---

*General Creighton Abrams succeeded Westmoreland as head of MACV in June 1968.

conclusion. It said that the arrested agents were a drop in the Cuc Ngien Cuu bucket.

Just then Doug Parry showed up with his initial report. He'd been down in the district to visit AID headquarters' Public Safety Division, which handled the Washington end of South Vietnam's identification-card program. "You'd never think that a laminated piece of paper could be such a touchy subject," Doug said, "but apparently it is. With my first question, the Public Safety chief looked like he wanted to dive under the table." I asked Parry what he'd found out.

It was a lot. Until late 1968, Saigon had been running a program under which seven and a half million ID cards were issued. However, these cards were easy to fake (which I already suspected because of the VC forging cell document), and large numbers had been lost or stolen by the VC. During the Tet Offensive, for example, the communists had assigned teams of cadres, including self-defense militiamen, to go door-to-door in the cities to collect government ID cards. The old system was so fouled up that President Thieu had decided to start up a new one. Saigon began distributing the new cards in October 1968. By 1 May 1969, the number of new cards issued was 1.5 million.

"Excuse me," I interrupted, "but it looks like most people still have the old cards."

"Right," said Parry.

"OK, then, how do you get a new one?"

"By presenting the old card to the local police," he replied, "or by showing them a birth certificate or proof of residency. Of course these are easy to forge too, and in any case, the requirement is normally waived for people who have lost them. I mean, there's a war on, and if somebody's house is burning down, one of the last things he thinks about is rescuing his identification papers. The police realize that."

"Another question, how do you join the South Vietnamese army?"

"By presenting an ID card to the recruiting officer."

"Very well, what's to prevent a Vietcong cadre from going to a government police station, telling them he lost his ID card, getting a new one, and then walking down the street to the post office to join the army?"

"Nothing." said Doug.

"In other words, becoming a VC spy . . ."

"Is like rolling off a log," he completed my sentence. I told Doug he was cooking with gas, and to please find out what the South Vietnamese government did to screen applicants for sensitive jobs, such as cryptographers, officer candidates, special branch policemen, and staffers in President Thieu's office. Once again he disappeared.

Parry's findings would have been important even in normal times, but at this moment they were downright explosive. The reason was Klein. While the above conversations were going on, he was flipping through MACV bulletins. He had discovered almost at once that his first fifth columnist, the DIOCC lieutenant, was anything but unusual. Mentions of VC agents appeared in all kinds of documents: after-action reports describing how fifth columnists had helped in Vietcong attacks; notices of awards for especially good agents; and records kept by military proselyting sections, which sometimes included rosters of spies—as usual, by cover name only. Among the latter were extensive records captured in the VC province of Ben Tre. Ben Tre was roughly the same as South Vietnam's Kien Hoa Province, a notorious hotbed of communist activity in the Delta. In this short period of time, Klein's count of military proselyting agents in South Vietnamese ranks had grown to four hundred.

"Four hundred!" I exclaimed in late June. "Before Tet the CIA had only a single spy in the VC."

"This is only a third of the bulletins," he said. "If noi tuyens keep showing up at this rate, we'll have more than a thousand."

We agreed that even a thousand was a small fraction of the total, or as Klein put it, "the tip of the iceberg." Furthermore, what they were was even more impressive than their number. We must have gone over his list of VC agents a dozen times. It included eight South Vietnamese radiomen, including three sergeants and a corporal; a warrant officer attached to Saigon's naval headquarters; two civilians working in intelligence at an airfield; a sergeant serving in a quartermaster depot at Danang air base; a platoon leader of a government anti-guerrilla formation; a Vietnamese employee of the CIA; two soldiers of unidentified rank working for Saigon's chief of ordnance; a second lieutenant who served as assistant chief of the spywar section of a Marine battalion (and who had recruited three other Marines in the battalion); and eleven South Vietnamese officers, aspirant through "captain," stationed in a single district in Kien Hoa. This last group—which came out of a report from a district proselyting section to VC province headquarters—was hard to swallow. I tried it out on Bill Johnson.

"If they have as many agents as this report claims, they must be running the entire district," he said. "Maybe that's so and we don't realize it, but there's no way to tell without a full-scale investigation. If I were you, I'd be very careful with a report like this. Vietcong agent handlers are doubtless like ours—subject to wishful thinking, and apt to exaggerate their accomplishments. For example, this 'captain' here; maybe the proselyters asked him to sign up as a fifth columnist, and he agreed to do it just to keep them out of his hair. Or to take out insurance in case the VC win. Mind you, I'm not saying that this report is necessarily all wrong. Maybe it's true, or, more likely, partly true. My advice is to proceed with caution."

This was my own instinct, and I handed him a copy of Klein's list. Then I wrote up a memo about it for Ron Smith. Reflecting Johnson's advice, it said the agents "should not all be taken as active and committed penetrations. Some probably are fence sitters, some nonexistent (the VC are prone to pad what they don't have to account for), and some may have had their sympathies misinterpreted by VC reporting officers. However, the documents indicated that some also were actively committed agents. Others, including a share of fence sitters, might become active under different conditions (e.g., U.S. troop withdrawal). In any case, Mr. Klein's efforts seem to be highlighting a problem of considerable scope."

"'Considerable scope' is putting it mildly," Ron Smith said after reading the memo. "But unfortunately, I haven't had much success in inserting your paragraphs about spies into Fourteen Three. There's a big brouhaha going on upstairs over communist logistics. I haven't been able to get a word in edgewise." The meetings on Fourteen Three, 'Sixty-Nine were already in session. I wasn't allowed to attend them, because—as Ron had told me—of "that business back in 1967." He said he'd try to arrange a private briefing, however, so I could argue my case in front of James Graham. Mr. Graham was the estimate's chairman, just as he'd been on the one before Tet.

All this had begun to get annoying, but it was hardly a surprise. Over the past week or two, I'd made the rounds to test the reactions of various offices toward Vietcong espionage and subversion. The Office of Current Intelligence was predictable. They had no one to spare to look into the matter, everyone being too busy on the Sitrep; besides, chasing spies was the DDP's business. The reaction of the DDP's Vietnam desk was similar. When I told the desk chief that the number of communist agents might run into the several thousands, he said: "For God's sake, don't open that Pandora's Box. We have enough trouble as it is." The only person who seemed to give a damn about them was Bill Johnson.*

Ron Smith finally arranged my briefing for James Graham in early July. About ten people crammed into a tiny room on the seventh floor to hear it. They included Ron, Paul Walsh, some DDP officials, and of course, Mr. Graham. With Klein and Parry as backup men, I shot off both barrels—that is, Bob's list and Doug's cards. The briefing fell flat. Always polite, Mr. Graham said: "Thank you, Sam, that was very interesting." A DDP desk man gave a short talk on Pandora's Box. But when Fourteen Three's latest draft arrived at the VC Branch on Monday, 7 July, it had no mention whatsoever of Vietcong military proselyting. The main subject was still the enemy supplies.

---

*The DDP's Vietnam Desk oversaw the Saigon Station's espionage and covert action programs. The Counterintelligence staff, of which Johnson was a member, was organizationally separate from the Desk, and in another part of the building.

That was absurd, so I wrote some comments on the draft. Vietnam was a political struggle, I said, not a race between stevedores. Communist intelligence—which allowed them to attack or hide when and where they saw fit—largely negated our vast superiority in materiel. The draft wasted too much ink on "the minutiae of logistics." On receiving the comments, Ron said, "Well, anyway, we tried." I knew it wasn't his fault, and began drafting a cable to the Saigon Station. It laid out Klein's findings from the documents, and asked whether the Allies were using them to catch agents. The draft concluded: "Request information on, and assessment of, efficiency of [South Vietnamese] programs against military proselyters."

Shortly thereafter, an incident occurred that became a major milestone on the downhill road of my career. At the time I didn't even realize it was important. What happened was that I became involved in the "minutiae of logistics." It began innocently enough around noon on Friday, 11 July, when Ron Smith came back from the morning session of Fourteen Three.

"Christ," he said, "the fur's flying up there."

"What about?" I asked.

"A Navy commander named Roy Beavers—he represents the military—is slugging it out with Paul Walsh. Beavers says the CIA estimate of Vietcong weapons expenditure is much too low."

"He's probably right," I shrugged.

"Maybe so," said Ron. "Someone claimed that if you believe the agency tonnages, the VC aren't even using as much ammunition as the Biafrans."

"Has anyone checked that out with the Africa Division?" I asked.

"Hell, no," he said, "that'd be asking for trouble."

"Well, why don't I? I used to work in Africa. It would be a cinch to find out."

"If I were you, I'd leave well enough alone," said Ron. He laughed, and we went separately to lunch.

Although I thought logistics was an overworked subject, Ron had aroused my curiosity. The province of Biafra in Nigeria was then engaged in a rebellion against the federal republic, and the Nigerian analyst was an old acquaintance, stretching back from my days on the Congo. So after lunch, instead of going to the VC Branch on the third floor, I went up to my old African office on the sixth. After a few minutes' gossip with my ex-boss, Dana Ball, I sat down in the chair next to the Nigerian desk. The analyst's name was Bill.

Bill and I discussed Biafran logistics for about fifteen minutes. It seems that our intelligence on the subject was superb. There was only a single supply route to the rebels, an airfield, and one way or another, the DDP had found out the precise load of ammunition on each incoming plane. "Pretty much down to the last bullet," said Bill.

"How many tons is it a week?" I asked.

"Depends on the week."

"Average."

"One hundred fifty tons. It's been averaging about one hundred fifty tons a week for several months now," Bill said. "I'd say that's accurate within a few percentage points."

I jotted "150 tons" on the back of an envelope, and took the elevator down to third floor to the Office of Economic Research Logistics Branch, a few doors down the hall from the VC Branch. It still being lunchtime, the Log Branch had only two analysts in it, one named John Cole. Fortunately, Cole was the man who'd supplied the agency's estimate of VC weapons expenditures for Fourteen Three.

"John," I asked, "How many tons of munitions do the communists use up each week in South Vietnam? What's that number you put in Fourteen Three?" He did some figuring on a pad of paper.

"Seventy-seven tons a week," he said.

"My God!" I exclaimed, "The Biafrans use a hundred and fifty! That's a hard estimate, too."

Normally stolid, Cole burst out laughing. "It doesn't look right, does it," he said. "I mean the little old Biafrans shooting off twice as much as the big bad VC."

"It sure doesn't," I replied.

"How did you come up with seventy-seven tons?"

"I'd hate to tell you," Cole said, at which the other analyst spoke for the first time: "Let's just say it's a soft estimate. Soft."

Logistics had become interesting. I ran back upstairs to Africa to tell Bill. He also started to laugh. "That's crazy. No wonder we're losing the war." I had some more questions. It turned out that the Biafran army was one-tenth as big as the VC's, but that it used similar tactics: much bushwhacking, few large battles, no artillery barrages of the type that eat up large weights of ammunition.

Armed with the two sets of numbers, I returned to the Vietcong Branch to write a paper about them. Only two pages long, it compared Biafran and VC weapons expenditures, and made this observation: "Thus if we accept the above statistics . . . it would appear that the Biafran army, which is in the order of one-tenth the size of the communist army in Vietnam, consumes about twice as much tonnage in arms and ammunition. This seeming anomaly raises the following possibilities . . ." They were: (a) That Biafran soldiers fired twenty times as many bullets per capita as the VC; (b) That the CIA way overstated Biafran munitions expenditures; and (c) That the CIA way *understated* VC munitions expenditures.

Since the first possibility was unlikely and the second was against the evidence, that left the third as the most probable. I concluded that "the problem bears looking into."

The weekend was at hand, and the subject was unimportant—or so I thought. In any case, I told Beverly she'd get the draft first thing Monday morning to type, and took off for home, unaware my memo wasn't about Biafra, or Vietnam either. It was about Cambodia.

Monday was the fourteenth of July, Bastille Day. Ron was late for work. He stopped by my desk at ten o'clock. In the most casual kind of way, I handed him the Biafran memo. Just as casually, he glanced at the title. When he saw it, he stiffened.

"Adams," he said, "you're sticking your pecker in a pencil sharpener."

"What do you mean by that, Ron?" I asked.

"I told you to stay out of logistics. It's Paul Walsh's turf. If he sees this, he'll flip his lid."

"But why?"

"Look, this tonnage fight's between him and the military. Specifically between him and Roy Beavers. Leave it alone."

"The military's right on this one. Probably has been all along. The VC are using more ammunition than we think. What's the big deal? A few more truckloads a week, that's all."

"There's more to it than that," said Ron.

The argument grew hotter. It became a matter of pride. I began insisting that the Biafran memo go straight to Paul Walsh. "I'm no big admirer of military intelligence," I said, "but this time they're right." Smith relented. OK, he'd forward it, he said, but *watch out*. For the rest of the day the VC Branch atmosphere was positively electric. A fellow analyst, Joe Stumpf, said: "What's the matter with you, Sam, anyway, you got a death wish or something?"

Finally, I walked down the hall to the Logistics Branch to ask why the fuss. Surely it amounted to more than a few truckfuls of ammunition. I was right.

"You just blundered into the Sihanoukville dispute," a Log analyst told me.

"What's that all about?" I asked. I knew that Sihanoukville was Cambodia's main seaport, about two hundred miles due west of Saigon, but I didn't realize it was the subject of a dispute.

He told me the story. The CIA and the military had been fighting for the last two and a half years over how many weapons were coming through Sihanoukville bound for the VC. The military said a lot. The CIA said no, the Ho Chi Minh Trail through Laos provided virtually all the weaponry the communists "needed." Right now the arguments centered on what was meant by "needed." The CIA said the Vietcong's needs were seventy-seven tons a week countrywide, and that the Ho Chi Minh Trail was able to provide them. The military (including Commander Beavers upstairs) thought the Communists' needs were far more than seventy-seven tons, and in fact exceeded the Trail's capacity by a considerable margin. Thus the communists "needed" a supplement to the Ho Chi Minh Trail. The supplement was Sihanoukville.

"This is where your damn memo about Biafra comes in," said the analyst. "The agency has other arguments as well, but the Biafran memo makes our principal one—the one about 'needs,' which is another word for 'munitions expenditures'—look absolutely ridiculous. By implying that the CIA 'way understates VC munitions expenditures,' it supports the military's side of the Sihanoukville dispute."

8 CAMBODIAN REPLAY

Publisher's note: Adams intended to include a long section about intelligence on Cambodia in his book, but never completed it. What survives is a draft of a magazine article, never placed, on which this chapter is based; a chronology of events, and notes for a study of the controversy over military munitions imported through the Cambodian port of Sihanoukville, briefly described in the previous chapter. Adams did a huge amount of research on this subject, which included a highly circumstantial story of espionage and agent handling in the classic mode, but he failed to turn his notes into finished text, perhaps realizing that he had commenced what was properly a second book. In telling the Cambodian story, Adams changed the names of some CIA employees in order to conceal their identities.

MOTIVES SEEMED LACKING to keep close tabs on the number of Cambodian rebels until March 1970. Analysts within the CIA who worked on Cambodia agreed there weren't very many, and that in any case the so-called Khmer Rouge posed little threat to Prince Sihanouk's government in Phnom Penh, and none at all to either us or our South Vietnamese allies.

Then on 18 March a right-wing coup unseated the prince. Chaos ensued. Sihanouk, away when the coup took place, announced his support of the rebels; the new government in Phnom Penh joined the Washington-Saigon alliance; the Vietcong invaded the Cambodian interior; and U.S. troops sallied over the frontier into Cambodia, where they stayed the months of May and June. While there, they captured some munitions and unearthed several boxes of papers belonging to the Vietcong high command.

By the late summer of 1970, Indo-China began to simmer down. Although a malaise persisted that the Vietcong could kick over the traces in Cambodia if they saw fit, the smart money bet they wouldn't. Some reports told of enemy doings in the villages, but the Cambodian war seemed at bottom a contest between communist invaders, all Vietnamese, and government defenders, all Khmer. Since Khmers and Vietnamese are ancient rivals, the theory took hold that the communists would fail to gain a native following beyond the small band of Khmer Rouge rebels extant before the coup.

In late 1970, I had worked on the Vietcong for five years, mostly trying to figure how many there were. Then they transferred me to a small staff to write a history of Cambodia's rebels. The history had a low priority. Other offices had the more important task of recording current events in Cambodia. One called the Manpower Branch had the job of keeping count of communist forces there.

My employment as chronicler of Khmer insurgents began in early 1971. Knowing little about them, I started from scratch, and spent the next several weeks gathering paper from the archives that crowd the CIA's lower floors. In short order I had stuffed a number of safe drawers with old reports, including a musty study done by French army intelligence in 1953. The study described the communists' rebel army in Cambodia in the early fifties, and the types of soldiers it had.

In mid-April, I thought to look at more recent stuff, including the documents taken from Vietcong headquarters in Cambodia in 1970. Unfortunately, the CIA's filing system, as good as it is for some things, had foundered at the prospect of sorting out by subject the cartloads of captured documents that showed up weekly from Indo-China. There was only one thing to do, plow through the lot and pick out those having to do with Cambodian rebels. I found a more or less complete set of Indo-Chinese documents—stored in large, brown, cardboard boxes in the CIA's first-floor archives—and went through two years' worth. It took three weeks.

In a few days' reading, the extraordinary story of what the communists had been up to in Cambodia began to emerge in detail. In the months after Sihanouk's fall, the Vietcong invaders had assembled a large and complex advisory system, bent on fielding a Cambodian rebel army to compete with Phnom Penh's. Some documents told of chains of command, of radio nets, of hospitals and training schools. Others mentioned artillery companies, commando battalions, infantry regiments, even a division. The dimensions of the new army were unclear, but the number of documents and the complexity of the system they described suggested it was very big. I assumed its existence was well known.

I found shortly that it wasn't. In mid-May, a just-published CIA memorandum about Cambodia arrived on my desk; it stated that the number of Khmers in the communist military structure in Cambodia lay in the range of five thousand to ten thousand. In light of what the documents said, the numbers seemed so uncommonly small that it struck me at once that something was wrong. Where had the numbers come from? I set out to inquire.

The DDI had three offices that dealt with the war in Cambodia. Neither the first nor the second could say where the numbers arose; furthermore, they asserted, they didn't get the documents. The third office was the Manpower Branch, which still had the job of tallying communists in Cambodia. The branch got the documents all right, but apparently hadn't sorted them out. Asked for its files on the Khmer communist army, a branch analyst proffered a thin folder that contained a dozen or so low-level agent reports—but no documents. There was also an internal memorandum, dated late April 1971, which stated the branch had done virtually no research on the Communists in Cambodia for almost a year. A check of CIA cables from Phnom Penh, Saigon, and Bangkok turned up the same story: no research on Cambodian numbers.

Thereupon I called the Defense Intelligence Agency in the Pentagon and asked for its Cambodia shop. A Sergeant Reisman came to the phone and said he was the person charged with keeping files on the Cambodian rebels. The range of five thousand to ten thousand, he declared, had come from the Cambodian government's army intelligence (G-2) a year earlier. DIA had tinkered with the number, then left it alone because it seemed "reasonable." DIA had never done an in-depth study on the matter, he said. "There's no one at DIA to do a study," he declared; "they hit us with too much shit." I thanked the sergeant and hung up. The time was five o'clock in the afternoon of 28 May 1971, a Friday.

So that was the story. U.S. intelligence had neglected to inquire whether our enemies in Cambodia had raised an army. I had happened upon it while looking for something else. Four hundred and thirty-six days had passed since 18 March 1970, the day Cambodia joined the war.

I began in earnest on Saturday morning to write a paper gauging the size of the Khmer communist army. Since the evidence was at hand— hundreds of captured documents, prisoner-of-war interrogations, and CIA field reports—the next step was to determine whom to count. I merely followed the criteria of the Cambodian G-2, whose range of five thousand to ten thousand the year before had included the communists' three types of soldiers: those in the main forces, the local forces, and the guerrilla-militia. They are the same categories the communists have in Vietnam and Laos, and, according to the French army study exhumed from the archives, the same ones the Khmer rebels had in 1953.

Writing the first draft took a week. It dealt with the categories one by one, and, using the same methods the CIA had earlier employed in estimating Vietcong numbers, came up with separate figures for each type. On Friday, 4 June 1971, the three estimates were complete, the line drawn at the bottom, and the total arrived at. They were:

Main forces	20,000 − 30,000
Local forces	20,000 − 30,000
Guerrilla-militia	60,000 − 90,000
Total	100,000 −150,000

This sum, the draft observed, was from ten to thirty times higher than the one carried on the U.S. government's official books. The reason for the discrepancy, the draft pointed out, was that American intelligence had missed the phenomenal growth of the rebel army from not having looked.

The draft explained at length who was in each category. The main forces, it said, were the communists' mobile reserve, and consisted of large numbers of independent companies and battalions and about a dozen infantry regiments—all but one of which the CIA memo of May had missed. The local forces, akin to the U.S. National Guard, fought in each of Cambodia's nineteen provinces and more than one hundred districts. The guerrilla-militia were local partisans who defended communist-held villages and hamlets. Poorly gunned in most places, they were armed to the teeth in others. The Vietcong guerrilla-militia had caused about one in four of all U.S. casualties in South Vietnam.

Experience told me that the Cambodian draft might run into heavy weather. As the CIA's only analyst on Vietcong strength in 1966 and 1967, I had written a series of studies presenting evidence that the Vietnamese communist force in South Vietnam was closer to 600,000 than the 280,000 then carried officially on U.S. books. The studies fared badly. Some were pigeonholed, others killed outright. But the evidence they advanced was so abundant that it was hard to overlook, and pressure mounted throughout 1967 to raise the official estimate.

American intelligence chose instead to rearrange the books to keep the Vietcong numbers low. Following guidelines form General Westmoreland's headquarters in late 1967 to maintain the Vietcong estimate below 300,000, his intelligence staff used two methods to do so. The first was to remove from the books categories of Vietcong who had been there all along. The second was to employ "conservative" techniques—such as omitting troops in small units—in accounting for types of soldiers supposed to be on the lists. And instead of going up, the Vietcong estimate went down—to about 240,000.

When the Tet Offensive hit in January 1968, large numbers of soldiers missing from the estimates popped up in the middle of South

Vietnam's cities. Two months later, the CIA, which had winked at the military's pre-Tet wiles, reversed itself and vowed officially that there might be as many as 600,000 Vietcong. But it took Tet to get the agency to reassess, then accept the evidence of 1966, an exercise, an analyst later wrote, "in counting Indians after they'd come through the window—not so much intelligence as a sort of morbid curiosity."

Fearful that my Cambodian draft might go the way of some of the papers before Tet, I determined to see that it got widely read within the government, even if it meant handing out copies myself. Before leaving the CIA that Friday, I told Bud, deputy chief of the staff to which I belonged, that I had written a paper on the Khmer communist army, and would do a final draft over the weekend. He looked up distractedly from his typewriter and nodded.

The final draft, handwritten, was complete one Sunday evening in June 1971. It took most of that Monday to type the thing up. When done, it came to about forty pages, with a hundred or so footnotes that referred to some twice as many sources. Late that afternoon I called an acquaintance on Kissinger's staff and told him of the paper's existence. He asked for a bootleg copy. That evening I stopped by the Executive Office Building (next to the White House) and handed him a Xerox copy in a manila envelope.

Arriving at work on 8 June, I gave the original to my boss, Mr. Pontiac, the staff chief, to whom Bud was deputy. Mr. Pontiac said that he would read it later. I went upstairs and showed the draft to various functionaries who dealt with Cambodia, including George Carver, chief advisor on Indo-China to the CIA's director, Richard Helms. Mr. Carver glanced it over, declared that 100,000 to 150,000 seemed to him too high, and suggested that "45,000 to 50,000" sounded better. When I returned to my office, Mr. Pontiac, who by this time had read the draft, said that under no circumstances was it to leave staff channels.

Mr. Pontiac spent a good part of the next day discussing the paper, I was told, with the DDI hierarchy, including its deputy, Mr. Walsh, and perhaps its chief, Mr. Proctor. After the consultations Mr. Pontiac called

Bud and me into his office. It was 3:00 P.M. He declared the paper was "unconvincing," that it was written "hurriedly and in anger," that it was "lacking in integrity," and that, moreover, my writing it had been a "clandestine operation." Were I to write another like it, he asserted, I would find myself "out on the streets." When he saw me taking notes on his remarks, he told me to stop. Whereupon he instructed Bud to come up with a more acceptable draft, and dismissed us both. I said to Bud as we left that I didn't think the draft was a clandestine operation because I'd told him about it the Friday before. "Yes," Bud replied, "but you didn't tell about the troll under the bridge."

The Kissinger staffer called on the tenth to say that he and a colleague had read the draft and thought it a good job. He suggested sending a bootleg copy to the Defense Department, which was apparently unaware of the problem. The following day Mr. Pontiac convened a meeting at 11:00 A.M. to discuss the draft. I was not invited. Nine other CIA officials who worked on Cambodia showed up. Mr. Pontiac told them that the draft was for "internal use only"—it was not to leave the building—that they couldn't see the original but would get copies of Bud's revised version when it came out. He also stated that the DDI front office had decided to turn over the revised version to the Manpower Branch for "action" since the branch was still the agency's official tabulator of communist numbers.

When Bud completed the revised version, it had two main changes from the original: the phrase "100,000 to 150,000" was amended to read "as many as 100,000, or more," thus making 100,000 seem the midpoint rather than bottom end of the estimate; and all statements which implied that the CIA hadn't done its homework were deleted. Otherwise unscathed, the revised paper made its way, footnotes and all, to the Manpower Branch.

On 18 June, the Manpower Branch chief, Mr. Tate, assigned a newcomer to the branch, Herman Dowdy, to supervise the Cambodian project. Unschooled in the labyrinths of communist army organization, Dowdy had never before worked on estimates of enemy strength. A few days later I received an under-the-table copy of Dowdy's first written foray into the business of estimating communist numbers. It was a memorandum commenting on Bud's revised version. The memo stated that the revised version was structurally unsound, and that it wrongly implied that the Khmer rebel army offset the government's.

Early in the morning of 22 June, Mr. Dowdy told a Manpower Branch analyst that neither earlier draft "would ever see the light of day." This was officially confirmed at a meeting, chaired by Mr. Tate, at 10:30 A.M. on the CIA's seventh floor. Mr. Tate announced his branch was going to scrap both early drafts and write an entirely new one. Asked how long it might take, Tate would not say.

Not long after the 10:30 meeting, I plodded disconsolately down a gray stairwell to the Manpower Branch to see what could be salvaged. As I arrived, a branch analyst named Peter Snider emerged from Tate's inner office. Tate, he said, had just put him on the Khmer communist army project under Dowdy's supervision. Like Dowdy, Snider was new to the branch, and had had little experience in dealing with communist numbers.

I asked Snider if I could help. He replied that he needed the references—documents and so forth—mentioned in the footnotes of the just-killed paper, since the Manpower Branch hadn't yet got them. I offered to show him where they were in the archives.

Snider then sat down at his desk, and remarked casually that his forthcoming study was unlikely to come up with more than thirty thousand Cambodian Communist soldiers; nor would it find less than ten thousand, he said. He stated that one of the reason for this was that his study would include only two of the Communists' three types of soldiers: the main forces and the local forces, but not the guerrilla-militia.

Perplexed, I began to advance reasons for keeping guerrillas in the estimate. In the first place, I said, the Cambodian G-2 had included guerrillas in its year-old range of five thousand to ten thousand, and for the CIA to drop them now would mean that Washington and Phnom Penh had separate definitions of who the enemy was. Then, of course, the Manpower Branch had included VC guerrillas in its Vietnam estimate, and the Cambodian guerrillas performed exactly the same tasks next door. And finally, they were a clear military threat—witness our losses to Vietcong guerrillas—since thousands bore arms, and nearly all were trained how to fight. But Snider shook his head and said they were too "amorphous" to count.

He then stated that he wasn't going to include service troops either. Again taken aback, I declared that ordnance sergeants, medics, and such like, where were an integral part of the main and local forces, were just as valuable as combatants: in some cases more so, since they took longer to train. Besides, I said, when the CIA reported the size of Phnom Penh's army, it always included the government's service soldiers—so why not the rebels? Counting them on one side and not on the other distorted the odds, since almost half of Phnom Penh's force consisted of service troops. Snider repeated his resolve to exclude rebel logisticians.

By this time I was filled with misgivings. Here was another case, I suspected, of the game before Tet: supply subordinates with a maximum number of enemy soldiers to count and let them figure out how to do it. In late 1967, it was three hundred thousand Vietcong. Now it looked like thirty thousand Cambodian rebels.

So I asked Snider if Tate had given him the number. Snider shrugged but did not answer. (But when a friend of mine who worked in the Manpower Branch later asked Snider the same question, he answered simply, "Yes." I repeated the query 10 May 1973, just before I quit the agency. Snider told me that Tate had given him the components to count and that in his opinion this amounted to the same thing. He also said that his immediate boss, Dowdy, had told him that morning that his job was to "refute" the numbers in the earlier drafts.)

On 23 June Snider informed me that the Manpower Branch had put the Cambodian project on the back burner, and not to expect anything before Labor Day. Hearing this, I clambered upstairs to see Helms's assistant, George Carver. I told Mr. Carver that the Manpower Branch planned to proceed all ahead slow on the Khmer communist army

paper, and intoned something to the effect of "Damnit there's a war on."
I also asked Carver if Helms knew what was going on. Carver replied he
would look into the matter.

At 4:30 P.M. the following day, Mr. Pontiac, flushed with what looked
to me like embarrassed anger, called me into his office, along with Bud.
He inquired what my "frustration factor" was. I replied that a certain
Snider had already been handed a number to come up with—30,000,
without benefit of evidence—told not to bother about speed, and that
the whole thing reminded me of the manipulations before Tet. Mr.
Pontiac heard me out, then said that the DDI front office had just told
him of my visit the day before to George Carver, and had said that the
visit showed that Mr. Pontiac didn't know how to control his under-
lings. This was not the case, Mr. Pontiac declared, since he (Pontiac) had
"sent people packing" before, and wouldn't hesitate to do so again in
my case. Thereupon he advised me to work after hours and on weekends until my still far-from-complete chronicle of Cambodian rebels
was done. He added that the front office had decreed that I remove
myself from the Cambodian numbers business. (I followed the former
instructions but not the latter; that is, I spent my weekends that summer
at CIA headquarters as a historian—muttering to myself about being
punished for discovering an enemy host—but continued to do sums on
Cambodian rebels.)

Recalling the suggestion of the Kissinger staffer to send a bootleg
copy of the original paper to the Pentagon, I called an old friend, David
Siegel, of the Defense Intelligence Agency's Estimates Staff. We dined at
noon at a Pentagon cafeteria, and I slipped him a copy of Bud's revised
version. Siegel swore secrecy as to whom he got it from, and promised
to make several copies for DIA analysts, including Sergeant Reisman,
still keeper of DIA's Khmer rebel files.

In August, Bud summoned me to his cubicle to tell of an irate phone
call he had just gotten from the DDI deputy chief, Mr. Walsh.
Apparently Snider had visited Sergeant Reisman in the Pentagon and
spied on the sergeant's desk a Xerox copy of Bud's revised version. On
his return to the CIA, Snider reported the observation to his boss, who

relayed the news to the DDI hierarchy. Mr. Walsh ordered Bud over the phone to track down who it was that was leaking papers to the Pentagon about enemy armies. Bud looked me in the eye and asked if I was responsible. I replied uneasily that I was not.

Hearing at last that Snider's draft was almost complete, on 12 November I asked Bud whether I, as an interested party, could follow DDI practice and review the paper before it went to press. Bud said the decision was up to the Manpower Branch. Later, the word arrived that I was not to see the paper before its publication. (Snider snuck me a draft anyway, but since I couldn't admit I had it, and since he had to stay below 30,000, my furtive lobbies for higher numbers got nowhere.)

Toward the end of the month I received, through regular channels, a copy of Snider's just-published paper. Affixed with the agency's seal, and with the classification "Secret Special No Foreign Dissemination," it went to those in Washington with proper security clearances and a need to know. The paper stated that the number of Khmers in the communist army in Cambodia was in a range of from 15,000 to 30,000 men; or within the limits given Snider on 22 June, the day he got the assignment. Having puzzled over it for several months, he at last settled on the same method the military had used in lowering the Vietcong estimate before Tet. He marched two whole categories out of the order of battle and "scaled down" what was left. The range of 15,000–30,000 became the U.S. government's official estimate, and shortly appeared in the press.

On 1 December Mr. Pontiac, who said he spoke for the DDI hierarchy, put me on six months notice to find another job. (Nothing came of it.) Putting aside my saga of Cambodian rebels, I began to write a critique of Snider's paper to suggest what was missing.*

The Manpower Branch received my critique of Snider's paper on 27 December 1971. It cavilled once more at the absence of guerrillas, then

---

*On the track of a particular communist unit, I once called the Defense Intelligence Agency for help. A Captain White answered the phone, saying he worked with Sergeant Reisman. He didn't know about the unit, but when routinely asked how DIA arrived at its Cambodian estimate, the captain replied, "First they give you the number, then they tell you to prove it." He did not elaborate.

dwelt on omissions in the main and local forces. The critique noted, for example, that Snider had included some main forces soldiers who belonged to regiments, but none in the myriad smaller units such as battalions and companies. The shortchanging of small units, the critique observed, was a device that the U.S. command in Saigon had used on the Vietcong estimate before Tet. In early January, at Tate's behest, Snider wrote a short rebuttal to the critique, which never left the building. That ended the matter.

With nothing else to do, I returned to my history of the Cambodian rebels. I traced them back to 1947 and discovered that in 1954, some three thousand had gone to Hanoi for training. I also found that a full-scale communist-run rebellion had started in Cambodia in 1968, and that the head of the Cambodian rebels was an obscure Khmer named Pol Pot. None of the facts had been known at the time, not even that the VC called the Cambodian rebels the Red K, and that the Cambodian rebels called the VC, Friend Seven. Increasingly glum, I turned in my history in February 1972. Its concluding paragraphs ended with this prediction:

> Finally there is the question of the party's position in the communist world. Here the evidence strongly suggests that the Cambodian party, although formed in North Vietnam, had a mind of its own. There are already clear indications that its leaders have flirted with China to offset Hanoi . . . Although the Khmers' short-term interests are clearly with Hanoi, the party leaders probably regard their dependence as temporary.
>
> In fact, what evidence there is points to friction in the future. A KC document of late last year was already referring to the "Vietnamese problem." A more recent document talked of difficulties the Khmer hierarchy was having with Friend Seven . . . And a COSVN assessment of October 1971 suggested that in some areas relations between the Cambodian and Vietnamese communists had grown "steadily worse."
>
> Whatever the problems may become eventually, they seem unlikely to get out hand in the immediate future. The two parties have

more pressing near-term goals . . . to gain Saigon and Phnom Penh, respectively, but it would not be surprising if at some more distant time, the ancient hatred between the Khmers and the Vietnamese publicly reemerges in the trappings of communist dialiectic.

Those were the last words I wrote that were published by the agency. The events they foretold have since come to pass. After their publication, I was told to work on Communist China.

On 13 March, however, a fresh CIA memorandum arrived on my desk again fixing the Khmer numbers at 15,000 to 30,000. I called Snider to ask why the range was unchanged. He replied that the Manpower Branch had stopped research on Cambodian numbers after the publication of his paper in November. He also mentioned in passing that as far as he knew no one in CIA headquarters kept a card file on enemy units. Hoping that a new volume of evidence might reopen the issue of size, I fished from my desk a cardboard box and a stack of three-by-fives, and reported to Bud's cubicle to ask if I could work upstairs for a while on "filing." Busy as usual at his typewriter, he replied absently that it was OK with him. That afternoon, I sat down at an unoccupied desk in the Cambodian Section of the DDI's Office of Current Intelligence, filling out index cards on communist units. (Since I still had to do my job downstairs with the staff, the project was slow going, and took upwards of a month.)

On 31 March, the CIA sent a memorandum to the White House stating that the Vietnamese communists were unlikely to launch a really large-scale offensive in South Vietnam in the next few months. The memo, which followed an earlier CIA brief to the White House that the main Vietcong attack had fizzled in February, once more put the Khmer numbers at 15,000 to 30,000. The top end of the range was now nine months old. The next day Hanoi launched its Easter offensive in South Vietnam, its biggest since Tet 1968. Apparently sure that the Khmer rebel army was large enough to hold its own, the Vietnamese communists began to march their combat units from Cambodia to South Vietnam. As the Vietcong bolted through the Vietnamese countryside, I started to shuffle my three-by-fives in preparation for another study on enemy strength in Cambodia.

"What are you trying to do—get all three of us fired?" Bud asked, evidently referring to himself, Mr. Pontiac, and me. I had just handed him the study based on the card file. The study listed by title an aggregation of Khmer communist units unaccounted for in the official estimate (and also noted that some forty Vietcong battalions were absent from the lists.) Despite his perturbation, Bud sent the study at once to the DDI front office. It responded shortly by instructing him to stop me from working on Indo-China altogether; and then it killed the memo. That evening I found that it had also packed me off to bureaucratic Coventry. A researcher from the Office of Current Intelligence telephoned my home to tell me—morose already—that Mr. Lehman, the office head, had passed down the official word to OCI analysts—some of whom had helped on the card file—to stop abetting my endeavors.

9 THE CROSSOVER POINT

THE EASTER OFFENSIVE was the last straw for me. As usual, it was a complete surprise, and I decided that something, goodness knows what, had to be done about American intelligence. I knew that my old friend, Gains Hawkins, had retired to Mississippi, so I determined to track him down. Eventually, I discovered he had bought a house in the small farming town of West Point. I called him up, he said he'd be glad to see me, and I flew down from Virginia. On a hot June afternoon in his backyard, he told me how, right before the Saigon conference of September 1967, he'd been given a number for the OB—and told not to go above it. He felt that the number he was given was unreasonably low, and that General Westmoreland was probably the person behind it. Hawkins agreed that an investigation was in order, and that Congress ought to do it. He particularly recommended the head of the Senate Armed Services Committee, John Stennis of Mississippi. Hawkins was taking a big risk. In agreeing to talk to the Senate, he was putting his pension on the line. Retirees are subject to the Uniform Code of Military Justice.

I returned to Virginia, and later in the year gave Stennis' committee a thirteen-page paper that listed names, dates, and sequences of events. A staff assistant told me it was an interesting document, but he doubted that the Intelligence Subcommittee would take it up because it hadn't met in over a year and a half. I gave up on the Senate and tried the House. The House was likewise unresponsive.

Despairing of Congress, I tried the U.S. Army and CIA Inspector General. Neither would investigate my charges.

With the arrival of additional reports that the Khmer communist army had continued to grow, I called upon the office of the CIA's Inspector General to lodge a formal complaint about the agency's research on enemy strength in Cambodia. The date was 4 December 1972. Scott Breckenridge, who had handled some earlier grumbles of mine to the inspector about the mischief over the Vietcong estimate before Tết, scribbled notes as I related my story about Cambodia. Mr. Breckenridge later informed me that William Colby, then the CIA's executive director, had learned of my complaint, and said, "Let the chips fall where they may." It was the last I heard of the matter.*

This curious story of numbers poses several questions, the first of which is whether it really mattered. The answer of course depends on one's point of view, but for American intelligence it must be yes. Because some time back—in McNamara's day, I suppose—the U.S. government decided to measure its wars statistically. It follows that when the numbers are cockeyed, the conclusions drawn from them tend to be skewed as well. Had the computers gotten the data of late 1970, for example, that the Khmer rebel army was growing rapidly, we might have concluded far sooner than we did that the conflict in Cambodia was fast becoming a civil war, not unlike the one in South Vietnam.

---

*Broadcasting by radio from Hanoi on 9 April 1973, Prince Sihanouk stated that the number of soldiers in the Khmer rebel army's "offensive" units, presumably meaning those in the main and local forces, had "now reached 120,000 men." On receiving word of the broadcast, the CIA announced in its daily bulletin on Indo-China that Sihanouk's claim was clearly exaggerated since the U.S. official estimate then stood at 40,000.

This estimate of the rebel's strength clearly sprung from the mold set on 22 June 1971. It excluded guerrillas and service troops, who numbered in the many additional tens of thousands, and failed to account for legions of the main and local forces it purported to include. A study from the field put the number of such combatants as high as 90,000, not all that far from Sihanouk's claim. But the study (which also omitted guerrillas and logisticians) remained unofficial. The true size of Khmer forces could have exceeded 200,000 by a considerable margin.

A second question is why anyone bothered at all to cook the Cambodian books. Although in the case of the Vietcong numbers before Tet everyone concerned knew that the main reason for the adjustments was to keep aglow the light at the end of the tunnel, the motives for doctoring the Khmer estimate are more obscure. Certainly the agency had reason to hide its fifteen-month delay in asking whether our Cambodian foes had recruited an army; but as a sole cause, it seems farfetched. Perhaps the real motive lies hidden in the rubble of the American policy for Cambodia, which held that the problem there was caused by Vietnamese, not native, communists. This was an argument Washington used to justify the bombing of Cambodia.

A third question is who was responsible. In the absence of a proper inquiry, it's impossible to say. But clearly the agency officials with whom I normally dealt were anything but sinister. Snider, for example, was a cheerful and usually candid young analyst from southern Virginia, who sometimes slipped me documents supporting higher numbers, and who often complained about what he thought was Congress's airy neglect of the CIA. Bud was a quiet, careful, Far Eastern scholar whom I considered more a protector than adversary, and who, when adrift from his typing machine, was a sometime poet. (Once, on being asked to display an example of his scholarship in the agency library, he submitted a literary review opened to one of his poems; on the page opposite was some verse by Robert Lowell.) Mr. Pontiac was a dignified, rather kindly man—when not assigning penance on weekends—who in the previous decade had helped write some of the CIA's darker reports on Vietnam, which made their way into the Pentagon Papers.

Of the agency's higher reaches I was scarcely in a position to judge from my post at the bottom of the well. But I knew that Messrs. Helms, Carver, Proctor, Walsh, and Lehman had all involved themselves, one way or another, in the CIA's acceptance of Westmoreland's suspect numbers before Tet. So for them to diddle once again with an estimate—this one on Cambodia—would not be out of character. I have no proof, however, and in any case am unpersuaded that they were villains in the grand manner. I doubt, for example, that any one of them snarled, "OK, Tate, go falsify those books." Rather, there must have been a series of nervous consultations in which numbers popped up and down like soybean futures, broad hints passed, and finally, guilt sloughed downwards.

So the question of accountability seems to me unresolved. Perhaps the trouble is that the answer is too diffuse, and that the best explanation I've heard of the problem came from one of the agency's burnt-out elders on Indo-China.

His name was Edward Haskins, and he had a grey crew cut, perhaps left over from World War II when he was with the U.S. mission in the hills of China with Mao. In the first half of the sixties he had run one of the CIA's research groups that had repeatedly warned of our deepening Vietnam commitment. In 1966, he had despaired of being listened to, stopped working on Indo-China, and gone on to another assignment.

I forget when it was that he made his remarks about the problem of responsibility. As I recall, it was during a conversation in which he was recounting examples he'd seen in the last decade or so of official humbug. He mentioned the faked progress reports on Diem's strategic hamlets, the whoppers the Air Force told when it first started bombing the Trail, and the habit that senior editors had of changing modifiers and dropping paragraphs to water down predictions. But what struck him most, he said, was not that there were scoundrels topside (this he assumed) but that it took so many people to practice the deceits. Because like all else in the U.S. government, tampering with evidence is a cumbersome thing to do. The generals have to pass the word to the colonels, the colonels to the majors and lieutenants, the lieutenants to the corporals. Then the supervisors must sort it all out, and the analysts and statisticians somehow glue together the wildly misshapen parts. Finally, the secretaries type it up, and the clerks store it away in the archives. And there it stays until months or years later (always too late to do any good) when some misfit complains aloud.

At this I joined in and the conversation spun toward its logical end. It seemed to us—I paraphrase—that the whole country, not just the government, had laid aside its normal pursuits and danced off to disport itself in a puddle of flummery, that we had become a nation of petti-foggers, of smalltime tricksters, a padded Lilliput whose citizens had simultaneously forgotten how to tell the truth. That the itch to equivo-cate had become as widespread and as irresistible as the temptation to fudge on taxes—and so on and so forth.

At last it must have seemed to Mr. Haskins that the talk had crossed the line from the pompous to the goody-goody, because he leaned back in his chair and burst out laughing. "Maybe," he said, smiling broadly as if the problem was certain to evaporate, "maybe they've put something in the water."

By mid-January 1973 I had reached the end of the road. I happened to read a newspaper account of Daniel Ellsberg's trial in Los Angeles, and I noticed that the government was alleging that Ellsberg had injured the national security by releasing estimates of the enemy force in Vietnam. I looked, and damned if they weren't from the same order of battle that the military had doctored back in 1967. In late February I went to Los Angeles to testify for the defense. Naturally, it was overjoyed to see me. When its lawyers heard my story, however, they decided to send for Colonel Hawkins. I knew this was more than the colonel had bargained for when he had agreed to an investigation. I tried vainly to dissuade them.

When Hawkins arrived in California a short while later, he looked at me as if I had betrayed him. "Stennis," he said, "not Ellsberg." I shared the colonel's distaste for Ellsberg. (The first I had heard of the defendant was from George Allen who had recalled Ellsberg's emotional pleas in Saigon in 1965 to send more troops to Vietnam. "Every year a new hobbyhorse," said George.) I felt my position was untenable. In volun-teering for Ellsberg, I was now jeopardizing the pension of a person who had gone out on a limb for me.

The matter came to a head as I was preparing to mount the witness stand. The colonel came up to me and said: "Sam, this is the end of our friendship."

I pleaded: "Please, Colonel, not that."

He hesitated for perhaps ten seconds and said: "Well, I suppose you know what you're doing. Go on up there and give 'em hell." We shook hands. The rest of the trial was an anticlimax.

When I returned to Washington in March, the CIA once again threatened to fire me. I complained, and, as usual, the agency backed down. After a decent interval, I quit. The date was 17 May 1973. It was the first day of Senator Sam Ervin's hearings on Watergate.

APPENDIX

Publisher's note: After several years of research into the military's side of the OB controversy Adams wrote an outline of what he believed had happened. The text which follows—"A Number to Live With"—was apparently written about 1980 or 1981. It is unsupported by footnotes or other source references, but the factual claims made in it were the substance of the CBS–Westmoreland trial and are all discussed repeatedly and are abundantly supported in the trial transcript. All are discussed, as well, in one of the books about the trial, Vietnam on Trial: Westmoreland vs. CBS *(Atheneum, 1987), a thorough and carefully written account by Bob Brewin and Sydney Shaw. With the exception of the four officials named in the first paragraph, Adams interviewed all those cited in the text of this appendix. Adams believed that the OB was falsified in Saigon for political reasons, since there was no way to change the OB without informing the press, and there was no way to double the Vietcong forces in the OB while continuing to claim the sort of success required to continue the war. But Adams felt it was unfair to lay the blame for this falsification solely on General Westmoreland, whom he grew to like in the course of the trial. In Adams's view MACV as a whole, Westmoreland included, was coerced by officials in Washington to suppress anything that might be interpreted as bad news. Adams believed that these Washington officials understood what was at stake in the OB controversy and deliberately exerted the pressure which resulted in falsification of the numbers. What mattered to Adams was not identification of those responsible, but reaffirmation of the importance of the integrity of intelligence. The whole sordid web of deceit which followed MACV's refusal to accept an increase in the OB was the result of trying to make the evidence support the conclusion. In*

Adams's view, all might have been avoided—the controversy, the trial, conceivably even the military disaster of the Tet offensive—if only the CIA had insisted on telling, and officials had been willing to listen to, the truth.

A Number to Live With

WHAT FOLLOWS IS A DETAILED ACCOUNT of how General Westmoreland's intelligence staff—with White House encouragement—falsified the Vietcong strength estimates before the communist Tet Offensive of January 1968. It is by far the most heavily researched portion of the book. My sources include forty military and twelve civilian intelligence officials, voluminous files of official reports, and other correspondence, such as letters home. I have yet to interview the four persons still living whom I believe chiefly responsible for the falsification: General Westmoreland himself, General Philip Davidson (Westmoreland's J-2 after McChristian), Mr. Robert S. McNamara, and Mr. Walt W. Rostow. I plan to approach them before the book goes to press, in the hope that they will shed further light on what happened, including the extent of President Johnson's involvement.

As already noted, MACV discovered its vast underestimate of Vietcong numbers in late 1966. Westmoreland's then J-2, General Joseph A. McChristian, although embarrassed, admitted his error, and by early 1967 was pressing for a higher order of battle. At this point, the main resistance against one came from the Pentagon, including the office of the secretary of defense, Robert S. McNamara. As McNamara explained to an aide in late January, he realized the official OB was all wrong, but that he was not yet prepared to tell Congress. He meant what he said. On 6 March 1967, he briefed a Congressional committee using the official numbers, the same ones he knew to be low.

McChristian's response to the Pentagon's foot-dragging was to adopt a second set of books. Kept informally by his OB chief, Colonel Gains B. Hawkins, the second set listed the lesser three of the OB's four parts.

The total for its most important component—the VC's main battle forces—remained public knowledge. To MACV strength analysts (mostly unaware that a controversy existed) the compromise was satisfactory. None of them felt much pressure to raise or lower their numbers for any reason other than evidence.

Incredibly, General Westmoreland during this period seems not to have grasped what the full public impact might be of the higher numbers. Furthermore he had neglected to add them all up. He received his first detailed briefing on the second set of books, with their big sums totaled, in May 1967. General McChristian and Colonel Hawkins conducted the briefing in Westmoreland's private office. Using a flipchart, they reviewed the OB's four components one by one, and when they reached the bottom line on the flipchart's last page, Westmoreland— according to my source—"almost fell off his chair." "What will I tell Congress?" he gasped. "What will I tell the press?" On recovering, some minutes later, he turned to McChristian and said: "General, I want you to take another look at those numbers."

McChristian took this as a suggestion to tamper with the second set of books. This he refused to do. He was sent home on 1 June 1967, protesting vigorously. At least some of his chagrin arose from the fact that his replacement was his archrival in the Army, an old West Point classmate, General Philip Davidson.

Davidson was more amenable than McChristian to manipulating the unofficial books. Among his first acts on 1 June was to lobby with the agency's DDI representative in Saigon to drop from the OB one of its main subcomponents, the so-called self-defense militia (or tu ve). Davidson's suggestion flew back and forth between Saigon and Washington for over a month. It came up at a meeting between Westmoreland and McNamara in Vietnam on 9 July, and again when the general and the secretary saw President Johnson at the White House on the thirteenth. Exactly what transpired at these meetings I have yet to find out, but what happened thereafter is clear.

MACV strength analysts began to suspect that someone was doctoring the order of battle. Among the first to harbor this suspicion was

Lieutenant Joseph Gorman, chief analyst for the VC main battle forces in IV Corps, which comprised South Vietnam's southernmost and most populous quarter. One of his jobs was to warn J-2 headquarters each time he discovered a new VC unit, so that J-2 could add it to the OB. During this period, however, he found the headquarters increasingly reluctant to enter new units on the lists. At first he thought that J-2 had tightened its "acceptance criteria," but as the summer wore on its reasons for disallowing new units became more and more frivolous. One VC battalion was turned down by J-2 because Gorman's request form had a typographical error; another because the form's cover sheet was not centered; a third because the sheet lacked the proper red-pencil markings. A second analyst, Lieutenant Richard McArthur—assigned in June to keep track of VC guerrillas countrywide—wrote his parents on 26 July that he had found that the guerrilla number for II Corps was "completely false," and that J-2 was "feeding people nonsense figures with no documentary evidence." He added, "I can't believe half the things I'm digging up."

Meanwhile, pressure continued to build on the order of battle. At the Board of National Estimates conference on Fourteen Three—convened in Langley in June—the CIA was still insisting on higher numbers. By August, its sessions had reached an impasse, and the principals had agreed to meet at an OB conference at Westmoreland's headquarters in early September—with CIA, DIA, and MACV attending. The purpose of the conference was to come to an agreement over VC strength.

MACV's preparations for the conference were both above board and below it. In one of the war's most unusual messages, dated 20 August, MACV deputy General Creighton Abrams cabled Washington, with Westmoreland's approval, the old request to drop the self-defense militia from the OB. What made the cable so extraordinary was the frank reason he gave for wanting to do so. To leave the militia on the lists, he explained, would contradict the "image of success" MACV had been lately building, and would provoke the press into drawing "an erroneous and gloomy conclusion" over the progress of the war. The message was widely distributed in official Washington.

MACV's below-board measures were also unusual. No longer content to exclude units from the OB, J-2 now began to cut down the size of units already in it. Marshall W. Lynn, a lieutenant charged with keeping tabs on six regiment-sized VC formations near Saigon, has explained how it was done. One morning shortly before the start of the scheduled conference, a colonel from J-2 stopped by Lynn's desk with the suggestion that the strengths at which Lynn was carrying his six VC units were "way too high." Lynn denied it, at which the colonel simply picked up Lynn's strength sheet, crossed out the numbers by each regiment, and penciled in new ones, on the average one-third lower. To Lynn's amazement, a unit which he had carried with 3,100 men became "1,900" instead. As for J-2's acceptance criteria for new units, Gorman remarked that by early September, "you could march a VC regiment down the hall, and they wouldn't put it in the OB."

The conference, which I describe at length in Chapter 5, ended with the CIA caving in on the first day, 11 September. And the order of battle, instead of doubling—to reflect the evidence discovered in late 1966—actually fell, from about 290,000 to just over 240,000. As Chapter 5 points out, the drop was accomplished by marching the subcomponent, the self-defense militia, from the lists (as well as another whole category, the so-called political cadres) and by a general acceptance of J-2's "scaled down" numbers. Among those dismayed by the proceedings was DIA's chief order-of-battle analyst, Captain Barrie Williams. Captain Williams felt "the whole session was painful. It was clear we were double-dealing."

Thinking that the conference had laid the VC numbers dispute to rest, official Washington was pleased with the result. Almost at once, however, new problems replaced the old ones. On his return from Saigon to his desk at the Pentagon, DIA's Captain Williams got his first whiff of what the new problems were. An order had arrived from Secretary McNamara's office saying that McNamara wanted the newly agreed-upon OB number of some 240,000 to be "retroactively readjusted." Apparently the secretary needed the VC strength figures for previous years so he could plot them on the same graph with the latest sum. Completely at a loss on how to "retroactively readjust" a number he thought fake to begin with, Williams went to his boss, Colonel John Lanterman, for advice. Lanterman was sympathetic. He felt that since MACV J-2 had come up with the number of 240,000, it ought to produce the earlier numbers as well; and he dropped the problem in MACV's lap. Williams flew back to Saigon to monitor what they did with it.

The "retroactive readjustment" took place in the third week of September in a conference room outside General Davidson's office. The readjustment was simple. A J-2 officer chalked a curve on a black-board.* On the right-hand end of the curve he wrote the number agreed upon at the Saigon conference—241,200—and the date of the last official OB, August 1967. Then he wrote "August 1966" at the top of the curve, and "August 1965" at its left-hand end. He stepped back to look at the curve from a distance, then returned to the board to write "285,400" next to "August 1966" and "204,700" next to "August 1965." This done, someone suggested that McNamara might want the OB's components (now three in number) readjusted as well. The components were figured out so that they would of course add up to the totals on the curve, the J-2 officer chalked them in, and Captain Williams copied them down for the secretary's benefit. The numbers from the board were as follows:

	August 1965	August 1966	August 1967
VC main forces:	73,000	126,300	117,900
VC guerrillas:	92,700	109,000	86,300
VC service troops:	39,000	50,100	37,600
Total:	204,700	285,400	241,800

They henceforth became the official U.S. intelligence estimate for enemy forces in South Vietnam for the times mentioned, and became the basic starting point from which later J-2 estimates were derived. The J-2 officer assigned to take them over was a West Pointer, Lieutenant Colonel Everette S. Parkins, head of a branch within the Order of Battle

*This turned out to be CINPAC's Lieutenant Colonel George Hamscher.

Section called OB Studies. On 25 September (about a week after Captain Williams' departure from Saigon with the readjusted numbers) Parkins was given a deputy to help him out with his computations. The deputy was a U.S. navy commander by the name of James A. Meacham.

As might be expected, demands for the official numbers started almost at once. In early October, for example, the American Embassy in Saigon, in preparing a message for the State Department, asked MACV J-2 for the latest figures on VC strength. OB Studies supplied them and the embassy cable—classified "Secret, Limited Distribution Only," and addressed to Dean Rusk with special instructions that he pass it to Rostow—noted that our effort in Vietnam was making "solid progress." To back up the assertion, it cited, among other facts, the drop in VC main force strength from "126,000 in August 1966 to 118,000" a year later—statistics clearly gotten from the curve on Davidson's blackboard. The cable was dated 7 October 1967, and that evening, the man who supplied its numbers, the newly assigned Commander Meacham, wrote his wife: "Once in a while I sit back—mentally—and consider the place and the rules of the game objectively, and then I look around for the Mock Turtle and the March Hare."

Meanwhile, pressures were building once again on the order of battle. As usual, they built from opposite directions.

On one side the pressure was exerted from Washington. It came from a series of meetings convened in October in the Executive Office Building of the White House by President Johnson's main Vietnam advisor, Walt Rostow—the same Rostow to whom Rusk had passed the embassy's cable of 7 October. The Gallup Poll readings for Johnson's handling of the war had reached their lowest point thus far, and the meetings (called Measurements of Progress) were designed to come up with information that showed that the Vietnam struggle had gone better than was generally thought. Thus when the OB question came up at the meetings, the context was not whether the numbers were too low, but whether they were too high. Rostow took the latter position, and as one of his aides later confided to a friend, "we really leaned on the OB." Contrary information was discouraged. When the CIA's George Allen, who'd always thought the OB was too low, mentioned unfavorable statistics, Rostow complained, "I'm sorry you won't support your president."

On the other side the pressure came from Vietnam. There the Vietcong, preparing for their Tet Offensive, were engaged in the greatest buildup of the war. Their preparations included the formation of hundreds of new units—battalions, companies and platoons—and the beefing up of units already in existence. Although MACV strength analysts were well aware of the buildup, it was unreflected in the OB. The policy of J-2 to disallow new formations in the OB was in effect.

In November the pressures increased. President Johnson's Success Offensive was now in full swing, and there were almost daily briefings on how well the war was going. On 11 November for example, Westmoreland gave Davidson a surprise order to brief the press in Saigon, and Meacham was pulled from lunch to fill Davidson's briefing folder. Among the papers he put in the folder was a graph showing the curve drawn on the general's blackboard in September. Davidson called in the press at two in the afternoon, and the next day the *New York Times* reported on page one that "US Aides Say Foe Is Weakening Fast," noting in the text that VC strength had fallen from 285,000 to 242,000 men. Westmoreland used the same numbers at a larger briefing at the Pentagon on 22 November with similar results. Earlier in the month, Davidson's curve was also used to brief President Johnson's "wise men"*—eleven distinguished citizens brought together to advise him on the war. On hearing the good news, the wise men concluded that the war was proceeding satisfactorily. They advised the president to keep fighting.

On 27 November, an odd cloud appeared on the horizon. It was a memo sent to Washington from Saigon, composed at the CIA Station by its Collation analyst, Joe Hovey. In his daily reading of captured documents, Hovey had noticed the VC were up to something big, but he couldn't tell just what. When he finally put the documents together, it

---

*Dean Acheson, George Ball, General Omar Bradley, McGeorge Bundy, Clark Clifford, Arthur Dean, Douglas Dillon, Abe Fortas, Henry Cabot Lodge, Robert Murphy, and General Maxwell Taylor.

became clear. As his memo put it, the Vietcong were planning "a political and military offensive utilizing all VC assets," its target to include "all major cities" in South Vietnam. The person who typed his memo was the Collation secretary, Betsy Gibson.

Hovey's paper created a modest stir. For almost three weeks it travelled around CIA headquarters, gathering comments. It went to the White House on 15 December and President Johnson read it the next day. But as comments on it pointed out, the paper always raised the same question: Why would the VC be planning an offensive "utilizing all their assets" when it was clear from the OB that their "assets" were going rapidly downhill? The most sensible answer, although none too convincing, was that the VC had become suicidal. In any case, five days after reading the memo, President Johnson explained in a briefing that the VC seemed to be planning a "kamikaze attack."

New Year's passed, with MACV's Order of Battle Section awaiting the go-ahead to finish its year-end OB—the one dated "31 December." On about 3 January , the OB Section chief, Marine Colonel Paul Weiler (who had replaced Colonel Hawkins in mid-September) received the OK from General Davidson's office, along with instructions to lower the estimate—which had dropped to 235,852 at the end of November—by 11,000 or so more men. Having already shaved a thousand-odd soldiers from the VC main forces, Weiler had about 10,000 more to go. He informed Meacham—now chief of OB Studies instead of Parkins—and their prearranged plan went into effect. If the estimate was to drop, they had decided, the component to absorb the loss would be the one they thought was the OB's "softest"—the guerrillas. They had already programmed the main computer to pare down guerrillas by province, to whatever loss total Davidson decreed. The appropriate buttons were pushed. The computer made the cuts: 500 guerrillas from Quang Nam, 50 from Quang Ngai, 400 from Long An, 450 from Vinh Long, and so forth. The results were entered into the order of battle. Thus MACV's year-end estimate for VC strength became 224,651. It was the last monthly order of battle before the Tet Offensive.

Among those oblivious to the proceedings was MACV's guerrilla analyst, Lieutenant Richard McArthur. Never shown the official OB, he kept track of VC guerrillas by province on a plexiglass toteboard next to his desk. He based his entries on reports from the field, and updated them with captured enemy documents. His toteboard showed VC guerrilla strength going up. McArthur's morale was low, and he was drinking a lot. Many of his OB colleagues were also unhappy, and for many reasons. Not the least of them was that MACV now kept, not two sets of books, but three.

The first set was the official OB, sent to Washington—and used in Saigon by such nonmilitary analysts as Joe Hovey. The second set belonged to the OB analysts themselves. It tended to be informal, displayed on maps, which showed increasing numbers of battalions that were labeled "unofficial." The third set, an amalgam of the first two, went to General Westmoreland, and was very tightly held. (One of its keepers was an Army lieutenant colonel named David Morgan. I have yet to approach him, but I know where he is—Bonita, California, retired. He is said to be ashamed of his role and may be willing to talk. But maybe he won't, fearing the loss of his pension.)

If January was a bad month for Richard McArthur, it was even worse for Joe Hovey. He had written what he felt was the most important paper of his life in late November and he was on pins and needles whether his prediction would come about. He was in an increasing quandary. All the most recent evidence confirmed his forecast of an enormous countrywide offensive—all the evidence, that is, except the order of battle. "How'll they pull if off?" he kept asking himself; "Where'll they get the men?"

The Tet Offensive started on 30 January 1968. It was a big attack all right, but to Hovey's puzzlement, all the action was in the northern half of the country. The southern half was quiet. That evening most American intelligence officials in Saigon went to bed at their usual times and places: Colonel Weiler and Commander Meacham to their rooms in the senior officers' BOQ near Tan Son Nhut; Joe Hovey to his lodgings downtown. None was aware that several Vietcong battalions had already stolen into the city or that VC sappers were screwing detonator caps onto bombs they hoped to use to blow their way into the United States Embassy.

The VC sappers attacked at 2:47 in the morning. The Saigon docks erupted at 3:58. By 5:00 A.M. guns were firing all over the city, Hovey was wondering whether to hide under his bed. Weiler and Meacham— neither of whom had remotely suspected a big offensive was in the offing—were manning a machine gun on the BOQ roof. To his horror, Meacham discovered that the machine gun's ammunition was all tracer. To shoot tracers was to reveal their firing position. Weiler said: "If we shoot this damn gun, we'll get a B-40 rocket smack in the puss." It takes only one man to fire a B-40 rocket. As chief of the MACV Order of Battle Section, Weiler's scope of interest in enemy strength had considerably narrowed . . .

Sam Adams's text ends here. Whether he intended to add anything further is not known.—Publisher's note.

SOURCES AND NOTES

CHAPTER 1: THE SIMBAS

Sources

This chapter springs mostly from memory, as refreshed by then-current periodicals, interviews (see below), and two books: *Congo Mercenary*, by Michael Hoare (London: Robert Hale, 1967), and *One Hundred Days in Stanleyville,* by David Reed (New York: Harper and Row, 1967). Among the people I interviewed were Dana Ball and his wife, Janet Ball (then Southern Africa's Mozambique analyst), both now retired in New Hampshire; Colleen King, contacted under her married name in Minnesota; and three current employees of the CIA. As to the chapter's dialogue, I can vouch for its substance, but not its exact wording.

Notes

1. Lumumba was assassinated in January 1961, apparently on orders from the Katangan politician, Moise Tshombe. There was "no evidence of CIA involvement" in his death—according to a report by a Senate Select Committee to investigate the CIA—but the agency had laid plans to kill him the year before. These plans were unsuccessful. Suspecting, when I joined the Southern Africa Branch in 1964, that the agency might have had a role in Lumumba's death, I asked the CIA's Congo analyst of the earlier period whether the Eisenhower administration had ever plotted to kill him. "I doubt it," the analyst replied. "They wouldn't have been that dumb." The analyst was probably as ignorant as he seemed of the plot, which was very tightly held. For an account of the CIA's tries at Lumumba, see: U.S. Congress. Senate. Select

Committee to Study Governmental Operations with Respect to Intelligence Activities. *Alleged Assassination Attempts Involving Foreign Leaders.* (Washington, D.C.: Government Printing Office, 1976) p. 13–70.

2. A factor in the early collapse of the first rebel regime in Stanleyville was a CIA operation carried out in 1961 by the Khartoum Station in the Sudan. The station had learned that a courier carrying the payroll for the Congo rebel army was en route from Cairo to Stanleyville by way of the Khartoum airport. Apparently unaware of airport procedures, the courier debarked from his plane, and, clutching a brown leather briefcase, entered the main waiting room, where a CIA operative—more familiar with Khartoum's procedures—awaited his arrival. The public address system made the usual announcement: "Will the passengers on flight such and such from Cairo please report to immigration." Not wanting to show up at immigration with a bag full of hot money, the courier shoved the briefcase under a waiting-room seat, and dashed off in accordance with the announcement. After the courier had disappeared, the CIA man slid the briefcase from beneath the seat and walked off with it to a waiting car. As he climbed in the front seat next to the driver, the theft was discovered, and pandemonium broke out in the terminal as the courier, the Sudanese police, and intelligence agents from other countries (which, as it turned out, also knew of the payroll) scurried about to discover what had happened. Flustered by the noise, the driver was unable to start the car. Eventually he succeeded, and when at last the briefcase was opened, it was found to have a false bottom, under which was $387,000 in American currency. Told of the heist, President Kennedy—still angry at the CIA for the Bay of Pigs—was "extremely pleased." The CIA man received a letter of commendation, and (as he later told me at lunch) a "small monetary award."

3. My only distinction at the Farm was to write the class skit, entitled, "How to Succeed at Espionage Without Really Spying."

4. The suspicions were probably correct (see note 1). Tshombe also died under suspicious circumstances. Abducted to an Algerian jail, he succumbed— according to prison authorities—to a "heart attack."

5. The DDP's initials have since changed to DDO, which stands for "Deputy Directorate of Operations." For an outline of the CIA's organization in 1964, see U.S. Congress. Senate. Select Committee to Study Governmental Operations with Respect to Intelligence Activities, Final Report. *Supplementary Detailed Staff Reports on Foreign and Military Intelligence; Book IV.* (Washington, D.C.: Government Printing Office, 1976) p. 100.

6. I learned later that the CIA had attached to the southern column a small team of Miami Cubans, whose job was to rescue the consular officials. The

Cubans arrived in Stanleyville too late, the Americans having been saved already by the Belgian paratroops. For an account of the Stanleyville operation, including its use of Cubans, see Michael Hoare's *Congo Mercenary,* chapters 7 and 8.

7. See *"Che" Guevera On Revolution,* edited by Jay Mallin (Coral Gables, Florida; University of Miami Press, 1969) p. 35. Among the lessons Havana derived from its fiasco at Fizi was that intervention in Africa needed more muscle. About two dozen Cubans were with Che at Fizi. There are now (1983) some 40,000 Cubans in Africa, supported by helicopters, tanks, jet fighters, and armored personnel carriers.

8. President Johnson shared Mr. Lehman's belief about the relative importance of the Congo and Vietnam. The index of his memoir, *The Vantage Point* (Holt, Reinhart, & Winston, 1971) has no entries on the Congo. Entries for Vietnam and related subjects total sixty-one inches.

CHAPTER 2: THE SITREP

Sources

I refreshed my memory about events described in this chapter by rereading the *New York Times* and the *Washington Post* for the period between 1 August 1965 and 10 January 1966, and by interviewing people I then worked with. These included Edward Hauck, Mary ("Molly") Kreimer, and four current employees of the CIA.

Notes

1. As in Chapter 1, the conversations in this chapter are accurate in substance but not necessarily wording. However, this, my first conversation with Ed Hauck, was so memorable that several phrases are verbatim. I distinctly recall him saying that the war might last "ten years, maybe twenty"; that Americans were an "impatient people"; and there were to be "riots in the street's." Saigon fell on 30 April 1975, just three months before Hauck said it might.

2. *The World Almanac and Book of Facts for 1965.* (New York: New York World-Telegram and Sun, 1965) p. 419.

3. I also read my copy of the *Encyclopaedia Britannica,* the renowned 1911 edition. It describes the South Vietnamese, whom it calls the Annamese, as follows:

> "The Annamese is the worst-built and ugliest of all the Indo-Chinese who belong to the Mongolian race. He is scarcely of middle height and is shorter and less vigorous than his neighbors. His complexion is tawny, darker than that of the Chinese, but clearer than that of the Cambodian; his hair is black,

coarse, and long; his skin is thick; his forehead low; his skull is slightly depressed at the top, but well developed at the sides. His face if flat, with highly protruding cheekbones, and is lozenge-shaped or eurygnathous to a dgree that is nowhere exceeded . . . his mouth is large and his lips thick; his teeth are blackened and his gums destroyed by the/constant use of the betel-nut, the areca-nut and lime. His neck is short, his shoulders slope greatly, his body is thick-set and wanting in suppleness. Another peculiarity is a separation of the big toe from the rest . . ."

4. For an excellent account of the pre-Starlight "jungle crap," see Philip Caputo's *A Rumor of War* (New York: Holt Rinehart, and Winston, 1977). The fighting that Caputo described turned out to be far more typical of the Vietnam war than that which took place during Starlight.

5. There are four sources for Operation Starlight: the *New York Times* of 19–28 August 1965; the *Washington Post,* of the same dates; Starlight's "After Action Report," submitted by Commanding General, Third Marine Division (Reinforced) to COMUSMACV, on 5 October 1965 (Reporting Officer, Colonel O.F. Peatross, commanding officer, 7th Marines); and the article "Application of Doctrine: Victory at Van Tuong Village," also by Colonel Peatross, in *Naval Review,* (Annapolis, Md.: U.S. Naval Institute Proceedings, 1967) p. 2–13.

6. The *Washington Post,* 13 September 1965.

7. "Vietcong Morale: A Possible Indicator of Downward Drift," CIA Office of Current Intelligence, (OCI No. 2390/65), 20 October 1965, p. 1.

8. The *Washington Post,* 29 October 1965, p. A–16. For an account of a fierce battle that took place near, and shortly after, the Special Forces officer made his remark about the VC, see "Fight at Ia Drang," in John A. Cash's *Seven Firefights in Vietnam.* (Washington, D.C.: Officer of the Chief of Military History, United States Army, 1970) p. 3–40. On 20 October 1976, Lieutenant Colonel George McGharrigle (U.S.A. Ret'd) of the U.S. Center of Military History told me that in a related one-day battle, a U.S. Army battalion suffered 276 casualties out of an estimated 443 men present for duty. This represents a 62-percent casualty rate, arguably the highest for one day suffered by an American battalion during the entire war.

CHAPTER 3 THE PUZZLE OF VIETCONG MORALE

Sources

Details for this chapter came from my letters home; from three-by-five index cards on which I recorded the names of, and conversations with, the people I talked to in Vietnam; from five-by-eight index cards on which I kept my notes on VC morale; and interviews of twenty-one Americans in Vietnam. Of these, one worked for Rand, three for MACV, and the rest for CIA. The most prolific source was Joseph Hovey, and ex–Collation Branch member whom I interviewed for a total of sixty hours in Los Angeles in March 1976. Hovey also sent me several letters. I was unable to locate Travis King. Paul Anderson died in a motor accident. I do not know what has happened to either Co Yung or Lieutenant Lam. For background information—and to jar my memory—I used Jeffrey Race's excellent study *War Comes To Long An* (Berkeley and Los Angeles: University of California Press, 1972), and Gerald Hickey's study, *Village in Vietnam* (New Haven: Yale University Press, 1964). The footnotes contain only representative samples from the above sources.

Notes

1. The description is based on a letter I wrote on 16 January 1966.

2. This explosion temporarily blinded the CIA station chief, Peer de Silva. For a description of the blast, see his *Sub Rosa: The CIA and the Uses of Intelligence* (New York: New York Times Book Co., 1978) p. 266–272. On page 266, he said the bomb weighed 350 pounds. Most other sources say 250. Take your pick. Mr. de Silva has since died of other causes.

3. As copied from five-by-eight notes on the provinces. Some notes were verbatim, others paraphrases of the USAID reports. Anyone interested in finding the reports should seek them under their original title. "USOM," which stand's for "United States Operations Mission," the early designation for USAID in Vietnam.

4. Quoted—with slight emendations—from *Songs of Saigon,* of which I have a copy.

5. Westmoreland, William C., *A Soldier Reports* (Garden City, New York: Doubleday and Company, 1976) p. 159–160. Hereinafter referred to as *A Soldier Reports.*

6. Interview, Major General Joseph McChristian (USA, Retired) to author.

7. *A Soldier Reports,* p. 160.

8. Memorandum of instructions to General Westmoreland, "1966 Program to Increase the Effectiveness of Military Operations and Anticipated Results Thereof," Top Secret, 8 February 1966, drafted by William Bundy and John McNaughton. General Westmoreland supplied a copy of the orders to Brigadier General Douglas Kinnard (USA, Retired), who was kind enough to let me see them on 15 March 1978. *A Soldier Reports* also refers to the orders on p. 161.

9. From my notes, made at the time.

10. Two months after this action, the head of the VC's Central Office of South Vietnam (COSVN) said the 506th Battalion was the "best one in the entire region," (See Race, p. 137). The "region" referred to was Vietcong Region III, comprising the provinces of the upper Delta.

11. From my notes, made at the time.

12. See Gerald Hickey's *Village in Vietnam.*

13. And Lieutenant Lam almost certainly killed a great many VC. A later name for his counter-terror team was the "Provincial Reconnaissance Unit," (PRU) generally considered by far the best government formation in Long An. I believe Lam appears in the eleventh photograph following p. 134 in Race's *War Comes to Long An,* but I'm none too certain. For a description of the PRU's activities, see Race, p. 212n, 213, 231, and 238. On p. 265, Race notes that the government programs best adapted to Long An "all shared a common organizational parentage in the Central Intelligence Agency."

14. From my notes, quoting an agency FVS report dated 9 February 1966.

15. From my notes, quoting MACV document CDEC Log #01-1504-66.

16. From my notes, quoting an agency FVS 12,625 dated 9 February 1966.

17. From my notes, quoting MACV document CDEC Log #02-1174-66.

18. My notes on Captain Plowman's reports reveal that in his statistics for the four-month period ending in February 1966 showed that US Marines in Vietnam had picked up 2,344 Vietcong suspects. Through interrogation it was found that 16 belonged to the main and local forces, 48 were guerrillas, and 48 were self-defense militiamen—that is, close to the same ratios that I'd found among defectors at the Long An Chieu Hoi center.

CHAPTER 4: BULLETIN 689

Notes

1. MACV Combined Document Exploitation Center Bulletin 689, of 19 July 1966 (date of issue by CDEC). Note that the Bulletin took a full month to make its way from the Tax Building in Saigon to Room 5G44 in Langley.

2. Layton's memo to Smith, dated 18 August 1966, was entitled "Vietcong Guerrilla and Militia Strength." It noted that the then-current guerrilla-militia estimate had "come to be used more by convention than conviction," and that Bulletin 689 suggested that the office estimate was "too low, perhaps grossly so."

3. CIA's "An Analysis of the Vietnamese Communists' Strengths, Capabilities, and Will To Persist," 26 August 1966. The last-minute caveats about the guerrilla estimate appear in the text (section II, paragraph 5, p. 2, 3), and in a footnote to Table IV-5 of Annex IV.

4. MACV translation report, CDEC Log Number 04-1354-66, issued on 29 July 1966, p. 2.

5. MACV translation report, CDEC Log Number 01-1593-66, issued on 7 February 1966, p. 8.

6. MACV, CDEC log number 04-1371-66 of 29 April 1966.

7. Draft paper, "The Strength of the Vietcong Irregulars," 22 August 1966. "Irregulars" was one of the many variations of "guerrilla-militia."

8. Draft paper, "The Strength of the Vietcong Irregulars," 29 August 1966.

9. CIA Draft Working Paper, entitled "The Strength of the Vietcong Irregulars," 8 September 1966.

10. New York Times, 7 October 1966, p. 16.

11. Based on notes of my conversation with Major Blascik of 10 October 1966. Ex–Marine Corps Captain Philip Caputo, who served in Vietnam in 1965 and 1966, has also commented on the subject. "We were making history: the first American soldiers to fight an enemy whose principal weapons were the mine and booby trap. That kind of warfare has its own peculiar terrors. It turns an infantryman's world upside down. The foot soldier has a special feeling for the ground. He walks on it, fights on it, sleeps and eats on it; the ground shelters him under fire; he digs his home in it. But mines and booby traps transform that friendly, familiar earth into a thing of menace, a thing to be feared as much as machine guns or mortar shells. The infantryman knows that any moment the ground he is walking on can erupt and kill him; kill him if he's lucky. If he's unlucky, he will be turned into a blind, deaf, emasculated, legless shell. It was not warfare. It was murder." From Philip Caputo, A Rumor of War, (New York: Holt Rinehart and Winston, 1977, p. 288.) Another source: "I think the most terrifying feeling is knowing you are going through a mine field, because it's kind of like being in the dark, knowing there is a step there, and afraid to walk. You have to almost force every foot down because your knees just don't want to react. Just that type of emotion—every step of the way." The source was Lieutenant William L. Calley, Jr., (convicted of murder for his participation in the My Lai massacre of March 1968) as told to Hearst reporter Patrick Sloyan, in 1971. Shortly before the massacre, Calley's platoon had lost several casualties to mines and booby traps. Correspondent Seymour Hersh, whose reporting on My Lai won him the Pulitzer Prize, has pointed out that more than 80 percent of American casualties in the My Lai area were caused by such devices.

12. "Operations of U.S. Marine Forces, Vietnam" (Fleet Marine Force, Pacific, June 1966, p. 8.)

13. Based on notes of my conversation with George Allen, undated.

14. COMUSMACV report number 6-075-7739/66, 18 October 1966.

15. Internal CIA paper, "Vietcong Irregular Strength," 7 November 1966.

16. CIA cable, Saigon Station to CIA Headquarters, 9 November 1966.

17. Based on notes of my conversation with George Allen, undated. In another conversation, Allen told me that the person who hired him from DIA was Richard Lehman.

18. Defense information report 6-075-8866-66, 4 November 1966.

19. MACV CDEC log number 09-1509-67 contained in Bulletin 7216, of 13 September 1967.

20. I made no record of this conversation. However, later on the same day, I related it to a fellow DDI analyst, who unbeknownst to me, jotted down what I said. The analyst later gave me the notes, which form the basis of this passage in the book. Still an agency employee, the note-taker, who became very prolific, is hereinafter referred to as the DDI analyst.

21. Internal CIA paper, "The Strength of Vietcong 'Main Force Support Personnel,'" (another name for "service troops") 2 December 1966. On file with the CIA Inspector General.

22. Internal CIA paper, "New York Times article Concerning VC Defections and Desertions," 18 December 1966. On file with the CIA Inspector General. The paper points out that VC desertions came out of a force of 600,000, rather than out of the 280,000 then listed in the OB. On 21 November 1966, the DDI analyst recorded my mention of "600,000" VC on that day. The analyst noted it was "very Catch-22."

23. CIA cable, CIA Headquarters to Saigon Station, 13 December 1966.

24. The agency's Cartography Division published the map in January 1967, as CIA map 64529 1-67. I hasten to note that both MACV J-2 and the CIA Collation Branch in Saigon used VC maps; but these maps had not found their way to CIA headquarters. Likewise, the National Security Agency—which analyzed VC communications—had compiled an enemy map; but it was so highly classified, that it was seldom looked at outside NSA.

25. Mr. Moore later recalled this conversation in an interview I had with him in late 1975.

26. MACV Order of Battle, 31 December 1966.

27. CIA memorandum prepared for Secretary McNamara by the Office of National Estimates, 9 January 1967.

28. An example of the range of services provided me by the Purcellville Library was its two-year quest for the derivation of the phrase *catbird seat*. Eventually one of its librarians found me its likely origin: "(probably from the

bird's habit of singing from a high perch) an enviable position, as of power."
My thanks to Mrs. Virginia Haley, and her husband, Pete.

29. Internal CIA memorandum, special assistant for Vietnamese Affairs
(Carver) to the DDI, 11 January 1967. On file with the CIA Inspector General.

30. Internal CIA memorandum, 13 January 1967. On file with the CIA
Inspector General.

31. Memo from the chairman of the Joint Chiefs of Staff to DIA, 19 January
1967.

CHAPTER 5: FOURTEEN-THREE

Sources

The documents cited in this chapter are generally from two sources: either
the batch I gave Representative McCloskey in May 1975, or the collection that
the CIA turned over to the House Intelligence Committee in December 1975.
The latter documents include a complete set of "Vietnam Situation Reports"
for the period 23–30 January 1968 (of which the 29 January edition appears in
facsimile) and various other reports connected with the CIA's "Post Mortem"
on Tet.

Among the books I consulted were Don Oberdorfer's *Tet!* (Garden City,
New York: Doubleday & Co., 1971); an unpublished manuscript on Tet by
ex-CIA analyst Patrick McGarvey: U.S. Marine Captain Moyer S. Shore II's
The Battle For Khe Sanh (Washington, D.C.: USMC Historical Branch, 1969):
W. W. Rostow's *The Diffusion of Power: An Essay in Recent History* (New York:
Macmillan Company, 1972), whose pages 462 and 463 quote extensive pas-
sages of the cable Saigon Station wrote in November 1967 predicting the Tet
Offensive: and Bernard Fall's *Hell In A Very Small Place* (New York: Vintage
Books, 1966).

Supplementing these sources were several interviews, and of course, my own
personal recollections.

Notes

1. The account of the first meeting on Fourteen Three is based on memorandum for the record "N.I.E. 14.3-67, the USIB Representatives Meeting 23
June 1967," which I wrote the same day, and later filed with the CIA Inspector
General. The numbers quoted in this differ slightly from those listed in the
memorandum of conversation. The latter's numbers were often expressed in
ranges (e.g., 456,000–541,000 in the case of the CIA's estimate for the total
number of VC), while the book uses a single figure, normally in the range's

middle. My motive is simplicity. I feel the order-of-battle dispute is complex enough as it is, without my inflicting on the reader two sets of numbers rather than one. I have followed the practice of using a single number instead of a range throughout the entire chapter.

2. Interestingly, everyone I talked to who worked with George Fowler liked him, for example, David Siegel, who was Fowler's subordinate at DIA, described him admiringly: "The ultimate bureaucrat. The finest harrumpher I've ever known."

3. CIA cable, Saigon Station to CIA Headquarters, 10 July 1967.

4. Davidson succeeded McChristian as MACV J-2 on 1 June 1967.

5. CIA memorandum, "The Viet Cong Security Service," July 1967. It contains 125 pages and 391 footnotes.

6. Unpublished memorandum, "Research On The Vietcong: A Proposal For A VC Study Group," 2 August 1967. Filed with the CIA Inspector General.

7. (May memo, re documents. Get citation later. [This citation was not supplied—Ed.])

8. Based on ranges copied from the slide. Once again, I use a single number rather than the range. In addition, I have corrected some minor mathematical errors on the slide, which was evidently put together in haste.

9. The countrywide guerrilla total, by VC region, as listed in MACV Bulletin 4,530:

Region 1	2,500
Region 2	24,485
Region 3	30,561
Region 4	2,487
Region 5	103,884
Region 6	6,434
Total	170,351

10. The document referred to is translated in CDEC log number 06-1038-67, which lists 11,235 Guerrillas in Quang Da, the VC designation for the government's Quang Nam Province. Confusingly the Vietcong also had a Quang Nam Province, covering roughly the same area as the government's Quang Tin.

11. The Estimates staffer was David Laux.

12. The problem of strength accounting is even more complex than appears here. Normally the VC listed their units in one of three ways: The T, O and E, or ideal, strength (which for a VC Division was around 10,000 men); the "assigned" strength, usually less than T, O and E, which listed the number of

men actually assigned to a unit (which in a VC division could be, say, 7,500 men); and "present-for-duty" strength, which lists the number who actually showed up for morning muster (in the same VC division, say, 6,000). The difference between assigned and present-for-duty strengths reflects the men who are away. (For example, the above division has 1,500 fewer men present for duty than assigned; the 1,500 absentees include men on sick call, deserters not yet stricken from the rolls, and soldiers in special training camps or on leave.) Civil War buffs are familiar with the problem. Union regiments with a T, O and E of a thousand men sometimes fought with a present-for-duty strength of 150.

13. CIA cable, Saigon Station to CIA Headquarters, 19 August 1967. Although Komer was using the station's communications facility, he was not at this time an agency employee. In Saigon, he worked for General Westmoreland.

14. MACV cable, MAC 7840, of 20 August 1967. Another addressee of the cable was Admiral Sharp, who, as CINCPAC (Commander in Chief, Pacific), was technically Westmoreland's boss.

15. MACV cable, MAC 7859, of 20 August 1967. Apparently, Westmoreland was away from Saigon when MAC 7840 was sent, and Abrams was minding the store.

16. The firm no longer exists.

17. Graham and Morris had accompanied Davidson to Saigon from Honolulu in June. Sidle had taken over the PR slot on 13 August.

18. Lieutenant Colonel Graham's remarks are based on notes I took at the conference.

19. Here are the actual service troop numbers involved:

	MACV figure in August	MACV figure in September
National level	10,795	9,500
Region level	10,082	7,600
Independent units	4,178	0
Province level	9,489	6,600
District level	0	5,000
Total service troops	34,544	28,700

Clearly, to make up for the 5,000 district troops added in September, MACV "scaled down" the national, region, and province levels, and did away with the "independent units." Source: CIA memorandum for the record "History of Strength Estimates of the Communist 'Administrative Services,'" of 2 April 1968.

20. His note survives.

21. The lieutenant colonel was David Morgan, now retired.

22. The document about Long Dat is translated in CDEC log number 06-1409-67. Source: CIA memorandum for the record "History of Strength Estimates of the Communist 'Administrative Services,'" of 2 April 1968.

23. The lieutenant colonel was Everette S. Parkins, now retired.

24. Unfortunately, no copy of this note survives (so far as I know). However, a number of interviewees recall it, including the chief order-of-battle analyst for the Defense Intelligence Agency, then-Captain Barrie Williams, U.S. Army, who was present at the conference.

25. CIA cable, Saigon Station to CIA Headquarters 12 September 1967. Conceivably, this was sent the next day. The cable was classified "RYBAT," meaning it was considered especially sensitive.

26. *The English Works of Thomas Hobbes of Malmesburg* (London: Longman, Brown, Green, and Longmans, 1839) Vol. 7, p. 73.

27. As taken from Carver's memo to Ambassador Bunker of 15 September 1967, relaying the already-worked-out agreement.

28. William Hyland later became chief of State Department intelligence.

29. Memorandum for Mr. George Carver "MACV Press Briefing on Enemy Order of Battle," from Paul Walsh, then acting deputy director of the Office of Economic Research, 11 October 1967. Among the other words and phrases Walsh applied to the proposed MACV briefing were "nonsense," "truly impossible," "unbelievably cavalier," "shocking," and "wanton." Mr. Carver also received derogatory comments about the briefing from William Hyland and Dean Moor.

30. Memorandum for the Honorable Philip Goulding, assistant secretary of defense for public affairs, "Transmittal of Requested Comments," from George Carver, CIA 13 October 1967.

31. Cable, Saigon Station to CIA Headquarters, "Summary of Vietcong Activities in Chuong Thien Province During September 1967," of 17 October 1967.

32. Internal memorandum for the DDI, "N.I.E. 14.3-67, Capabilities of the Vietnamese Communists for Fighting South Vietnam," of 23 October 1967, drafted by Paul Walsh.

33. Cable, from Ambassador Bunker to the White House via CIA channels, of 23 October 1967, Serial Number: "Bunker 325."

34. CIA cable, Saigon Station to CIA Headquarters, 3 November 1967.

35. The document appears in MACV translation report 03-1499-67 of 20 September 1967. As Mr. Parry suggested, see p. 10.

36. Although sent out under a Board of National Estimates letterhead, the Introductory Note was at "the request of one director." Dated 3 November 1967.

37. Memorandum for the record "Comments on the Current Draft of the Introductory Note and Text of National Intelligence Estimate 14.3-67" by the author, on 9 November 1967, p. 7 and 8.

38 SNIE 14.3-67, Serial Number 186035, 13 November 1967, then classified "Top Secret, Controlled Dissem. Limited Distribution."

39. The Estimates staffer William Hyland snipped this headline out, and posted it over his desk.

40. Westmoreland's briefing of 22 November failed to mention the exit of the militia. Neither did an earlier briefing which he'd given in Saigong on 11 November. At that time, he'd ascribed the drop in the VC army from 285,000 to 242,000 to "heavy casualties" and "declining morale." A third press briefing on the numbers, given at the Pentagon on the 24th, did mention the militia's disappearance, but with one exception, the press failed to catch its significance. The exception was Andrew Hamilton, who wrote about it in the *New Republic* magazine's edition of 16 December 1967. When Ambassador Komer read the article in Saigon later in December, he angrily cabled Washington, saying, in effect "See what happens when you tell the truth? I told you we shouldn't have done it." See his cable of 19 August 1967.

41. Mr. Allen's comments were directed at an internal memo which contained the same numbers as those in the newspaper articles.

42. MACV Bulletin 7,872, published under CDEC log number 11-1166-67 in early November 1967.

43. The first version of the cable, like later versions, was divided into three parts: An "Overview," the "VC Winter-Spring Campaign," and a part concerning negotiations. The key part was part two.

44. Quotes are from the version that went to the White House on 15 December 1967.

45. OCI's comments were prepared by the newly appointed head of its South Vietnam Branch, Thaxter Goodell. Although a good analyst (who'd gained a solid reputation during the Cuban Missile Crisis), he had virtually no experience in Indo-China. His appointment resulted in part from OCI's preference of "generalists" over "specialists." See remarks of OCI's deputy chief, Mr. Lehman concerning a specialist namely Molly at the end of Chapter 1.

46. My remarks were dated 14 December 1967. They noted that the Vietcong main battle forces are "considerably larger than we give them credit for. The order of battle omits myriad small, but elite units; it frequently

underestimates the size of units it does carry; it does not take into account many North Vietnamese soldiers who are already in the south." They went on to say the service troop number was "fraudulent," that the guerrilla number "overlooks major VC documents which indicate it is much higher," that the OB also omits "over 100,000 self-defense militia, tens of thousands of assault youths" (a category which this book skips), "scores of thousands of armed political cadres, and goodness knows what else."

47. Memorandum for the Honorable Walt W. Rostow, special assistant to the president, entitled "Papers on Vietcong Strategy" from George Carver, of 15 December 1967. Quotes are from Carver's cover sheet.

48. CIA memo to Secretary McNamara entitled "A Review of the Situation in Vietnam," dated 8 December 1967.

49. MACV Order of Battle, 31 December 1967.

50. As noted in the last MACV "update" message for the end-of-year OB. The message was sent on 4 January 1968.

51. Whether Helms actually gave the briefing, I don't know.

52. Memorandum of conversation, between Colonel Hawkins and the author, dated 16 January 1968. (The conversation, held on 12 January, was witnessed in its entirety by Mr. Ronald Smith of the Office of Economic Research, of whom more later.)

53. MACV Order of Battle 31 December 1967.

54. This document is unavailable. However, a second document, taken in February 1968, lists the same units. See CDEC log number 02-1261-68. The second document's date of information was 24 September 1967.

55. See CDEC log number 07-3050-67, one of several captured near Danang in July 1967 concerning the T89 Battalion.

56. NSA study 2/0/VCM/R32068 of 25 January 1968.

57. DDI memorandum "The Situation in Vietnam," SC number 00895/68, 29 January 1968.

CHAPTER 6: N-DAY

Sources

The documents cited in this chapter are from the same general sources as Chapter 5's. They include the CIA's Central Intelligence Bulletins for the period of 30 January 1968 through 8 February 1968; the Vietnam Situation Report for 30 January 1968; additional reports connected with the CIA's Post Mortem on Tet; and a chronology I maintained during my various attempts to get an investigation started. The reader will observe that in the footnotes below, I state that certain conversations were "based on" notes or memorandums of conversation I wrote either during or shortly after they occurred. The reason for the phrase "based on" is that parts of the conversations—as they appear in the book—are not verbatim quotes. Kept for legal purposes, notes and the memorandums of conversation tended to be dry. In the book, I have tried to re-create the original phraseology. I feel the result is reasonably accurate.

The following books were again used for background information: Don Oberdorfer's *Tet!*; the unpublished manuscript about Tet by Larry Pennsinger, then an analyst in MACV J-2's Strategic Research and Analysis Branch; Peter Braestrup's *Big Story: How the American Press and Television Reported and Interpreted the Crisis of Tet 1968 in Vietnam and Washington* (Boulder, Colo.: Westview Press, 1977) 2 vols; and Dr. Stephen T. Hosmer's *Vietcong Repression and Its Implications for the Future* (Lexington, Mass.: Heath Lexington Books, 1970). My involvement with Dr. Hosmer's book is discussed in Chapter 7.

Supplementing these sources are several interviews—including ones with Thomas E. Becker, Joseph Hovey, Robert Klein, and Robert Appell—and as usual, my memory.

Notes

1. Based on my interview with Thomas E. Becker. It is quite possible that some readers would recognize Becker if they saw him after resigning from the CIA, he appeared as an actor in the movie about Vietnam, *The Deer Hunter,* which won the Academy Award for Best Picture in 1978. Becker played an extremely unsympathetic army doctor—so well, that Eleanor, who was sitting beside me when he came on the screen, remarked: "Typical Army." I said: "No, no, that's old Tom Becker. He's a nice guy." As to the movie itself, I, like many others who saw or heard combat in Vietnam, found it harrowingly realistic. The scenes of torture by the Vietcong—which raised the hackles of some Americans who had been against the war—to me rang true. I have read too many accounts of Vietcong brutality to feel otherwise. For me the scenes brought to mind an individual: Mr. Minh, the chief interrogator of COSVN, who shot prisoners "while trying to escape."

2. CIA's Central Intelligence Bulletin, 30 January 1968.

3. Draft cable, from which I quoted in my testimony to the House Select Committee on Intelligence on 18 September 1975.

4. Check stub, dated 30 January 1968. I include this in as an example of the information I used to compile my chronology.

5. I can't recall who the dignitary was. Another person who was there seemed to think it was Nicholas Katzenbach. Don Oberdorfer's *Tet!* recounts the same episode.

6. Memorandum for the Honorable Walt W. Rostow, special assistant to the president, entitled "Papers on Viet Cong Strategy," from George Carver, 15 December 1967.

7. Buckslip, initialed by Drexel Godfrey, also quoted in my testimony to the House Select Committee on Intelligence, 18 September 1975.

8. Memorandum for the record, 31 January 1968, from S. Adams to George A. Carver, Jr. Mr. Carver later turned the memo over to the CIA Inspector General.

9. *Washington Post,* 1 February 1968, p. 1.

10. *Washington Post,* 4 February 1968, p. 1. Interestingly, Peter Braestrup's *Big Story* pooh-poohs Arnet's story, saying that "Tet was less a demonstration of Vietcong efficiency than the result of a kind of mass escapism by the Saigon regime" (vol. 1, p. 194). Generally, I agree with Braestrup's criticisms of the press. Not this one. It was a good story, which made several fascinating observations.

11. CIA's Central Intelligence Bulletin, 3 February 1968.

12. There was a vast discrepancy between the U.S. aircraft losses as reported in the situation room (a total of 1,200 destroyed or damaged), and the U.S. aircraft losses which MACV admitted publicly (58 destroyed and 239 damaged, for a total of 297). There is no question in my mind that "1200" was the approximate number I saw in the situation room, since on 26 February 1968, I mentioned this figure to the so-called DDI analyst, who duly recorded it. George Allen later told staffers of the House Select Committee on Intelligence that he had seen a message from General Westmoreland requesting 500 aircraft to "replace those lost during Tet. This suggests that the total of 1200 is in the right ballpark, since damaged aircraft doubtless outnumbered destroyed. The question arises: How come the discrepancy? I recall discussions at the time, that MACV was jiggering with definitions of what constituted "destroyed," and what constituted "damaged." My recollection is that for an aircraft to be publicly reported as "destroyed," MACV required that it be virtually obliterated, and for an aircraft to be publicly reported as "damaged," it had to have suffered severe structural damage. Aircraft which suffered only light or moderate damage went unreported, at least in public. Two problems arise. The first is that many—if not most—aircraft publicly reported as "damaged" *never flew again,* leading one to question MACV's definition of "destruction." The second problem is that the numbers still don't track. (That is, even if one postulates that *all* of the 297 aircraft publicly reported as "destroyed" or "damaged" were permanently grounded, the number is still some 200 short of the 500 General Westmoreland requested as replacements.) I have since heard allegations that

MACV changed the tail numbers of aircraft to conceal the extent of the losses. I was told this involved taking a new plane and giving it a destroyed plane's tail number. This leaves the question unanswered of how MACV explained the disappearance of the new plane's number. I leave it to someone else to track down what really happened. Meanwhile, the "official" losses—as put forth by Lieutenant General Daniel O. Graham in his testimony to the House Intelligence Committee on 3 December 1975—are still 297 aircraft

13. MACV Order of Battle, 31 December 1967. MACV J-2 skipped the 31 January 1968 OB because of the exigencies of Tet.

14. My memorandum for the record, "Suggested Topics for Research," 5 February 1968.

15. MACV CDED Log Numbers 01-1988-68, 01-1998-68, and 01-1999-68. These documents were captured before Tet, warning the defenders of Pleiku that an attack was coming. Despite the warning, the VC got into town, and destroyed large numbers of U.S. helicopters in the process. A visitor to Pleiku shortly after the attack recalled seeing long lines of wrecked helicopters. I do not know whether MACV classified these as "destroyed" or "damaged." Vietcong losses in personnel were very heavy at Pleiku.

16. Based on my memorandum for the record "George Allen's Remarks about the Communist Force Commitment," 10 February 1968.

17. I have been unable to locate the citation for this document. However, another document—CDEC log number 05-1131-68—mentions the presence of VC self-defense militia units in Hue.

18. Based on my memorandum of conversation with Mr. George Carver, Jr., 11 February 1968.

19. CIA cable, CIA Headquarters to the Saigon Station, 13 February 1968.

20. CIA cable, Saigon Station to CIA Headquarters, 19 February 1968.

21. CIA cable, CIA Headquarters to the Saigon Station, 19 February 1968. This answered the cable cited in Note 20.

22. During this same trip, I went over the OB with Colonel Hawkins. Again, we had no major disagreements. I wrote up a memorandum of conversation on the following day, 28 February 1968. In it, I made this comment: "Colonel Hawkins, as usual, was candid and thoroughly aware of the OB problem. Personally, I feel he is one of the most competent officials in the U.S. intelligence apparatus. Not only does he seem extraordinarily honest, but he obviously shares my belief that intelligence and politics should not be mixed. I wish there were more like him."

23. Blascik's cover sheet to his secretary read: "This memo must: 1) Be read by Sam Adams, 2) Go to Carver for approval, 3) Be finalized, 4) Go to the

director this P.M., 5) Courtesy copies to Paul Wash, Dean Moor and Ron Smith. Have Fun. DWB."

24. CIA cable, CIA Headquarters to the Saigon Station, 26 March 1968.

25. Joint memorandum (CIA and DIA) "The Attrition of Vietnamese Communist Forces 1966–1969," 30 March 1968.

26. Based on notes I took while talking to Mr. Andrews, 1 April 1968.

27. Based on notes I took at the conference, 10 April 1968.

28. The final conference report went to the director in a memorandum entitled "Results of Community Negotiations on Enemy Strengths in South Vietnam," under serial number SC 09739/68, from Paul V. Walsh, 2 May 1968.

29. My memorandum to the CIA Inspector General, "Complaints About Research on the Vietcong," 27 May 1968.

30. My memorandum for the record "Comments on the Current Draft of the Introductory Note and Text of National Intelligence Estimate 14.3-67," 9 November 1967, p. 8.

31. Based on notes I took during my conversation with Mr. Stewart, 28 May 1968.

32. Based on notes I took during my conversation with Mr. Stewart, 5 June 1968. Mr. Douglas Andrews was also present. I relayed the conversation to the so-called DDI analyst, who duly noted it down. The analyst's account agrees with mine.

33. The ex-chief of the Saigon Station, Gordon Jorgensen (see Chapter 3) also took part in these discussions. He was slightly bemused, but otherwise his same old self—direct, and Cagney-like in his manner of expression.

34. A VC document putting the number of victims at 3,000 was translated under CDEC log number 06-2049-68.

35. Quoted from Dr. Stephen Hosmer's *Viet Cong Repression and Its Implications for the Future* (Lexington, Mass.: Heath Lexington Books, 1970) p. 49. He got the account from the *New York Times* edition of 1 May 1968. An earlier account of the massacre appeared in the *Times* of 28 March 1968. See Dr. Hosmer's book, p. 45–51. I later talked to a CIA case officer, who was present when the first bodies were unearthed. He said that it was the most horrible sight he had ever encountered.

36. Based on notes of my conversation with Messrs. Breckenridge and Gier, 1 August 1968.

37. Based on notes of my conversation with Mr. Stewart, 22 August 1968.

38. Headquarters notice NH 20-363 of 13 September 1968.

39. Based on notes of my conversation with Mr. Ueberhorst, 17 September 1968.

40. Based on my memorandum of conversation with Colonel Lawrence K. White, 20 September 1968. I took especially careful notes on this occasion, so that much of what Colonel White said is verbatim.

41. My memorandum to Colonel Lawrence K. White "Accuracy of a Draft Memorandum of Conversation," 23 September 1968.

42. Based on notes of my conversation with Colonel White, 23 September 1968.

43. Based partially on memory, but also on notes I made after my conversation with Mr. Helms, 8 November 1968. I took no notes on the incident concerning Earl McGowan, but I remember it distinctly.

44. Thomas Powers was kind enough to give me a copy of the chronology he compiled in preparation for writing his book.

45. Based on notes of my conversation with Messrs. Proctor and Smith, 19 November 1968. George Carver was also present.

46. My letters to Taylor and Rostow, 18 November 1968, sent with a cover letter, to Helms.

47. Memorandum from Admiral Rufus Taylor, deputy director CIA, to S. Adams, 20 November 1968.

48. My memorandum "Intelligence Failures in Vietnam: Suggestions for Reform," 24 January 1969.

49. Memorandum from Admiral Rufus Taylor, deputy director CIA, to S. Adams, 31 January 1969. It was among the last official documents the admiral ever produced. He retired from the government that afternoon.

50. *Washington Post,* 6 April 1969, the Outlook Section, p. B1 and B4. The interview originally appeared in *L'Europeo,* a magazine published in Milan, Italy, by the Rizzoli Corporation. Ms. Fallacci, whose reporting I greatly admire, described Giap as chubby, about five feet tall, "slightly bloated," and with "an infantile little round nose. But his eyes are among the most intelligent I've ever seen, and also the most crafty, the most cruel." In one of the more significant passages of the interview, Giap bragged about the Vietnamese beating the Mongols in A.D. 1200. Although 800 years old, it's an event that all Vietnamese apparently savor.

INDEX

A NOTE ON THE AUTHOR

Sam Adams was a graduate of Harvard College (1955) and spent ten years (1963–1973) as an analyst for the Central Intelligence Agency. After leaving the CIA he wrote, raised beef cattle in Virginia, testified before Congress, and helped to produce a CBS television documentary about American intelligence failures in Vietnam. He was completing an account of his time with the CIA when he died suddenly of a heart attack in 1988. He is survived by his wife Anne and two sons, Clayton and Abraham.

A NOTE ON THE BOOK

This book was composed by Steerforth Press using a digital version of Bembo, a typeface produced by Monotype in 1929 and based on the designs of Francesco Griffo, Venice, 1499. The book was printed on acid free papers and bound by Quebecor Printing ~ Book Press Inc. of North Brattleboro, Vermont.